Kill Everyone

Kill Everyone

Advanced Strategies for No-Limit Hold 'Em Poker Tournaments and Sit-n-Go's

Lee Nelson
Tysen Streib and Kim Lee

Foreword by
Joe Hachem

Huntington Press
Las Vegas Nevada

Kill Everyone
Advanced Strategies for
No-Limit Hold 'Em Poker Tournaments and Sit-n-Go's

Published by
   Huntington Press
   3665 S. Procyon Ave.
   Las Vegas, NV 89103
   Phone (702) 252-0655
   e-mail: books@huntingtonpress.com

ISBN: 978-0-929712-47-5

Cover Photo: Copyright IMPDI 2007 for the WSOP
Design & Production: Laurie Shaw

Acknowledgments

There are a number of people we'd like to thank for making this book possible. This includes our fabulous editor, Deke Castleman, our publisher Huntington Press and Anthony Curtis, and the production team led by Laurie Shaw. We thank this group for the expeditious professional way they got this book from pen to press.

We thank WPT and WSOP Champion Joe Hachem for the kind words in his Foreword. Besides being a world-class player, Joe is an incredible human being and a fantastic ambassador for poker.

We'd like to thank Blair Rodman, the co-author of *Kill Phil*. While his primary focus moved to other areas (primarily Elimination Blackjack and the Ultimate Blackjack Tour) after the publication of *Kill Phil* and he elected not to devote his efforts to another poker book, his review of the *Kill Everyone* manuscript and support of this project have been invaluable. In fact, Blair acknowledges having incorporated some of the concepts in *Kill Everyone* into his no-limit arsenal, which proved strong enough to win a bracelet and more than $700,000 in the 2007 World Series of Poker.

We sincerely acknowledge the contributions made by our

poker readers: Dennis Waterman, Joe Brandenburg, Matt Davidow, and Andy Bloch.

We thank Dan at propokertools.com for his simulation results.

Our thanks to Lee's wife Pen for her typing and to Tysen's wife Allison for her proofreading, and to all our wives for putting up with the incredibly long hours of our office sequestration that they uncomplainingly endured.

Finally, we want to thank all poker players for their support of the game we love.

To all of you, our heart-felt thanks.

Contents

Part Three: Other Topics

Part Four: Online Short-Handed No-Limit Hold 'Em Cash Games

Appendix 1

Appendix 2

Appendix 3

Appendix 4

Appendix 5

Appendix 6

Index

Foreword

I first met Lee Nelson about seven years ago at my "home" casino, Crown, in Melbourne, Australia. I actually knew Lee by reputation long before we first met. I think we'd all heard about this American-born Kiwi tearing up the tournament scene and it was great to finally meet Lee in person.

For someone who hadn't played tournament poker seriously until in his mid-50s—he once described himself to me as a "retired gentleman looking for a hobby"—it's hard to appreciate the scale of Lee's achievement in compiling the best tournament record of any Australasian player since the turn of the century.

I've learned some important lessons from Lee. It was Lee who taught me the importance of patience in the bigger tournaments, which was underlined watching Lee make final table after final table after final table. His nickname "Final Table" is certainly apt.

He is admired by all the top pros in Australia and abroad for being a great poker player, astute analyst, and a true gentleman of the game. All poker players would love to emulate Lee's level of tournament performance.

Just months after winning the main event at the 2005 WSOP, I had the pleasure to play with Lee during the third day of the 2006 Aussie Millions' main event. We made a pact to play our best poker and make the final table together where we would battle for the coveted prize. Unfortunately, I bombed out, but Lee went on to dominate the final table with an almost uncanny read of the game with which few individuals are gifted, and celebrated the biggest win of his career. It was a masterful poker performance, which will be remembered for a very long time.

In *Kill Everyone*, Lee has teamed up with Tysen Streib and Kim Lee. Although I do not know Tysen and Kim personally, I know they are extremely astute poker analysts. Tysen has written a number of excellent articles for *2+2 Magazine*, and Kim Lee is a university professor.

Their mathematical understanding and analysis of the game are obviously sharp, clear, and insightful. Combining their analytical prowess with Lee's practical experience is a formidable combination that has resulted in *Kill Everyone*.

Together they show you how to accumulate chips in tournaments, and provide detailed mathematical analyses of key concepts, not only for multi-table tournaments, but also for Sit-n-Go's and satellites.

There is a lot of information in *Kill Everyone* that the pros don't want you to know. There is no doubt in my mind that mastering the concepts in this book will make you a formidable player.

Lee and Blair Rodman, along with Kim Lee, tantalized us with some tasty morsels in *Kill Phil*, but *Kill Everyone* serves up a sumptuous main course. For those who thought *Kill Phil* hit the mark, be prepared to have your socks blown off by *Kill Everyone!*

Kill Phil was a hit, but I fully expect *Kill Everyone* to surpass it in every respect.

I hope you enjoy *Kill Everyone* as much as I did.

Joe Hachem
Melbourne, Australia
July, 2007

Introduction

A lot of things have changed since Blair Rodman, Kim Lee, and I (Lee Nelson) wrote *Kill Phil*.

Poker has continued to boom as more and more talented, young, Internet-honed players enter the fray. The 2006 World Series of Poker (WSOP) had an astounding 8,773 entrants—a prize pool of almost $88 million—making it, by far, the biggest sporting event in history. Even with the current U.S. legislation (against which a backlash has begun), the 2007 WSOP Main Event drew 6,358 entrants, much more than the early predictions of Las Vegas oddsmakers.

Poker is spreading around the globe. In Australia many pubs offer tournaments. The Sydney APL, a pub poker club, has more than 170,000 members and is reportedly growing by 5,000 members weekly. The 2006 Aussie Millions Main Event, the biggest poker tournament Down Under and one of the biggest outside the U.S., had 418 entrants with a first prize (which I was fortunate enough to win) of US$1 million ($1.3 million Aussie). The 2007 Aussie Millions had an astounding 748 entrants, nearly double the 2006 turnout. For 2008 they're expecting more than 1,000!

I predict that by the time you read this, poker will have

spread through Asia faster than bird flu. In November 2006 the first Asian tournaments were held in the Philippines and Singapore. This year (2007-2008) will usher in Asian poker tournaments that will probably include destinations such as India, Macau, Korea, Japan, Vietnam, and almost certainly both the Philippines and Singapore. If poker, with its TV celebrity status, catches on in Asia, and I see no reason why it won't, the number of players there could be huge. Many online sites are already viewing this lucrative potential market with covetous eyes; it's just a matter of time.

Meanwhile, the game itself continues to go through a metamorphosis. As Blair and I predicted in *Kill Phil*, the new breed of Internet-spawned young Turks are playing ultra-aggressive poker, moving in more frequently and calling more all-in bets with weaker hands than seasoned pros can imagine. Having played literally thousands of hours online, they've developed skills and played more hands than a brick-and-mortar-based pro could play in 20 years! Make no mistake, a lot of these young guns, many of whom aren't yet even 21 years old, can play. And as they continue to come of age and emerge from their online cocoons, they're taking down big prizes.

Jeff Williams, an American not yet old enough to enter a U.S. casino, won the 2006 European Poker Tour Grand Championship event in Monte Carlo with its €900,000 (euro) (US$1,084,000) first prize, and 19-year-old Jimmy Fricke took down $1,000,000 Aussie (US$810,000) as runner up to Gus Hansen in the 2007 Aussie Millions Main Event. When I travel the international poker circuit, I see quite a few of these 18- to 20-year-old poker prodigies in Europe and Australia, where you only need to be 18 to play, and heaps of 16- to 17-year-olds are coming up who'll be forces to be reckoned with in the near future.

The hallmark of winning tournament play continues to be fearless controlled aggression. While some of these young phenoms may be short in the control department (thank God, or old guys like me might never win a tournament), they can never be accused of lacking courage. Though it started as a predominately Scandinavian innovation, a plethora of tough, aggressive, young players now seem to have cropped up universally. I'm continually seeing baby-faced kids turning up the heat on more established players. Granted, often those who play a bit too rashly sometimes find themselves suddenly and unceremoniously relegated to railbird status, but those who have learned to slow down a bit when circumstances warrant a modicum of prudence are going deep into many events and winning quite a number of them.

Developing short-handed skills is essential in order to take down big prize money. In *Kill Phil*, Blair, Kim Lee, and I developed a simple basic strategy for no-limit hold 'em with a number of advanced refinements, based on a move-in or fold model. In this book, Tysen Streib, Kim Lee, and I show you how to approach the game at varying chip-stack levels, using a push or fold strategy when appropriate, but also incorporating other tactics to accumulate chips as you navigate through a tournament field. We also show you how to tackle a short-handed no-limit hold 'em cash game. We take you through ways to build your stack when the blinds are low, teach you how to modify your play as you approach the bubble, and provide detailed explanations for bubble play, final-table play, short-handed situations, and heads-up confrontations. We not only cover large multi-table tournaments (MTTs), but also Sit-n-Go's (SNGs), winner-take-all events, multiple-winner satellites, and short-handed cash games, including multi-tabling. We provide you with actual examples to help illustrate the principles. Finally, we focus exclusively on the game that, like it or not, has become synonymous with poker—no-limit hold 'em (NLHE).

Our approach in this book, as it was in *Kill Phil*, is to marry poker math with real-time experiences to provide a sound approach to recurring situations you'll encounter as you accumulate chips and approach the money. Then, once you're in the money, we show you how best to move up the ranks to big payouts. Intuitive concepts have been rigorously examined for accuracy and robustness by Kim, Tysen, or both. We supply you with some new weapons and show you how, and when, to use them.

As a bonus, Mark Vos, a top online cash-game player and 2006 WSOP NLHE bracelet winner, reveals how he beats short-handed online cash games. We're confident that an understanding of the ideas in this book will make you a better poker player.

—Lee

How This Book Came About

Lee has lots of practical tournament experience, both live and online, having won more than $2 million in live tournaments alone. Tysen has written many articles for *2+2 Magazine* on mathematical end-game situations and Sit-n-Go's, and has developed informative charts and graphs to illustrate key concepts. Kim Lee is an innovative math and finance expert with unique concepts for analyzing poker situations; more math means more money! Mark Vos is a big winner in short-handed online cash games and a WSOP bracelet winner in no-limit hold 'em.

The four of us have teamed up, combining real-world experience with math and computational horsepower, to produce winning strategies for multi-table tournaments, Sit-n-Go's, and satellites.

To allow the narrative to flow better, we use first-person examples throughout much of the text. In Parts 1 and 3, "I" refers to Lee. In Part 2, the first person applies to Tysen. And in Part 4, the "I" refers to Mark.

Part One
Early-Stage Play

1

NEW SCHOOL VERSUS OLD SCHOOL

Loose Aggressive

Accumulating chips in big MTTs is an art form and different players have various ways of accomplishing this critical feat. Old-school practitioners play tight, waiting for big starting hands (about top 5%), such as pocket 9s or better, A-Q suited, or A-K (preferably suited), and try to extract as much as possible with these hands. They use bets and raises to define their hands. Aggressively playing sound values is the hallmark of this approach.

Early in tournaments, however, other players are getting huge implied odds to play speculative hands, such as small to medium pairs and suited connectors. If they miss the flop, no big deal; the big pair wins a small pot. But when they flop two pair or better, they're now in position to bust a player who falls in love with aces or kings and can't get away from them.

If this is what you're patiently waiting for (you'll get aces or kings on average only once every 110 hands), you naturally might want to extract full value and may be willing to go all-in with them. This is exactly what today's predatory players are looking for. Get married to aces early in a tournament and you'll often have a great bad-beat story to tell your friends. Actually, it's not a bad beat at all, especially if you slow-play aces early on, as many players are prone to do. They're just asking to get busted and plenty of players around today will happily oblige them. The number of players I see crippled or eliminated early in tournaments due to slow-playing big pairs is staggering. Unless you're superb at reading hands and other players and have a great feel as to where you are in a hand, it's probably a mistake to slow-play aces, especially early when most players are deep-stacked.

In fact, sometimes drastically *over*-betting aces early in a tournament can pay off big time. A few years ago in the $25,000-buy-in WPT Championship event at Bellagio, where each player started with 50,000 chips, Jim McManus shoved in all 50,000 of his chips pre-flop with pocket aces. He was called by a player who had pocket queens and apparently thought they might be good, perhaps because no one in his right mind would bet 50,000 with aces when the blinds were tiny. When asked about this play, pro player Chip Jett responded, "I don't see anything wrong with it. Aces aren't part of my plan for accumulating chips anyway!" While Chip undoubtedly said this with tongue in cheek, it's true that today's new-school players aren't dependent on big pairs to build a big stack.

New-school practitioners play all kinds of hands in the early going in an effort to get their hands on some chips. Optimally, they do it with small-ball moves—small bets, raises, and re-raises that keep their opponents off-balance and guessing. When a player is capable of playing virtually any two cards, there's nearly always a possible hand he could have that will bury you. In fact, new-school adepts, such as Daniel Negreanu, James Van Alstyne, Alan Goehring, Patrik Antonius, and Gus Hansen (to name just a few), consistently show their opponents improbable holdings to take down big pots.

Here's an actual example from an April 2007 tournament at Bellagio.

At the 50/100 (second level) of a $3,120-buy-in no-limit

hold 'em event with 6,000 starting chips, Alan Goehring is the chip leader with 26,000 plus. Alan Cunningham, another great player, is second in chips at the table with about 13,000, more than double his starting chips.

Goehring has been playing many hands and taking a lot of flops, even when there's a raise before he acts. In this hand, Goehring limps under-the-gun (UTG) with 64 offsuit. Cunningham, seated three seats to the left of Goehring and holding A♣K♣, makes it 400. It's passed around to Goehring now heads-up and out of position with a top player; Goehring calls! The flop comes 5-3-2 with two clubs and one heart, giving Goehring the nuts and Cunningham the nut flush draw with 2 overcards. Goehring checks, Cunningham bets around 700, Goehring raises to 1,600 or so, and Cunningham calls; the turn brings the 4♠ and Goehring bets about another 1,600, taunting Cunningham to raise. Cunningham doesn't bite, despite the fact that he now has a wheel (a 5-high straight) to go with his nut flush draw. The river is the jack of hearts; Goehring now bets about 6,000 and Cunningham, after some deliberation, calls.

This hand cost Cunningham 9,600, leaving him with only 3,400, and catapulting Goehring to more than 35,000 chips, nearly six times his starting stack, and it was still only the second level!

Playing a lot of hands when deep-stacked makes new-school adepts extremely hard to read and unpredictable. Not only is it problematic to put them on a hand (they can have *anything*), but they can also smell weakness and steal a lot of pots. Creating uncertainty in the minds of their opponents, they find ways either to induce a desired call or to blow opponents off of better hands, often amassing a mountain of chips in the process. In my view, the best players in the game today play some variant of this loose aggressive (LAG) strategy.

Also in my view, a large part of the credit for developing this loose aggressive style goes to the Dane, Gus Hansen.

Coming from backgammon, Gus thinks in terms of equity. He realized that there's a vast difference between pre-flop and post-flop equity. Although AK is 67%/33% better than T3 (a hand now called "Hansen" by some) pre-flop, post-flop it's about a 30%/70% underdog if either a 10 or a 3 flop without an ace or king. If the flop comes A-T-3, the AK is nearly a 3/1 underdog, but he has a hand that may be strong enough to play for all his chips. Since pre-flop raises are generally small relative to stack sizes early in a tournament, Gus reasoned that he could play a lot of hands, especially in position; if he hit an unsuspected hand, he could stack his opponent.

Friends of mine recall that in season one of the WPT, at the Five Diamond Tournament at Bellagio in 2002, top players were buzzing about Gus having played an estimated 70% of the hands on his way to victory.

Other Scandinavians have followed in Gus' footsteps, further perfecting this style and taking it to new heights. The best around at this perspiring moment, in my opinion, is the Finn, Patrik Antonius. Patrik plays even more hands than Gus, has incredible focus, and is fearless and unpredictable. With a barrage of bets and raises, he puts tremendous pressure on his opponents.

Say you have AK early in a big tournament and raise it up to 200 in early position with blinds of 25/50. Antonius calls on the button. The flop is a pleasant A♣3♦4♥. You bet 400 into the 475 pot and get called. The turn is the innocuous-looking 2♥. You bet 1,000 and Patrik, in his inimical fashion, thinks for about a minute and raises you 1,500. You're pretty sure that if you call this bet, you'll be faced with a decision for most or all of your remaining chips on the river. What to do? What could Patrik have here? Pocket 3s or 4s? A3? A♥6♥? Actually, all of these hands are possible holdings and therein lies the rub. Against such players, you can't safely eliminate most starting hands, and he'll play very aggressively with a hand that may be second best at the moment, but can improve. So when he raises on the turn, you could be in mortal danger. That harmless-looking deuce might have made *him* a straight. Against more conventional players it would almost certainly be a blank, but Antonius is betting as though it helps him and his style prevents you from ruling out this possibility. You also know, and he knows you know, that he's fully capable of pulling the trigger on the river, either with the goods or on a total bluff. It's this uncertainty, combined with fearlessness, that's the strength of his game. This style of play is characterized as loose aggressive.

Suddenly, your tournament life is on the line. Do you risk it all with top-pair top-kicker when an expert player is telling you with his betting that he's got you beat? I've seen players move in in spots such as this with top pair, or an over-pair, and get called instantly and shown a set or a made straight. Exit stage left.

Playing against top new-school players who have position on you early in a tournament is similar to walking through a minefield. You take a step and it's OK. You take another—no problem. The third step you take and boom! You're on you way to the airport in a body bag.

If you're at the table and watch this play go down, you learn an important lesson—stay out of this guy's way unless you have a monster. But monsters are few and far between and it seems as though Patrik, and others of his ilk, are in an awful lot of pots, so they're difficult to avoid. This is why in *Kill Phil* we recommended that newer players overplay their big pairs and use a push (all-in) or fold pre-flop strategy with very specific guidelines, depending on stack size relative to the blinds, to neutralize the effectiveness of the "Phils" (and Patriks) of the world. When your chip stack is 10-times the cost of a round of blinds and antes or less, this strategy is close to optimal.

If you haven't read *Kill Phil* yet, we recommend you do so, as it provides a solid framework for concepts discussed in this sequel.

Play a Lot of Speculative Hands Early

If you've developed the ability to read hands and players really well, as many of these new-school experts have, you may be ready to employ similar tactics against your opponents. When you've got a deep stack, hands such as 64 suited or T7 suited can be played for a small raise. Also, you could see a flop by limping after several limpers with hands such as unsuited connectors or even hands such as Q♠5♠, if you're on or near the button. If you hit the flop big (2-pair, trips, a straight, or a flush), you can win a large pot and perhaps double up. No one will suspect that a flop such as 7-5-3 rainbow helped you. After all, you're not Alan Goehring, so it's unlikely other players will suspect that *you* might have flopped a straight. If they've got a big over-pair or the nut flush draw with overcards, you might just bust them.

Playing Tight Early to Establish an Image

If you're uncomfortable with this strategy of playing a lot of hands and seeing a lot of flops because you're afraid of being outplayed post-flop, there's an effective alternative strategy: Play very few hands early to establish a squeaky-tight image, so you can steal effectively later. With this strategy your range of playable hands might be as narrow as 55+, AQs+, and AK. Small pairs can be played for a small pre-flop raise, but you'll be done with the hand unless you flop a set. With 99, TT, or JJ, if the pot's been raised, you might consider just calling and trying either to flop a set or have a well-disguised overpair if three small cards flop. Play big pairs (QQ-AA) aggressively pre-flop by raising or re-raising.

Your objective with this game plan is to convince your opponents that you're really solid when you get involved. You might want to show them aces or kings a couple of times to reinforce your tight image. By the 4th or 5th level, they should be convinced. Now you can pick your spots and make some aggressive moves with a high probability of success.

For example, coming over the top of a late-position raiser, with or without a caller, is highly likely to be successful. For hours the other players have seen you play tighter than a clam, so it's unlikely they'll suspect that you're now stealing, until they see a marginal hand or two shown down. If this occurs (and you're still alive), go back into your shell for a while before stepping it up again.

Blind Stealing Early in the Tournament

It's important to distinguish between playing speculative hands early in the tournament and attempting to steal blinds with garbage. When the blinds are small, there's not much reason for most players to steal. Say you're playing in the WSOP Main Event with 10,000 chips and blinds of 25/50. You may have read somewhere that you should raise from the button with any two cards in an attempt to pick up the blinds. Adding that 75 to your stack represents a paltry 0.75% increase, so most players should avoid getting involved with trash hands for such a minimal return. Unsuited hands without high cards or straight potential should generally be mucked.

Notice that I say "most players." Some of the greats are an exception, but they have their sights set much higher than the 75 blinds. If the blinds give up, fine—they'll lock up the small profit. But if they raise to 150 and get called, now it's game on! Because these players are highly experienced and great hand readers, they'll try to outplay their opponents on the flop and beyond, perhaps garnering significant chips in the process. If their opponent checks, they'll bet virtually every time, instantly picking up the pot when their opponent misses on the flop (about 2/3 of the time). If they get resistance, they'll use small bets, raises, or check raises to pare down hand ranges. Once they have a good feel for what a foe has, they'll analyze the situation based on their extensive experience in similar situations. If they've got him beat, they'll take an approach to maximize their profits; if they determine that he's ahead, rather than turning tail and running for cover, they'll size him up and if they think they can make a bet that he can't call, they'll do so without hesitation. Conversely, if they conclude that they're beat and are unlikely to bet an opponent off his hand, they'll fold early in the hand. On occasion, the pro might give up a small pot, but he's much more likely to win far more pots than he loses.

The combination of a tournament expert's unpredictability (he can have any two cards), astute reads, betting power, fearlessness, and position is often insurmountable for intermediate players. Indeed, it's these characteristics that make him great. He realizes that deep-stack NLHE pre-flop play doesn't mean a lot. Expert players routinely give up pre-flop equity to get more value later in the hand. Intermediate players can't do this. So although that button raise with a hand such as 64o may represent negative pre-flop equity, if you're Alan Goehring or Patrik Antonius, it's worth giving up this small amount of negative pre-flop equity in exchange for positive post-flop equity in deep-stack play.

Poker is a zero-sum game. If one player has positive expected value (+EV), then another player must have an equal amount of negative expected value (-EV). If you're the best or second-best player at the table, playing hands such as 64o may represent value, but otherwise it's a losing play to get involved with such hands. Muck them and move on.

When I suggest playing speculative hands early, I'm referring to hands such as small pairs, suited connectors, 1-gap suited connectors, and suited aces. The Rule of 5 and 10 (see page 49) and 3 and 6 (see page 66) will help you determine how much to invest with these hands. Unsuited connectors can also be limped with from the button and small blind for a small percentage of your stack. Mere mortals should avoid attempting blind steals with trash hands.

Blind Stealing Later in the Tournament

After the first 5 or 6 levels, blind stealing becomes more lucrative. In fact, it becomes essential. This is especially true once the antes commence. Factors that influence the frequency with which you can steal include:

• Your chip stack relative to that of the big blind. Generally, the bigger his stack, the harder he'll be to steal from.

• The type of player in the big blind. Passive players who won't re-raise without a top 10% hand are best. Aggressive players who frequently re-raise are tough to steal from effectively.

• Your hand value. Obviously, the better your hand, the more likely you are to raise. Against better players who frequently re-raise, you need to upgrade the quality of your steal hands. Even so, against a frequent re-raiser you may need to move in with a hand such as 87s, 76s, etc. True, you'll feel sick if he calls and shows you pocket aces, but you sometimes have to take risks such as this to regain control of your table. Unless he's got a monster, your play will be successful.

• Your table image. If you've stolen the blinds a few times recently, you should only steal-raise with a hand that can stand a re-raise. It's sweet to wake up with a big pair or AK when you've stolen two hands recently. Most semi-aggressive players will play back at you the third time you raise.

• If the player in the big blind has just won a nice pot, he's a good candidate for a steal attempt. Players who have just won a pot and are now comfortable stack-wise are excellent targets. They'll rarely get involved right away without a premium hand. If that player is a pro, though, ignore this advice. Some pros like to "play their rush" and will frequently play the next hand after dragging a big pot. If you ever play with Doyle Brunson, you can count on this happening.

The Big Move

Sometimes early in a tournament, an opportunity presents itself to make a big move to build your stack. This may involve thinking outside the box. You need to know the odds of certain match-ups, have the courage of your convictions, and have a fair amount of risk-tolerance, but we'd argue that without these traits your chances of consistently doing well in tournaments is minimal anyway.

Early in the 2006 Aussie Millions Main Event, I encountered an unusual situation. I was seated at a tough table. Jason Gray, an Aussie pro, was seated on my left, followed by Mark Vos and a couple of accomplished, tough, online players. All players started with 20,000 in chips and there had been only minor fluctuations in the first hour of play when this hand come up.

With blinds of 50/100, I was UTG with 7♥6♥ and made it 225 to go. In early position, I like making small raises such as this with big hands and speculative hands alike. Jason Gray and Mark Vos both called, as did two of the tough Internet qualifiers. There was now 1,175 in the pot.

The flop was Q♥5♥4♣.

I checked and Jason bet 1,000. Surprisingly, Vos and the two other players all smooth-called the 1,000. The action was now back to me and I paused for over a minute before acting. I had a flush draw and an open-ended-straight draw. Nine cards would make my flush, plus another six cards that would make a straight (eight straight cards minus the two straight cards that are hearts and have already been accounted for). With 15 possible outs (if you're not familiar with counting outs, please read *Kill Phil*), I never considered folding.

Know the Odds

My first instinct was to call, but then I surmised that there was an excellent chance another player had the nut flush draw.

After all, four players had called a nearly pot-sized bet. If the nut flush draw was out there, then my outs would be dramatically slashed to the six non-hearts that would make the straight. I knew that my hand was at least even money against any outstanding hand except a set or a better flush draw. I reasoned that it was unlikely for any player, other than possibly Jason, to have a set, because with all the draws that the flop provided, it would be foolish for a set-holder not to protect his hand by raising on the flop. Remember, everyone in this pot was a good player. What would you do with my hand here?

With this background information, I came up with an action plan—I moved in. All 20,000! How did I arrive at this decision? First off, I knew the approximate odds of an all-in heads-up confrontation on the flop. I'd be:

- about 56% against an over-pair;
- just over even money against any 2-pair;
- about 40% against a set;
- about 37% against ace-little of hearts (A♥2♥, A♥3♥, etc.);
- about 35% against ace-big of hearts (A♥K♥, A♥J♥, etc.).

Paradoxically, the hands against which I would fare worst heads-up were the nut flush draws; I had to raise any flush draw out of the pot, if indeed a hand such as this was out, as seemed probable. These seemed easiest to knock out with an all-in bet. Experienced players would realize, I figured, that they would be only 35% against 2-pair, and a 2-1 underdog against a set, my most likely holdings, and it would be a very tough call to make. Once I eliminated better flush draws, and given the unlikely event that a set was out based on the betting so far, I liked the odds I was getting.

There was already more than 5,000 in the pot. Any opponent who called would add another 19,000, so I was risking just under 20,000 to win 24,000, *if called*. I would be getting 1.2- to-1 on my money against an over-pair, or 2-pair, against both of which I was a favorite. Sure, Jason, or less likely one of the other players, *could* have an unsuspected set and I'd be a 1.5-to-1 underdog and only be getting 1.2-to-1, but this underlay was a risk I was willing to take. Most players won't lay down sets, but in a situation such as this, some players might fold bottom set to an all-in bet this early in a major tournament, when they've only committed about 5% of their chips. Given my fold equity, a concept we'll be discussing in more detail further on, I became convinced that moving in was my best play. I realized that if no one had a set, there was a good chance they'd all fold, and if I was unlucky enough to run into a set, I still had lots of outs.

Now put yourself in each of my opponents' shoes as they decided what to do. Jason's actual hand was AA without the ace of hearts. Faced with my all-in and with three players yet to act behind him, he quickly (and correctly) folded. He realized that he was either up against a set or a huge draw and was probably an underdog. Given the fact that one or more of the other players yet to act might also have his aces beat, his decision to fold was easy.

Mark Vos' decision was even easier. Holding pocket tens, he quickly folded.

The next player was faced with a real dilemma. He had 54, two small pair. He went into the tank for 6 minutes and finally called time on himself! I've never seen anyone else do this. He wanted a self-imposed deadline to make his decision. In the end, he also folded. He probably figured out that his hand wasn't a favorite against the range of hands I could have and that he was virtually drawing dead if I had a set of queens. With only 1,225 invested and nearly 19,000 left, he reluctantly let his two pair go, rather than face possible elimination. By the way, if I'd had a set of queens I'd have played the hand the same way, so his trepidation over two small pair was warranted.

Playing both your big hands and your bluffs in the same way is a recurring theme of this book. Unpredictability is the hallmark of all expert tournament players. Played the same way, your big hands protect your bluffs.

The final player to act did, indeed, have the nut flush draw—the ace and a small heart. From his perspective, it probably seemed as though he was up against a made hand (he knew who had the nut flush draw), most likely a set, against which he'd be about a 2-to-1 underdog—an easy fold.

From my perspective there were a number of positive spinoffs from this hand. Not only did I increase my stack by 25%, a big step toward the pivotal early accumulation of chips, I also achieved some psychological advantages, most notably what we refer to as "fold equity" and "fear equity." The realization that all their chips might be threatened even this early in a tournament might make some of them think twice about entering pots in which I was involved. The combination of fold equity and fear equity is a powerful asset in no-limit hold 'em tournaments.

FOLD EQUITY

When you bet or raise, there are two ways to win. Either you pick up the pot right there when your opponents fold or you can show down the best hand when all the cards are dealt.

When you call, you have no instant win. Calling throughout the hand gives you only one way to win—show down the best hand.

Folding, obviously, relinquishes all claims to the pot. Whatever equity you had in the pot is gone. You've surrendered.

In hold 'em few hands are locks before all the cards are out. Say you have K♣K♠ and the flop is K♦9♠5♣ rainbow. Your opponent holds 7♥6♥ and can win only if he hits his gutshot straight draw and you don't improve, or if the turn and river produce both a 3 and a 4. He's drawing pretty thin, but he'll still win 15% of the time if this hand goes to a showdown. This 15% is his equity in the pot. If you bet on the flop and he folds, he loses this equity.

Pot equity is the expected value of the pot when dealt to showdown, with no more betting. Fold equity is the forfeited pot equity.

Here's another example: You have AKo on A98 rainbow, and you're up against 76—top pair versus a straight draw. Your opponent has around 34% pot equity. If you bet enough on the flop, he can't profitably continue. He forfeits his 34% and your share increases from 66% to 100%.

It's frequently possible to get your opposition to fold a better hand. The equity picked up by getting your opponent to fold is substantial. After all, if the cards were just dealt out, in situations such as this you'd lose more than you'd win. But by getting your opponent to fold the better hand, you've converted negative equity into a positive return. Having fold equity on your side is a significant asset in NLHE tournaments. This is one of the main reasons why aggressive players win tournaments—they consistently have fold equity working for them.

Now don't get us wrong. We're not saying it's incorrect to fold often. In the example we gave of the gutshot versus the set on the flop, it would be sheer folly for the player with the gutshot to continue when faced with a reasonable bet of perhaps 50% of the pot or more, unless both players have very deep stacks and the implied odds justify a call. Folding is often the correct play. In fact, in certain situations, it's correct to fold very strong hands when you have a good read on the opposition and you're convinced that you're beat. But as a general principle, it's good to have fold equity on your side as much as possible, and this means betting and raising more and calling less.

We also believe, and it's a major premise of this book, that in NLHE tournaments, especially in live events, many players play too tightly and fold too frequently. This is especially true in the latter stages of an event, when players are often moving in pre-flop.

In general, the bigger the bet (or raise), the greater the fold equity. The caveat to this general rule, as discussed later in the text, is that all-in bets, in some contexts, may now be regarded with more suspicion than pot-sized or smaller bets. Once other players realize that you're willing to commit all of your chips at any time, you'll begin to develop another kind of equity—fear equity.

FEAR EQUITY

One of the positive spinoffs of making big bets with monsters, bluffs, and semi-bluffs is what we call "fear equity." Your opponents will become very aware of the fact that your style can put all of your chips (and often most or all of theirs) at risk at any time. This realization has a definite impact on the other players.

Good tournament players are constantly scanning the table for easy marks. The ideal target is the so-called "weak-tight" player. This type of player is easy to read, because his play is straightforward. If he bets, he usually has something; if he checks, he has nothing and is ready to fold to a bet. Since each player misses the flop more than two-thirds of the time with unpaired hole cards, more than two times out of three a strong player can take the pot away on the flop. If a weak player won't call a bet on the flop with less than top pair, he'll fold to a bet on the flop the vast majority of the time. This type of player also won't stand any pressure later in the hand when a scare card, such as a third flush card, falls on the turn or river and you make a convincing bet after he checks. He's also a prime target for blind stealing. Moreover, because these timid players will rarely play back at you (raise or re-raise), they don't pose much of a threat. You just keep hammering on them and grind them down.

On the other hand, a player who shows that he's willing to put it all in relatively early in a tournament can be a menace. Players like this aren't good targets to steal from, because they're fearless and aren't shy about re-raising, often all-in. These players aren't easy to pound into submission, any more than pounding on nitroglycerine is a good way not to blow yourself up. Volatile unpredictable players are anathema to tournament gurus, unless the expert has a big hand with which he can trap. The pro won't try to steal much, but he will use plays, such as reverse steals (raises from one of the steal positions with a strong hand) and traps, if possible. Generally though, the pro will avoid tangling with aggressive foes who can severely damage him.

Other players also tend to avoid mixing it up with a player perceived to be aggressive and fearless. Unless they have a big hand, they'll duck for cover. That sense of trepidation that big-bet players instill in their foes is fear equity. After seeing a big all-in move from an aggressive player, there's often that niggling sensation that in any contested pot, the next bet or raise might be for all the chips.

As Kim Lee points out, a critical recurring theme in NLHE is that the value of tournament chips is nonlinear. It's analogous to a game where you must cash your own chips at a diminishing pay scale. For example, one chip is worth $100, two chips are worth $190, three chips are worth $279, etc. In this case people are rationally risk-averse and very tight about calling large bets. When they become tight, you should become aggressive.

Fear equity is a powerful asset to have on your side. It will stop a chronic blind-stealer dead in his tracks and minimize steal attempts during the play of a hand as well. Used effectively, fear equity helps a player control and dominate a table. The more chips he accumulates, the bigger weapon his chips become and the greater the fear equity. It's very tough to be effective at no-limit poker when you're afraid of going broke and your opponent has clearly demonstrated that he's not. If you can instill an element of fear into your opponents in the process of building your stack, you're well on your way toward making the money.

Winning a Lot of Small Pots

Small-ball artists are constantly firing out small bets and raises, often with the added benefit of good position. Pre-flop, they almost always bring it in with a raise with both their strong and speculative hands. This gives them several ways to win a hand.

First, they can flop a big hand or a big draw. For example, if the flop comes T-6-5 and they started with 65 suited, their pre-flop raise followed by a bet on the flop may well be interpreted as a continuation bet with a couple of high cards. An aggressive opponent may raise to try to force a fold, setting up a big pot situation where the 2-pair is likely to be good.

Second, they can also miss the flop, but bet or raise opponents out of the pot. For example, when an ace flops, they can represent top-pair strong kicker, even though they may have totally missed with a hand such as 65 suited.

And third, they can partially hit the flop and play accordingly, often picking up a small pot. For instance, after raising pre-flop with 65 suited, they might check a flop such as 9-6-2, representing 2 high cards, but raise if their opponent bets, now representing an overpair. This creates confusion in the minds of their opponents, even though the amounts of the bets and raises are typically rather small in relation to the pot size. *Unpredictable players are generally feared.*

Picking up a lot of small pots is a very good way to accumulate chips. There are many pots, especially those contested by only two players, where no one hits the flop. A bet on the flop or turn often wins these orphaned pots and as we've discussed, these guys aren't shy about betting. Betting makes good sense. If they can make a bet of half the pot and get you to fold more than one time out of three (highly likely), they're getting the best of it.

What if you pick up on this and bet first? These players generally don't run for cover. They'll often call and wait to see what you do on the turn. Do you have the courage to fire a second barrel? If not and they sense weakness, they'll bet and pick up that pot. Even if you do muster the courage to bet the turn, if they pick up any sign of weakness, they're not afraid to raise. Also, they're not afraid to represent a hand if a scare card, such as a third flush card, hits on the turn. They've got lots of ways to pick up small pots, many of which they're not entitled to based on the value of their hand, continually adding to their stacks without putting themselves in any significant jeopardy.

To be effective at this style of play, you must have a good idea where you're at in a hand. What starting hands do each of your opponents play and how do they bet them? Can you pick up any tells? Can you work backwards through a hand and see how bets, calls, and raises triangulate with the board, helping you to work out your opponents' likely hands? If you're proficient at these skills, then small-ball plays are a great way to get chips while controlling risks.

Winning a Few Big Pots

Another effective way to get your hands on a pile of chips is to pick up a few big pots that you'd normally not be entitled to win. This style is riskier than small-pot poker, but can also be quite effective. You may have heard the poker adage, "Don't play a big pot without a big hand." While this is generally true, it doesn't encompass all situations. The big bluff is one of those exceptions.

To be effective, bluffing should be congruent with the way

you've played the hand. Here's a simple example.

With blinds at 50/100, you call a pre-flop raise to 300 from an early-position raiser off a stack of 10,000. You're on the button holding 9♠8♠ and have around 10,000 in chips. The flop is A♥9♣3♥. Your opponent bets 500 into a 750 pot. Although he may have missed the flop and is now making a continuation bet, there's also a good chance the ace hit him; you call. The turn is the six of hearts, putting three hearts on the board. Now he checks and you bet 1,000. If his initial bet was a continuation bet and he doesn't have an ace, he'll likely give you the pot right here.

But say he has a hand such as an ace with a good kicker (AK-AJ) and calls your 1,000 turn bet, the river is the 3♠, and he checks again. Now you move in! Notice that each bet you made fits perfectly with the hand you're representing, in this case a flush. You called a raise pre-flop, but didn't re-raise. You flat-called a substantial bet on the flop when an ace and two hearts hit; you bet about 60% of the pot when a third heart hit and your opponent checked, and you moved in on the river for around 8,500. This is an extremely difficult bet to call, unless your opponent happens to be an Internet maniac sicko. I can tell you this—unless I've got a dead read on the player, I'm not calling here, nor are most other pros.

Since your opponent is representing (and probably has) an ace, which can't be a heart because the ace of hearts is on the board, your 1,000 bet on the turn was smart. He could possibly have a high heart, such as the king or queen, and decide to call a big bet on the turn with top pair and the nut flush draw (or second nut flush draw) if you moved in. Keeping the turn bet to 60% of the pot helped build the pot and put you in position to move in on the river, unless a fourth heart hit. If a fourth heart came and he made the nut flush, you'd probably hear from him. If he checked, you might still move in. Without the king of hearts (or possibly the queen), it's a very tough call for him to make.

One of the key questions that the best aggressive players in the game ask themselves is: "If I move in, what are the chances of this particular player calling with his tournament life at stake with the hand he's most likely holding?" If the probability of inducing a fold is greater than the risk being taken, then the move is profitable.

For example, let's say that there's 100,000 in the pot and a player moves in for 200,000 on a bluff. He's effectively laying 2-to-1 odds that his opponent will fold. If his opponent will call less than a third of the time, this play has positive expected value (+EV). If it means the tournament is over if they call and lose, most players need a very strong hand to call. Often, they need the nuts (the best possible hand) or something close to it to take such a big risk. This occurs far less than one time in three, so the all-in bettor is usually rewarded for his courage.

There are several important elements in a bluff such as this. First, you must select the right target. Better players are good marks for bluffs. They hate guessing and, unless they have a strong read, will usually fold when there's a good chance that they're beaten. The players you don't want to bluff are those who fall in love with their hands and can't bear to part with them. As more and more Internet players find their way to live tournaments, we're seeing more "calling stations" enter the fray. Against players such as these, you can stow all your clever bluffs. The best approach is not to bluff, but to overplay your big hands, as we recommend for online tournament play. Don't be afraid to move in with the nuts against players who can't release a hand. This is the easiest and best way to accumulate chips against this immovable breed.

At the final table of the 2006 Aussie Millions main event, after about an hour's play, none of the seven finalists had been eliminated. Shannon Shorr, an aggressive young American player who subsequently had a fantastic year and with whom I'd played for only a short while the preceding day, raised from around back (near the button); I called from the big blind with pocket sixes. I had about 1,000,000 and he had about twice that. The flop came 3♥3♣8♥. I took the lead, betting around 70% of the pot; Shannon called. The turn was a black king. Now I checked and Shannon fired a chunky bet of 200,000. I studied Shannon and, convinced that the king missed him, I called. The river was a repeat 8. The board now read: 3♥3♣ 8♥K♠8♦.

I was pretty sure Shannon didn't have either an 8 or a king in his hand. I put him on a pair, perhaps sevens, nines, tens, or jacks, or possibly a busted flush draw. I didn't think he could call an all-in bet with a medium pair (and obviously wouldn't with a busted flush draw), so I pushed it all in for nearly 700,000. He had me covered. If I lost this hand, I was history.

Shannon literally jumped in his seat as though he'd suddenly been given an electric shock. He was visibly upset. Then he went into the tank, an agonized look fixed on his face. From the way he was reacting, I expected him to fold, but after what seemed an interminable time (but was actually only a minute or two), he called! Yikes! Great call. As I rolled over my sixes, I thought my tournament was over. Shannon stared motionless at my now-exposed hand, like a deer caught in the beam of headlights. What was he waiting for?

I was sure I was beat. What hand could he have to call a huge all-in bet on the river that didn't beat my pair of sixes? Still, he gripped his cards tightly in his hands. "You're not going to slow-roll me, are you"? I finally blurted out. Slowly, he shook his head and mucked!

Until I saw this hand on television, I didn't know what Shannon had. In actuality, all he had was ace high! His hand was A♠7♦. He must have thought I was on a bluff with a busted flush draw and his ace high was best. The moral is, if a player like Shannon Shorr is willing to commit a substantial portion of his stack with this weak a hand, this is definitely not a player you want to bluff!

You may be wondering why I didn't just check the river

with the intention of calling any bet. At the time, I thought I could get him off some hands that had me beat. As you now know, whenever possible I like to have fold equity on my side. However, had I known that there was no chance of him folding a medium pair, I'd have been better off checking with the intention of calling, giving Shannon the opportunity to bluff on the river, although he might just have checked it down, thinking his ace could be good. As it worked out, my bluff turned out to be an unexpected value bet!

Besides selecting appropriate players to bluff and making bets that fit the hand you're trying to represent, it's important to consider your chip stack, your opponent's chip stack, and the size of the pot. Bluffs are most successful when you have more chips than your opponent and can put him to a decision that risks elimination. Bluffing a player who can't be significantly wounded if he loses is a recipe for disaster.

The Threat of the Set

This is a term we first heard from Blair Rodman—the threat of the set. Although sets occur infrequently, they can be tournament busters. Especially early in a tournament, players are wary about running into a set. This concern can be exploited by using the semi-bluff in an unusual way.

Let's say you call a pre-flop raise to 600 in the early going, with 6♥5♥ in the cutoff. The blinds are 100/200, your opponent started the hand with 11,000, and you have 12,000. The flop comes down: K♥8♥3♣.

You now have a flush draw and some backdoor straight possibilities, making you about a 3/2 underdog to AK. Your opponent bets 900 and you decide to call. If he doesn't have a king, you might have the best hand (you're a favorite over hands such as AQo), you have position, and his bet may be a continuation bet. Some players might move in here, figuring that there's a reasonable chance their opponent may fold and they've still got almost a 40% chance of winning, if called. Although this line of reasoning has some merit, many players will now read this for exactly what it is—a semi-bluff with a flush draw—and will call with top-pair top-kicker (or less). For this reason, we think calling on the flop is a better play.

The turn is the 7♠, giving you a straight draw, in addition to your flush draw with only one card to come. Although your chance of winning has dropped from about 40% to 34% now, your fold equity, should you decide to semi-bluff, has gone up considerably. If your opponent bets again, consider a big raise. A raise on the turn looks much more like a set (or 2-pair) to your opponent than a drawing hand. The turn is where set-holders generally make their move, so this is a deceptive time to semi-bluff with your draws. An all-in raise in a spot like this will most often take down a good-sized pot.

Notice how difficult it is now for your opponent to put you on a draw. With the current board, a drawing hand seems far less likely than it did on the flop. When you do get called, you'll still "get lucky" 34% of the time. The combination of your fold equity and the chances of winning a showdown, if called, can make this a positive equity play.

If, instead of betting, your opponent checks the turn, you have the option of either betting or checking and taking the free card. Bet if you read him as weak, otherwise take the free card. If the free card is a blank, be careful about pushing on the river. Your check on the turn is often read as weakness (correct) and the chances of an all-in river bet by you getting called have escalated (as exemplified by the hand discussed previously with Shannon Shorr).

Here are a few guidelines *for bluffing*.

One, if a player has already committed half his chips or more to the pot, he'll often be hard to bluff. Some players will feel "committed" to the pot if they have 35% or more of their chips already in the pot. With half their chips committed and getting over 3/1 odds, most players will call.

Two, if a player has a big stack and the size of your bluff bet won't significantly injure him, it's usually best not to bluff. Bluffs are most effective when your opponent's tournament life is on the line.

Three, the best players to bluff are those with medium stacks whom you have covered. If they call a big bet and lose, they're out. It's very difficult for most players to commit in situations such as this without the nuts or close to it. Players with chip stacks about equal to yours, or those with slightly larger stacks who would be crippled if they lost the pot, are also ideal candidates to bluff. Be sure that you have sufficient chips to make an imposing wager when you bluff. This requires thinking the hand through in advance and allocating chips for each betting round, so your bluff will be sufficiently threatening.

And four, although many players love to show bluffs, either for ego gratification or to put opponents on tilt, it's rarely a good idea.

Look at this hand sequence from the 2006 WSOP Main Event.

Having played down to just a few tables remaining, Jeff Lisandro, a strong pro, and Prahlad Friedman, a well-known Internet gun, were at the same table. Internet players might know Prahlad by his screen names of Mahatma and Spirit Rock. A dispute arose where Prahlad accused Jeff of not anteing; he wouldn't let it go, bringing it up on several occasions and finally saying, "Sir, I don't trust you." Finally, Jeff lost it and exploded in anger (the camera later showed that Jeff had indeed anteed and that Prahlad was off base). The tournament director told Jeff to play and the game was on!

A hand came up where Lisandro raised before the flop to 140,000 and Friedman called. The flop was: A♠K♣J♦.

Friedman checked, Lisandro bet 200,000, and Friedman folded. Lisandro showed Friedman his hand: 4♣4♥, a bluff. Jeff is a superb player in both tournaments and cash games and I'm confident that Prahlad's accusation was his reason for showing the bluff, but as you'll see, this may have been a costly mistake.

The very next hand, Jeff raised again to 140,000 from the cutoff and Friedman re-raised to 350,000. Lisandro called. The flop was: A♣J♣8♣.

Friedman now bet 500,000 and Lisandro folded. This time Prahlad showed Jeff his hand: 9♠2♦! Prahlad quipped, "Now we're playing poker!"

A while later, Lisandro limped for 50,000 and Friedman checked his option from the big blind.

The flop: K♠Q♣8♥.

Friedman checked, Lisandro bet 100,000, and Friedman called; the 7♥ on the turn was met with checks by both players. The J♣ on the river prompted Friedman to bet 225,000; after Lisandro folded, Friedman flashed his cards as he raked the pot: 6♥3♦.

In my view, it's generally imprudent to rub a good player's nose in a successful bluff. You might create a monster. Let sleeping dogs lie.

BET SIZING OF BLUFFS AND MONSTERS

Two interesting theories on bet sizing for big hands and bluffs abound in poker circles. One is to make small-value bets and small-bet bluffs, in classic small-ball fashion. Since the bet size is indistinguishable between bluffs and monsters, an opponent can't get a good read.

The second theory is to make big bets (often all-in) with both the nuts, or close to it, and with bluffs. Again, the bet size gives no clue as to hand value. Which is better?

Let's consider different strategies for a poker game that represents a common drawing situation. If a flush or straight draw gets completed, then it will probably win more than the current pot; it will also win future bets. These additional bets are called "implied odds." In addition to pot odds and implied odds, a drawing hand may also be able to win with a bluff. The equilibrium strategy combines sincere bets with bluffs to maximize the implied odds for the drawing hand.

In order to get these implied odds, it is essential that your opponent cannot tell whether or not you make your hand. This always happens in seven-card stud, because the final card is hidden. But it also happens in hold 'em with scare cards. In some cases you might be drawing to either end of a straight and your opponent can't tell which end. For example, on a board of A-T-9-2 rainbow, you might plausibly be drawing to a straight with QJ or with 87. In this case your opponent fears any Q, J, 8, or 7 on the river. Even if you missed your draw, you can bluff and represent a hand if any of these cards hits. Other boards combine straight and flush draws (see Mark Vos' example in the final chapter), such as A♠T♣9♥2♥. On this board you might be able to bluff with any spade, any heart, or any Q, J, 8, or 7 on the river. In contrast you won't be getting implied odds from a flush if your opponent can read it.

In this example it's common knowledge that your opponent is leading with one card to come. At the end of the round the pot is $100 and you have probability "p" of making your hand. I'll consider three strategies:

Strategy one: Suppose you bet $10 when you make your hand and your opponent always calls. Yippee, you win $110. For example, if p = 10%, then your expected win is $11. That's $10 pot equity, plus $1 from implied odds.

Strategy two: Consider instead a pot-sized bet when you make your hand, plus a few bluffs. You're getting even money on a steal, so your opponent must call half the time. Your opponent is getting 2-to-1 on his calls, so you should bluff p/2 = 5% of the time. In other words, you bluff half as often as you get a real hand. (Note that in flop games you should usually bluff only when a scare card hits.) Anyway, you break even on bluffs and your opponent breaks even on calls (this is a general equilibrium condition). On your good hands you win $100 half the time when you don't get action and you win $200 the other half. So you win $150 on average. In other words, your implied odds increase your expectation by 50%. This concept appears in *Pot-Limit and No-Limit Poker* by Stewart Reuben and Bob Ciaffone (1999).

Strategy three: Now suppose you move all in when you hit your hand. If your remaining effective stack is S, then your opponent needs to call 100/(100+S) of the time. For example, if S = 900, then your opponent must call 10% of the time to keep you honest and snap off bluffs. You'll bluff often enough to make him break even on calls. On your real hands you will take the uncontested $100 pot S/(S+100) = 90% of the time. But you'll win $100+S when you get called 100/(S+100) = 10%. So your EV is 100*S/(S+100) + (100+S)*100/(S+100) = 100*90%+1000*10% = $190. Asymptotically, as your stack is large this approaches $200. In other words, large stacks get implied odds that almost double their pot equity.

Comparing the three strategies, we see that the big-bet strategy extracts the most EV in implied odds. Note that it rarely gets called. But when it does, it wins a bunch. This resembles the situation of promotional casino match-play chips. You lose half their value when you bet on even-money wagers, because you lose the chip when you win. But if you bet them at high wagers on craps or roulette then you get most of their value. In both cases the big risky bet gets the most EV.

Here's a good application. Suppose your p = 24%, the pot is $100, and remaining stacks are $1,200. How much can you call? Well, the implied odds double your effective probability to almost 48%. And when you call, you retain equity in your bet. Surprisingly, you can call $200. This builds the pot to $500 with $1,000 stacks left. You're getting 2-to-1 on your bluffs, so your opponent must call you one-third of the time. This means if you make your hand, you'll move in and get action a third of the time, winning $1,500. You'll also win an uncontested $500 two-thirds of the time. Also, you'll bluff often enough on scare cards so that your opponent breaks even on his calls[1]. Your EV is 24% x 1/3 x 1500 + 24% x 2/3 x 500 = $200. So you break even by calling a $200 double pot bet, even as a large dog. Conversely, the leader must bet more than $200 to shut you out. The poker literature discusses betting two-thirds of the pot or the pot, but doesn't emphasize shutting your opponents out.

Phil Ivey utilizes the big bet with monsters/big bet with bluffs strategy *par excellence*. In a hand we'll discuss later in the book, Ivey was eliminated from the 2006 Aussie Millions Main Event when he was caught bluffing on an all-in river bet against Jamil Dia. After seeing that bluff, Jerry Fitt, an Australian player seated at the same table who had previously folded 9s full to Ivey's river all-in bet in a big pot with the board showing K-K-9-5-9, said, "I guess I should have called before." Sorry, Jer. In that hand Ivey had quad kings!

Optimal Bet/Bluff Sizing

An interesting counterintuitive trend has developed recently in tournament poker. All-in bets have become suspicious. They're frequently suspected of being bluffs. This is especially true among pros, where smaller than all-in bets often get more respect than pushing.

Why? The pro reasons that the smaller bet is more likely to be a "suck bet" than a bluff and acts accordingly. This type of reasoning is also starting to spread online where some players are now calling all-ins with a variety of marginal hands. Perhaps in part due to *Kill Phil* and a growing tendency for online

---

[1] In this example your opponent is getting 3:2 on his calls, so you should be bluffing 40% of the time when you bet. In other words 60% of the time you have a real hand and 40% of the time you are bluffing. This means you should bluff 16% of the time and bet your real hands 24% of the time, for a total of betting 40% of the time.

players to push more frequently in order to get fold equity on their side, the strongest bet you can make (all-in) may now be getting called more frequently than weaker bets.

Here's an example from the 2006 WSOP $2,000-buy-in NLHE event that illustrates this important point.

Nam Le, a great player and one of the hottest players on the tour in 2006, got heads-up with young Australian superstar Mark Vos. I know Mark quite well, having played with him in a number of tournaments in Australia, including the 2006 Aussie Millions Main Event. He also finished second to me in the Grosvenor's World Masters 1,000-British-pound-buy-in event in London. Mark is also a highly successful online short-handed cash-game player and has contributed a chapter in this book on this important aspect of poker. This kid can flat-out play!

They battled back and forth, then Vos took the lead, when this hand came up.

Vos raised to 90,000 from the button, and Le called with 6♣6♦. The flop was: Q♠8♠3♥.

Le checked, Vos bet 150,000, and Le called. Turn: 2♦; Le checked, Vos bet 250,000, and Le, once again, made the call. The river was the Q♦. Le checked again and Vos moved in. Le thought for quite a while, then called. Vos showed Q♣T♣ for trip queens and the tournament was over.

In the post-tournament wrap-up on the cardplayer.com Web site, referring to the last hand Le said that had Vos just bet again, he would have folded, but when he moved in, he called, thinking that Mark was bluffing.

Many top pros think this way. Freddy Deeb laid down a solid hand when Daniel Negreanu made a well-calculated, but less than pot-sized, raise on the river when they were heads-up at the Plaza Ultimate Poker Challenge in 2005. On TV Deeb commented, "Why such a small raise, Daniel?" before mucking his winning hand. Negreanu was bluffing.

Negreanu and Deeb locked horns again in season one of

"High Stakes Poker." Although now playing in a big cash game rather than a tournament, a similar situation arose. Pre-flop three players—Johnny Chan, Negreanu, and Deeb—got involved in a pot. The starting hands were: Chan ATo; Negreanu A♠7♦, Deeb T♦8♦. The flop was Q♠9♣6♦.

Chan, first to act, checked, as did Negreanu and Deeb.

Turn: T♠

Chan checked again, Daniel bet $8,000, Deeb called, and Chan, after a bet and a call, thought his tens were beaten and folded.

River: 5♠

Negreanu thought for a bit, then massively overbet the pot, betting $50,000! Daniel, holding the ace of spades, was representing the nut flush. Deeb now pondered. Did Daniel really make a back-door flush or was he bluffing? Deeb thought long and hard. Finally he asked, "Why so much, man? I've only got second pair and I'm thinking about calling." After a bit more agonizing, Deeb finally mustered up the courage to call.

After the hand, in response to a comment from Negreanu that the reason Freddy called was because he'd been bluffed already on several occasions, Deeb defended himself: "The way the hand came down and the amount you bet made me call … You bet $15,000 and I fold."

There are many more examples we could give of similar thinking. Is there a way to take advantage of this trend? We believe there is.

You can use the all-in bet for your monster hands, while making about pot-sized bets when bluffing. Although you might be able to get away with even smaller bets as bluffs, in some instances you'll be giving your opponents very good pot odds to call and some players won't be able to resist. A pot-sized bet gives your opponent only 2-to-1 odds, so unless they think you'll bluff over a third of the time (unlikely from their perspective), they'll be getting the wrong price to try to pick off a bluff. Notice that you'll still be making big bets with your bluffs and monsters, just that your bets with your big hands will be more than your big bets with bluffs.

A nice side benefit of this approach is that when your bluffs do get called, you won't be eliminated from the tournament in most cases. Naturally, if opponents start to pick up on this pattern, it will lose its effectiveness. For this reason it's best to mix it up a bit by occasionally making a pot-sized bet with a monster and moving in with a bluff. A good time to change it up is after a hand or two have been shown down in which you used this tactic.

The Scandinavian Mini-Raise Bluff

It will come as no secret to regulars on the international poker circuit that Scandinavia now seems to be cloning excellent young no-limit hold 'em players. Apparently, groups of players in these countries share information and collectively analyze situations, developing new tournament strategies. One particularly effective strategy that has evolved from this northern poker brain trust is the novel use of mini-raises in order to accumulate chips.

A mini-raise is a raise equal in size to the previous bet. Since it gives an opponent very good odds to call, it often represents a very strong hand. Because of its small size, it virtually begs for a call. The clear message is, "I've got a monster hand and I'm trying to get more money in the pot, so I'm choosing a minimal amount to raise to get a few more chips into a pot that I'll almost surely win." Some players use mini-raises, for example, if they've flopped a set, a straight, or the nut flush and an opponent bets into them. They're trying to build the pot without scaring off an opponent who's usually drawing pretty slim.

Chewing on all this, a clever strategy to accumulate chips evolved. Faced with an early-position pre-flop raise, some aggressive young players will call with a variety of hands when on or near the button. If the flop comes down with coordinated cards, especially if there's no ace or king, and the pre-flop raiser bets, as he most often will, he now gets mini-raised. If the original raiser has nothing and was just making a continuation bet, he'll often give up at this stage. If he decides to continue and checks the turn, the mini-raiser now moves in!

The young Turks using this move can have a range of hands. They can have anything from a strong made hand to a semi-bluff or even air (a bluff with almost no chance of winning if called).

Say you raise from UTG with pocket queens, get called by a loose aggressive player on the button, and the flop comes T♠9♠6♦. You bet 80% of the pot and get mini-raised the same amount. The mini-raiser will make this play with a set, 2-pair, a straight, a flush draw, a pair and a gutshot, or nothing at all. What do you do?

If you're either short-stacked or pot-committed, you'll probably move in. If you're both deep stacked, though, this mini-raise presents a problem. If you continue, there's an excellent chance you'll be playing for all your chips.

What most players do in situations such as this is to call the mini-raise and re-evaluate on the turn. However, unless you hit a third queen on the turn, you'll probably find it hard to bet again. The mini-raise freezes you into checking. Now, after due thought, the mini-raiser pushes.

There are lots of hands that beat you. Do you really want to risk your tournament on this hand? He represented extreme strength on the flop with his mini-raise and followed through with an all-in bet on the turn, and you're left with nothing but guesswork. This play is very strong, especially against good players who are loathe to risk their tournament on one pair, especially after this betting sequence.

How do you defend against this? You have to make a decision on the flop and, most importantly, be willing to go broke. If the player is Scandinavian and under 25, a pro friend of mine

says he leans toward pushing on the flop after the mini-raise, if
he has an overpair. If the mini-raiser is from the U.K. and 40
years old, it's a clear pass!

While this was said with a smile, there's a lot of wisdom in
this approach. Against young LAGs, knowing their range of
hands, sometimes you just have to make a stand. Lacking other
information, age and country of origin are as good a determi-
nant as any.

The Blocking Bet

A blocking bet is a small bet designed to prevent an opponent from making a larger bet. Although it can be made on any
street from the flop onward, it's most often used on the river
when the pot is already large.

Say you have a hand such as top-pair top-kicker against
one opponent, a possible flush card comes on the river, and
you must act first. If you check, your opponent can put you
to a tough decision by making a pot-sized bet or greater. He
might have made his flush or he might be bluffing, but if you
bet something like 35%-40% of the pot, it could prevent him
from making a larger bet. If he's made a flush that's not the nut
flush, he may now be afraid to raise for fear of being beaten
and your bet may also keep him from bluffing for fear of being
called. Blocking bets can freeze your opposition, saving you
valuable chips.

The problem with blocking bets is that if opponents notice
you make small bets with marginal hands and big bets with
strong hands, they'll start raising when you make small bets
and folding when you make large bets. If you use blocking bets
frequently, you'll need to mix in some bets with your big hands
that appear to be blocking bets.

For example, when a flush card hits on the river and you
make the nut flush after having led at the pot on each round,
consider making a bet that looks like a blocking bet. An ag-

gressive foe may have noticed your prior freeze bets and decide that it's time to test you with an all-in raise. Bad timing!

For a more complete discussion of blocking bets and the math behind them, see *No-Limit Hold'em—Theory and Practice* by Sklansky and Miller, pages 135-142.

Making Big Laydowns

A corollary to accumulating chips is not losing them in situations where you're likely beaten, even when you have a big hand. There are times when circumstances warrant laying down kings pre-flop.

David Chiu's classic laydown to super-tight Louis Asmo's all-in 3-bet at the original Tournament of Champions and Mike Matusow's and Phil Gordon's pre-flop fold of pocket queens and kings respectively to Phil Hellmuth's all-in 3-bet at a WSOP final table are classic examples of big folds. In both cases, Asmo and Hellmuth had pocket aces.

Making laydowns such as these are highly dependent on the situation. In the first instance, Chiu was certain that the only hand Asmo could have to move in with at the final table over a raise and his re-raise was pocket aces. He was so sure that he turned his kings face up when folding. Similarly, Matusow and Gordon were aware of how badly Hellmuth wanted to win that WSOP event and correctly reasoned that aces were the only hand Hellmuth could have, given that betting sequence.

Great players make great situational reads that often baffle others. There's probably no one better at this chip-saving art than Phil Ivey. Ivey is considered by many pros to be the best in the business. In the 2005 Monte Carlo Millions, they were down to two tables of seven each and Ivey, with about 450,000, was the chip leader. With blinds and antes of 2000/4000/500, this hand came up.

Victor Ramdin, a good player who's been doing well in recent tournaments and is a member of Team Poker Stars, raised to 12,000 from middle position off a stack of around 150,000. Ivey, on the button holding 63 suited, called. When he has position, Ivey calls a lot of raises, knowing that he can often outplay his opponent later in the hand. The pot size was now 33,500. The flop came down: 3-4-5 rainbow.

This was a very good flop for Ivey, giving him a pair and an open-ended straight draw. Ramdin checked and Ivey bet 20,000; Ramdin called. The turn was a jack and both players checked. The river was a 6, giving Ivey 2-pair, but putting four cards to an open-ended straight on the board. Now Ramdin bet 35,000, just under half the pot. Ivey deliberated for a while, then folded! Ramdin's hand was 7-7. As Ivey correctly deduced, Ramdin did, indeed, have the straight. Ivey told Ramdin that he folded 2-pair, to which Ramdin responded, "That's why you're the best."

In this instance Ivey correctly reasoned that there was no way Ramdin would bet 35,000 in this situation without having the straight. This money saved is equivalent to *winning* 35,000 and helped Ivey maintain his big chip advantage. Ivey went on to win this event and its $1,000,000 first prize.

To make big laydowns, you need to have a good understanding of your opponent's style and tendencies. At the 100/200 blind level at the main event of a big tournament in London, I raised to 600 pre-flop from middle position with A♦T♦ and was called by Simon "Aces" Trumper in the big blind. I'd played with Simon a couple of times before and knew that he was a solid player who's capable of making big folds. A bit earlier, I saw him lay down AK on a flop of K-7-2 when he was raised on the turn, after betting both the flop and the turn. Sure enough, his opponent showed him a set of deuces.

After Simon called my 600 pre-flop raise, the pot was 1,300. The flop came down: K♠J♦4♣.

This is a scary flop. Players should be aware that there's an increased probability of opponents flopping 2-pair or a straight draw on coordinated flops (two cards in sequence, or with one gap) or flops containing two high cards.

Simon checked and I bet 700; he called. At this point I was sure Simon had at least either a king or jack in his hand (or both) and I was prepared to check the turn when a beautiful queen hit the board, giving me the top (Broadway) straight. Simon checked and I fired in a pot-sized 2,700 bet. Simon called again. A repeat queen came on the river. The board now read: K-J-4-Q-Q with no possible flushes. The pot was now 8,100. Simon pondered a bit, then bet 5,000.

I went into about a two-minute dwell-up. For Simon to call my pot-sized turn bet would have required him to have at least 2 pair, I reasoned. His most likely hands, given the action to this point, were KQ or QJ, although a set was also possible. The queen on the river followed by his well-calculated 5,000 bet screamed of a full house. In fact, the more I thought the hand through, the surer I become that Simon had me beat.

Finally, I turned my hand face up and said, "You've got me beat; show me your full house." Sheepishly, Simon showed me KQ and asked, "Would you have called twenty-five hundred?" I just laughed. Knowing the player and correctly interpreting bets and calls made this play possible. It's probably not a play I'd have been able to make without having had a line on Simon's play.

It's interesting to ponder what I'd have done had Simon moved in or made a smaller bet. In both instances, I'd have been less certain about his hand than I was from the way he played it. The all-in could be a big bluff representing a made full house, while the smaller bet might have been interpreted as a blocking bet. In both instances, I'd have been more likely to call.

Summary

Accumulating chips early in tournaments is an art form. Some of the key factors are:

• When the blinds are low, play speculative hands trying to flop a big hand. I don't mind calling standard-sized raises of 2.5 to 4 times the big blind with hands such as small pairs or suited connectors, or limping behind several limpers with unsuited connectors. I'll call a raise up to 8% of my stack or a touch more. The better my position, the more of my stack I'll put at risk, but I generally won't exceed 10%. I'll also make small raises in early position with both speculative and big hands. This helps provide deception.

• One way to accumulate chips is to pick up a lot of small pots to which you're not entitled. Making frequent small bets, raises, and check-raises is an effective early tactic.

• If your game isn't suited to picking up small pots with the worst hand, chips can be accumulated by picking up a few big pots. This can be accomplished by a combination of well-timed big bluffs and by betting big with your big hands and getting paid off. In order to be effective, bluffs need to be congruent with the betting action and the board on each street.

• Chips saved are the same as chips won. Folding good hands when circumstances warrant helps preserve chips that have been accumulated.

2

SPECIFIC GUIDELINES FOR ACCUMULATING CHIPS

We've discussed several ways that winning tournament players accumulate chips. Now let's look at some practical pointers that you can add to your game.

Pointer 1—When First In, Bring It In With a Raise

I'll usually bring speculative hands in for 2-2.5 times the big blind from early position if I'm first in, 3 times the big blind in middle position, and 3-4 times in late position, just as I do with my big hands, although I'll occasionally limp with them if I'm under the gun or second to act (see below). Bringing it in for a raise with hands such as these allows me to represent AK when an ace or a king flops, while disguising the strength of my hand when I hit the flop. In today's game, many players put you on two high cards when you raise pre-flop, especially when you raise from early position. They're looking for small cards to flop to take the pot away from you. When a big card flops and you bet, they're usually done with the hand, but when small cards flop and you make what appears to be a continuation bet (around a half to two-thirds of the pot), they may put in a big raise.

If you raise with 6♥5♥, for example, and the flop comes something like T♣6♦5♠, a half-pot bet will often be misread and your opponent may raise. You can now win a nice pot either by immediately re-raising or check-raising the turn. If the board is connected or has two to a suit, I lean toward a big re-raise on the flop—pot-sized or perhaps all-in. On an unconnected flop against an aggressive player who's likely to bet again on the turn, I'd be more inclined to just call his raise on the flop and look to check, then make a big move after he bets the turn.

The reason I'll sometimes limp with pairs and suited connectors when first or second to act is that limping up front makes a lot of players nervous. This play is often made with aces (or kings) and many players are loath to raise, due to fear of being re-raised off their hand. Hands such as medium pairs are often content to just limp along and see the flop under these circumstances, rather than raise. Your limp will often attract multiple limpers, giving you great pot odds for your speculative hands. Also, if you hit the flop big, such as flopping a set, someone is probably going to like his hand well enough to play with you.

How often would I raise versus limping when playing speculative hands upfront? About 85% raise, 15% call.

My usual raise from early position is about 2-2.5 times the big blind, with no ante and with an ante, respectively. About 85% the time I'll make this raise with both speculative hands and big pairs, while limping in the other 15%. The more aggressive the table, the more I'm likely to limp with big pairs, especially if they've seen me limp a couple of times with speculative holdings. I'll also raise to 2-2.5 times the big blind from up front with hands such as AJs, AQ, and AK, as well as with big pairs. Mixing it up this way, observant players can't be confident about the strength of my hand.

Chen and Ankenman, in their book *The Mathematics of Poker*, present a solid math-based case for bringing it in with a raise, using smaller raises upfront and bigger raises as the action progresses around the table. This policy gives the big blind a difficult decision. The early raises generally indicate a stronger hand than the latter ones, so even though an upfront raise is small, the blinds are often up against a strong hand. Larger raises from near the button may represent weaker hands than upfront raises, but give the blinds worse odds to call. Of course, the tighter the blinds, the less the amount you need to raise. Pros probe for a minimum raise threshold, risking the minimum required to induce a fold. In some situations, this may be as little as 2-2.5 times the big blind, even from late position.

I'll usually raise with speculative hands only when I'm first in. If another player has raised, I'll call; if there's already been a limp or two, I'll limp along. I'm looking to flop 2-pair or better or a big draw. If I flop only one pair, I'll proceed cautiously. I don't want to get busy in a pot with only one pair and a weak kicker, even if it's top pair. This doesn't mean I won't bet it—I will—but if my bet gets called, I'm likely to slow down and keep the pot small by checking the turn, unless I improve further. This also provides the opportunity to pick off a river bluff, should my opponent decide to get frisky.

In deciding whether or not to call a raise when we have a speculative hand, we use the Rule of 5 and 10[2]. If it costs us 5% of our stack or less, we call; if it costs 10% of our stack or more, we fold. In between is a judgment call, depending on how facile you are at post-flop play, your position, and the quality of your hand. Lee almost invariably calls up to 8% of his stack, if he's near the button.

Notice that the bigger your stack relative to the blinds, the more likely you are to fall within the Rule of 5 and 10. This flexibility often allows the better new-school players to keep accumulating chips right up to the final table. Also notice, however,

---

[2] First suggested in *Pot-Limit & No-Limit Poker*, Stewart Ruben and Bob Ciaffone, page 65.

that when you have more chips than a target opponent, it's the size of *his* stack that this rule applies to. No matter how many chips you have, you can't win more than your opponent's stack, so implied odds applies only to the lesser of the two stacks.

If more than 10% of your stack is at risk if you call an early-position raise, this doesn't necessarily mean that you should fold. It just means that calling isn't your best option. Moving in or folding then become your optimal choices.

Pointer 2—Using Position

In big-bet poker, the importance of position can't be over-emphasized. When I'm on or near the button, my range of playable hands early in a tournament expands. I'll limp or call small raises with unsuited connectors and 1-gap suited connectors. If there have been several limpers, I'll limp and take a flop *in position* with hands such as T8 offsuit and the like. When the flop comes J-9-7 or 7-T-8, it will be difficult for my opponent to put me on the hand I'm holding and I can win a big pot. This is especially effective against opponents who limp with aces. I've had a number of tournament situations where I've doubled up with hands such as this when an opponent who has slow-played aces decides to make people "pay" for their draws by moving in on the flop. Then they run off and tell their friends how unlucky they were to have gotten busted with pocket aces! As discussed next, position also allows you to pick up more "orphaned" pots.

Pointer 3—Picking Up Orphaned Pots

In no-limit hold 'em, a lot of flops either miss everyone or give someone a marginal hand that can't stand much pressure. In a 3- or 4-handed unraised pot, if it's checked to you on the button and the flop is something like J♠5♣3♦, you should bet about two-thirds of the pot. Most players would've bet if they had a jack, so you'll usually pick up the pot on the flop. This applies to any rainbow flop with one high card and two small cards. If a player check-raises, you fold unless you have a solid hand. Sure, you might be the target of a check-raise bluff or semi-bluff from a player with a hand such as 6♠5♠, but if you pick up similar pots more than 40% of the time (and you will), you're ahead of the game.

Similarly, if you check a flop from early position and it's checked around, you should consider betting the turn, especially if a seemingly inconsequential card hits. All the players have acted as if they have nothing, so give them credit for having nothing and bet! You'll be amazed how often they'll all fold. This play is most effective when you're first to act. This is the most likely position from which to have slow-played a big hand. Betting out on the turn confirms this suspicion, even though you have nothing, and is often an effective way to adopt an orphaned pot. Force yourself to bet if the other players seem reluctant.

Pointer 4—Identify the Tight Timid Players

Be observant. As previously discussed, try to identify straightforward players who can be manipulated.

Pointer 5—Don't Get Busted with Aces Post-Flop in an Unraised Pot

This is one of the biggest and most frequent mistakes I see players make, especially online. They limp with aces (or sometimes kings, queens, or even jacks!), get called in several spots, and all the money goes in on the flop or turn. Much to their chagrin, they discover that they're up against two pair, a set, or a made straight. I see this time and time again.

As Doyle Brunson so aptly put it in *SuperSystem*, "Aces are going to win a small pot or lose a large one."

I try not to play a big pot with aces early in a tournament, unless I can get it all-in pre-flop. If I raise with aces and get re-raised, I'm likely to stick in half my chips right there, especially online. No matter what flops, I'll push the rest of my stack. Online, I'll often get re-raised all-in pre-flop by AK or a pair of tens or higher. If I get busted, and it *does* happen, good luck to them.

If I happen to have limped with aces, though, and no one raised, I'll proceed very gingerly on the flop. I'll probably bet two-thirds of the pot, but if called, check-call on the turn and again on the river. If another player makes a big move, I'll give that pot up. Bottom line—with aces in an unraised pot, I'm looking to play a small pot, not a big one. Even in a raised pot pre-flop, if I encounter resistance post-flop, I'll try to play a small pot, not a big one.

Keep in mind, I'm talking about early in the tournament, when a lot of speculative hands are getting the right implied odds to call standard pre-flop raises and are looking to bust a player who can't release a big pair. That's how I play and believe me, I'm not the lone ranger. Don't get trapped for all your chips!

Pointer 6—Play Medium Pairs Similar to Small Pairs

In the early going, medium pairs (77-JJ) should often be played like small pairs. In a raised pot, consider calling rather than re-raising with hands as strong as JJ. Remember, in the early stages your goal is to win some big pots. Flopping a very well-disguised set of tens or jacks is a good way to accomplish this. If three undercards flop, an overpair should be played similar to AA. Bet the flop, then slow down, trying to keep the pot small if you meet resistance and perhaps pick off a bluff later in the hand.

Pointer 7—Don't Over-Think a Weak Bet

Weak bets relative to the pot size generally mean weak hands. This is especially true in online tournaments. Consider raising. For example, with 25/50 blinds, a player raises to 150 pre-flop, you call with pocket fives, and everyone else folds. The pot size is now 375; the flop comes: Q♣8♥2♠.

Now your opponent bets 100. This usually means he's missed the flop and doesn't want to show weakness by checking his AK, but also doesn't want to risk as much as 200 by making a "normal" continuation bet. He bets 100, hoping that you'll fold or that he'll get a cheap look at the turn and, hopefully, catch an ace or king. If you raise on the flop, calling the 100 and raising around 300, there's no way most players will call without top pair or better.

Although it's true that occasionally you'll run into a big hand (such as AQ or a set of queens or eights, in the above example), the vast majority of the time you'll take down the pot on the flop. Your opponent will usually read you as having at least a queen and muck. You're risking 400 to pick up a 475 pot and you'll do so successfully far more than half the time. Stay aggressive with plays such as this, whenever you smell weakness.

Pointer 8—Don't Be Afraid to Commit All Your Chips Early if the Situation Warrants

There will be occasions during tournaments where your best play is to move in fairly early in an event. An obvious one is with pocket aces pre-flop in a raised and re-raised pot, but there are post-flop situations where you know you're either definitely or most probably a favorite, but not a lock, at the time all the money goes in. A typical situation would be when you flop a set against the nut flush draw with two overcards.

Say you raise pre-flop with 99 and get called. The flop is

J♠9♠8♦, giving you middle set. You bet your standard two-thirds-pot flop bet and get raised. Although a made straight or top set are possible, you're a favorite over the range of hands that your opponent is likely to hold. Hands such as A♠Q♠, A♠K♠, A♠T♠, JT, AA, KK, QQ, and 88 are all hands many players would raise with on the flop. I don't get cute in spots such as this—I move in! If he's drawing, as most often he will be, I want to tax him to the max. If I'm already beaten by top set or a made straight, all the money's going in anyway, and if he's got a straight, I still have 7 outs on the turn and 10 outs on the river.

Keep in mind that if he calls with a draw, my hand isn't a lock. I'm the favorite, but he's got outs. You've got to be willing to take calculated risks such as this if you want to win big events.

Also, an early all-in move creates fear equity. Other opponents will notice that you're aggressive and not afraid to commit your whole stack at any time. Knowing this, they're likely to give you a wide berth—viva la fear equity!

Pointer 9—Make Adjustments for Online Play

As a general rule, online play is looser than live tournament play, especially in the early going. This requires some adjustments. First and most importantly, you should tend to *over-bet your big hands and bluff less frequently*. Online players will call big bets, even (perhaps especially) all-in bets, which they often view as steal attempts.

I consistently see online players make calls with some very mediocre holdings. This means big bets with your big hands will get paid off more often than in brick-and-mortar establishments. It means that you'll get caught bluffing more frequently as well.

KEY POINT: In online MTT tournament play, overbet your big hands (both pre and post-flop) and bluff less frequently than in live contests.

Pre-flop, online players will raise and call raises and re-raises with a wide range of hands. In a live event, if there's a raise and a re-raise, unless I know the players very well, I'm likely to fold pocket jacks pre-flop and flat call with queens.

Not so online. Given the same betting sequence, I'll call with jacks and move in with queens. It wouldn't surprise me to get called by both opponents and to have them show down something like 77 and AQ suited.

Interestingly, when Internet players play live, often because they've won a satellite entry to a live tournament, they tend to tighten up.

It seems to me that there are a number of reasons for this. There's more investment involved in live tournaments. Not only are the buy-ins generally bigger in live events, but players have a considerable investment in both time and money just to get to many of them. Major live televised events are spread across the globe and players travel many hours to get to them. Once there and playing, they don't want to get knocked out, so they tend to tighten up. Live events, especially those that are televised, are fun. People are watching, cameras are whirring, and no one wants to be left out.

Furthermore, no one wants to be scrutinized for making a donkey-like play, especially in front of millions of people on TV. I refer to it as "the embarrassment factor." The anonymity of the Internet is a breeding ground for impulsive decision-making. It's so easy for players to push the call button or ramp up the bet meter to all-in, while playing naked in the comfort of their bedroom, without anyone knowing who they are. When they make a bonehead play that knocks them out, they don't have to face the discomfort of slinking out of a cardroom (the walk of shame), while the whole table stares at them with mixed looks of pity and disgust. Simply put, it's a hell of a lot easier to play badly online, since the element of social pressure inherent in live events is lacking.

Another factor favoring looser play online is the fact that it's easy to find another tournament to jump into. Players may even be multi-tabling, playing several tournaments simultaneously. If they get knocked out of one, it's no biggie—they're still alive in several others.

When I play online, I loosen up my standards. For example, let's say we're about midway through the big Sunday online tournament at PokerStars.com with blinds and antes of 100/200/25 and I've got 6,000 in chips in the small blind. A guy from mid-position makes it 600 to go off a stack of 4,000 and the next player, with a stack of 3,000, moves in and it's passed around to me.

Now, in live play, I'll muck pocket jacks in most cases, unless I have a good read on my adversaries. Queens would be a pivotal hand and I might move in with them or fold them, depending on other information; I'd move in with kings or aces and fold AK.

That's what I'd do live. Online, my pivot point drops to tens. After a raise and a re-raise, I'm calling with jacks and higher and I'll think about calling with tens or AK, depending on the circumstances. If there's been a third raise before the action gets to me, my fulcrum would move up to queens, sometimes calling, sometimes mucking. Online, it usually takes a 3-bet, before the action gets to me, to get me off jacks.

Online, players raise and re-raise with all sorts of garbage. With pocket jacks, you'll often be looking at one hand that has an underpair (such as 77, 88, or 99), while the other hand is AK, AQ, or even AJ or AT! Pocket jacks wins this type of match-up about 42% of the time and you're getting better than

2-to-1 odds. As you can see, calling with a greater range of hands online has value.

Because players play more loosely online, they also call more liberally. This makes moving in witha big pair pre-flop in raised pots an attractive option. It never ceases to amaze me when, early in a tournament, I push with pocket kings over a raise and re-raise and get called by AK and pocket 8s! I guess they put me on a couple of high cards and think they're in front. Why not? That's what they're used to seeing!

Bluffing, on the other hand, loses value online. I'm not saying to avoid taking stabs at orphaned pots, but I think you need to proceed more cautiously when representing straights or flushes that you don't have. Many players online will get married to top pair and you couldn't get them off it with a carload of dynamite. So when that third flush card comes on the turn and you move in, you should *expect* to be called.

Play your straights and flushes fast and you'll get paid off, but bluff and you'll proceed at your peril.

I still sometimes get hoisted on my own petard when I play in the Sunday tournament on PokerStars. Here's a hand that came up recently. About halfway through the event, I was in the big blind and was the chip leader at my table with 15,000. With blinds and antes of 300/600/30 (PokerStars has since changed the structure), an early-position raiser made it 1,200 to go off a stack of 8,100. Getting almost 4-to-1, I called the extra 600 with 7♣3♣. The flop was T♥7♥2♣, giving me middle pair and a backdoor flush draw. I checked and he bet 900 into nearly a 3,000 pot.

As we've discussed, weak bets far more often connote real weakness, rather than strength. His pre-flop mini-raise might have indicated a big pair, but his 900 flop bet with both straight and flush draws abounding belied this possibility. I read him as weak and raised to 2,700; he called. This surprised me, because I thought he was weak. The turn was the queen of spades. We both checked. I now put him on a medium pair such as 88 or 99, which would account for the betting sequence. I decided that if I made 2-pair or 3-of-a-kind, or if either a heart or a straight card hit on the river, I was moving in. The jack of hearts on the river provided the possibility of both the straight *and* the flush. The board now read: T♥7♥2♣Q♠J♥.

I paused for about 20 seconds, then pushed. I had him well-covered and his tournament life was on the line. He thought for about 3 seconds, called, and I was shown K♣J♠! How he called the check/raise on the flop for about 25% of his stack is a mystery. If he can call this, his river call was easy! After all, he finally made a pair. After the hand, I kicked myself for bluffing on the river. If he had the hand I put him on (88-99), I'm convinced that he'd also have called.

Bluff less and overbet your big hands and you won't go wrong. This is especially true until you approach the money. As the tournament progresses and the quality of the opposition tends to improve, bluffing a bit more in certain situations may become a more viable option.

Hopefully, the above tactics will provide you with a nice stack of chips as you approach the money and beyond. Let's take a look at some of the new considerations that this happy situation entails.

Part Two
Endgame Strategy

Introduction

The strategy for playing the endgame portion of a tournament is dramatically different from that of the early stages. There is no defined point where the tournament enters the endgame; it is usually more of a gradual change of playing conditions. In addition, certain players may inadvertently enter the endgame earlier than others. For example, if you lose 90% of your stack in the first five minutes of a tournament, you could be dealing with some of these situations right away. But in general, as the tournament progresses, the following factors will start to become more significant and will affect the way you play.

• The blinds will become larger in proportion to the stack sizes, often resulting in players going all-in pre-flop or on the flop.

• Your actual stack size and those of your opponents will become vital considerations.

• Prize-money-distribution considerations will become important, changing the situation so that simply relying on pot odds can often lead to the wrong decision.

• Play may become short-handed.

Winning poker requires both math and psychology. Skilled players are constantly scanning for information and marrying their impressions with math in order to make winning decisions. Proper endgame play is the most mathematical aspect of poker and it can be proven that some plays are technically superior to others. When the blinds are very large, there can even be a single "correct" play. That can never be said of early-stage deep-stack play where there can be many different ways to approach the same hand, and it's often difficult to mathematically prove which is best. While it's often said that the skill factor is reduced when the blinds get large, there's still plenty of room for skillful play. So while science becomes more important in endgame play, art doesn't disappear. Opponent reading and hand-range estimations weigh heavily in many of your decisions.

Proper understanding of endgame play is critical for tournament success and is often overlooked by the casual player. Many players without a lot of tournament experience get lost when play becomes short-handed or the blinds become very large. Knowledgeable players often run over those who are slower to adjust to the changing conditions.

Remember, while only a small fraction of the players are involved in the endgame, it involves 100% of the money. Different tournament structures require different strategies—this section helps you understand how to play this critical part of a tournament.

3

BASIC ENDGAME CONCEPTS

Looking at Your Stack: CPR and CSI

When you look at how big your stack is, it doesn't do any good to simply look at the number of chips. After all, 500 chips can be a large stack and 200,000 chips can be a short stack. What matters is the size of your stack compared to the blinds and antes. To figure this out, you must calculate two important numbers: the cost per round (CPR) and your chip-status index (CSI).

Calculating CPR: The cost per round, as originally described in *Kill Phil*, is the amount of money it would cost you to sit through an entire round of play as the button makes one orbit around the table. It's the total of both blinds and antes (if there are any). You can also think of it as the amount of money in the pot before anyone plays.

For example, if there are no antes and the blinds are 25/50, the CPR is 75. If the blinds are 200/400, the CPR is 600.

With antes you have to add in the total of all the antes, which means multiplying the ante by the number of players and adding that total to the blinds. So if there are 10 players with blinds of 400/800 and a 100 ante, the CPR is 400 + 800 + (10 x 100) = 2,200.

Calculating CSI: Your chip-status index is your chip stack divided by the CPR. Exact precision isn't necessary; an approximation will usually do.

For example, if the CPR is 1,100 and you have 8,000 chips, you don't need to know that you have a CSI of 7.27. Simply knowing that it's a little more than 7 will be fine. For CSIs greater than 20, even less precision is called for. The first level at the World Series of Poker Main Event has blinds of 50/100 and starting chips of 20,000. Your CSI is 133, but saying to yourself, "I'm well over 100," is good enough.

Actually, once your CSI gets over about 25 or 30, most of your decisions using CSI will be the same, so don't even bother making the calculation if you know it exceeds that.

Changing Your Play with CSI

Your chips are your weapons. The more weapons you have, the more options you have in attacking your opponents. A large stack provides flexibility in playing tactics. If you get reduced to a short stack, your choices will become severely limited and your attack will be reduced to the all-in move.

Always keeping track of your CSI and adjusting your play accordingly is the *single most important* aspect of endgame play. Make sure you fully understand this concept and all of its implications before proceeding; we'll constantly refer to it. You'll be rewarded if you master this concept and adjust your moves appropriately.

Why do you have to change your style of play depending on your stack size? There are three main reasons:

• As the blinds become larger in comparison to your stack, it begins to cost too much to wait for premium hands.

• Stealing the blinds becomes more valuable.

• You have smaller implied odds for your speculative hands.

The first two are fairly obvious, but the third one may be the most important. The profitability of speculative hands, such as small pocket pairs and suited connectors, depends on implied odds. They rarely make big hands, but when they do, they're really big. As a result, you generally prefer to see the flop cheaply with these hands and have enough left in your stack to get paid off if you hit. If your CSI gets too low, your payoff will be too small to make up for all the times that you fold these speculative hands when you don't improve.

A handy guideline is the Rule of 5 and 10, previously discussed on page 49. Use this rule when you're thinking about calling a raise with a speculative hand. As you'll recall, if your stack is less than 5% of the raise, then it's an easy call. If it's more than 10%, then it's an easy fold. If it's between 5% and 10%, then it's a judgment call. Be more apt to call if:

• You have position on the raiser. Position is very important with suited connectors, but not as important with pocket pairs.

• You have a medium pocket pair (77 or 88) rather than a smaller one.

• You have a no-gap suited connector, such as 7♠6♠ rather than a 1- or 2-gapper such as T♠8♠ or 9♠6♠.

• Your opponent is the type of player who rarely folds top pair or an overpair after the flop.

Note that if your opponent has a shorter stack than you, you need to consider the raise as a percentage of *his* stack rather than your own. His stack is the one limiting the implied odds. This is a very important point. For example, if your opponent has raised using 15% of his stack, you should generally fold, even if this raise represents only 5% of your stack. Any time a stack size is mentioned, it should always refer to the "relevant stack," that is, the biggest stack size that could come into play for you.

Of course, like any rule, there are exceptions. If I have position and have good control over an opponent (i.e., he's predictable), I may very well make this call, knowing that I'll often be able to take the pot away if I miss on the flop. The "rules" presented here are really guidelines. Table composition and fear equity need to be constantly evaluated. As you gain experience, opportunities may arise that may violate these guidelines. At times such as these, winning players will deviate from the suggested line of play, and so should you. However, don't kid yourself. Until the time when you're capable of making accurate reads of your foes, it's probably better to stick with the basic program.

Very speculative hands—suited 3-gaps like 95s, suited ace-low like A5s[3], unsuited no-gaps like 87o, and suited connectors where the high card is 4 or less, such as 43s, require even more implied odds, because they have fewer ways of making a big hand. Therefore, you need to use something more like a Rule of 3 and 6 for calling with these hands. Any raise more than 6% of the smaller stack is probably too high to call and see the flop. The best time to call with very speculative hands is in position, when there's unlikely to be a re-raise behind you.

The Rule of 5 and 10 ensures that you'll have the proper implied odds when calling pre-flop raises. But similar logic applies when there's no raise and you're thinking about limping into the pot. If your stack is too short, then frequently, even limping doesn't give you sufficient implied odds. It pays to be aware of the possibility of a raise behind you, which can destroy your chances of seeing a cheap flop.

The following table summarizes playing stages corresponding to different CSIs:

---

[3] Not all suited ace-lows are equivalent. A3s-A5s are the best for deep stack calling since they can also form a good straight in addition to the obvious flush potential. A2s, A6s, and A7s are weaker since they either can't form a straight with both cards, or in the case of A2s, only the bottom end of a straight. A8s and A9s are also fairly weak when deep stacked, but these are better than A6s and A7s. When we study short stacked situations, kickers will become much more meaningful so that a higher kicker is always better than a lower one (except that A5s is slightly stronger than A6s).

CSI	Stage	Implications	Advantage To Be First One In the Pot?
17 or more	Normal	Play normal poker. Obey the Rule of 5 and 10 (or 3 and 6) for calling raises.	Some, but position is more important.
12 to 17	Semi-Aggressive	Start raising more frequently. In early position, don't limp with small pairs and suited connectors.	More so than before, because of blind stealing
7 to 12	Aggressive	All pairs and suited connectors cannot be limped. Raise or fold with these hands. Raise more frequently than before.	Not as much (see next section)
2 to 7	Move-in	Every hand is all-in or fold pre-flop. Pairs and suited connectors become playable again.	Yes
0 to 2	Special	You have no fold equity. Someone *will* call.	No

As the blinds increase, you'll feel more and more pressure to make a move. A common mistake, especially in a fast-paced tournament, is to play too tightly when the situation calls for aggression. The problem with overly tight play is that you may get blinded away to such an extent that by the time you get a good hand and double up, you're still fairly short. Most professional players want to get out of the Aggressive and Move-in stages as quickly as possible. They don't wait for premium hands; they want to get their hands on some chips—or bust out trying.

To reiterate from our Rule of 5 and 10 discussion, if you're the chip leader of the remaining active hands at the table, you should act as if you have the CSI of your largest opponent who's still in the hand. For example, you're on the button with a CSI of 15, the small blind has a CSI of 6, and the big blind is 4. If someone before you comes in with a CSI of 22, you should continue to act as a CSI of 15. However, if it's folded to you on the button, you outchip both of your remaining opponents. You should therefore act on this hand as if your CSI were 6. Your extra chips will not be in play this hand, so you don't have the added flexibility of a deeper stack.

KEY POINT: Adjust your CSI to that of your largest active opponent in the hand and act accordingly.

Playing the Normal Stage

With a large stack, you can continue to play as we've advised in early-stage play. There are different phases of the normal stage, so it's best not to treat all CSIs above 17 the same. If your CSI falls into the low 20s, there's an increased risk in playing as freely as before. Calling raises with suited connectors or small pocket pairs might no longer be profitable. Calling a raise may be more than 10% of your stack, so you won't have a deep enough stack to justify calling for the long shot of making a big hand.

Playing the Semi-Aggressive Stage

As your CSI falls below 17, you need to start opening up your game a little more. You should raise pre-flop slightly more than you did before, since stealing the blinds and antes will become more significant. While raising with speculative hands still has value, since you can often pick up the blinds or take the pot away on the flop, calling a raise is often incorrect. With a shorter stack, your implied odds are further reduced. You can continue to limp with these hands, but only if you think the pot is unlikely to be raised. The best time to do this is in late position behind other limpers.

However, in early position you should probably raise or fold all of your suited connectors and pocket pairs, since there's a bigger chance of a raise behind you. In early position with a mixed table composition of tight and aggressive players, consider raising with pocket sixes or better and folding pocket fives and lower. At a tight table, however, consider raising with any pocket pair or suited connector. As discussed previously, in early position, we suggest raising to 2-2.5 times the big blind with these hands. We also make the same-size raise in early position with big pairs.

Lower your raising requirements with big cards as well, especially in late position. Medium-strong hands, such as AT, KJ, etc., become good candidates for raising from the button or the cut-off after a few limpers.

Example: Blinds are 100/200 and you have a stack of 7,500. You're in the cut-off with 8♠6♠. A solid player with 4,200 in early position raises to 700. You should probably fold unless you know that this player is particularly weak and you could take the pot away from him. Since he's the shorter stack, you need to apply the Rule of 5 and 10 to his stack. Although the raise is less than 10% of your stack, it's 17% of his. Since you can't get paid off enough to chase your speculative hand, fold.

Playing the Aggressive Stage

Now that your CSI has fallen below 12, you need to become even more aggressive. However, you're in a sort of a strange "in between" state that causes a few odd things to happen.

First, suited connectors and pocket pairs generally should not be just called in this stage. You can no longer limp with these speculative hands anymore and calling a raise with them is even worse. You should raise or fold, with few exceptions.

Another strange thing about having a CSI in this range is that it's no longer as attractive to be the "first-in" raiser. With deeper stacks or with shorter stacks, it's usually to your advantage to be the first one to raise pre-flop. With deep stacks, raising allows you to assume the role of the aggressor and take control of the hand. With a shorter stack, you can simply raise all-in and put your opponents to difficult decisions.

However, with this "in between" stack size, you have too many chips to go all-in when no one has entered the pot. If you make a smaller raise as the first one in, a re-raise by one of your opponents will essentially put you all-in. Now it's *you* who's facing the difficult decision. There's a saying in bridge (the card game) that goes, "Make your opponents take the last guess." The same can be said in this situation for poker. By being the first raiser, you give your opponents the opportunity to put you to the last guess.

Even though it's a slight disadvantage, if you're first to enter the pot, don't be afraid to come in for a raise. Taking down the blinds is essential. However, pay attention to your raise size. Make your standard-size raise whenever possible, but if that amount would be a third of your stack or more, go all-in instead. If you were to raise larger than a third of your stack, but not all-in, you'll often feel pot-committed if re-raised. Don't make the mistake of raising a smaller amount than your standard raise because you intend to fold to a re-raise; your opponents may pick up on this. Make the same-sized raise with your good hands and weaker hands alike, so that your opponents can't determine the strength of your hand by the size of your raise. If you can make your standard-sized raise for less than a third of your chips, do it. Otherwise, you should be going all-in.

> **KEY POINT:** Don't make a raise that will give you a difficult decision if someone re-raises after you. If your standard raise will commit a third of your chips or more, move in instead.

As a result, you may find yourself playing more like the Move-in stage if your CSI is around 8, especially in late position. Let the style of your opponents determine how you should proceed with the hand. If your opponents frequently re-raise from the blinds, it may be best to push all-in right away when your CSI is below 8.

Even though it's not as attractive for you to be the first to enter a pot, it's now more attractive when you're on the other side of a raising war. Your opponent raises as the first one in the pot and now you can re-raise *him* all-in. Now he must make the last guess. Every time you put your opponents to a decision, there's a chance they will make the wrong choice. Every time they make the wrong choice, you make money. Consistently having fold equity on your side is *critical* for tournament success. We've mentioned this previously, but it's worth repeating:

When you bet, raise, or re-raise, there are two ways you can win the pot—your opponent folds or you win when all the cards are out. When you call, there's only one way to win. That's why I sometimes call the Aggressive stage of 7 to 12 CSI the "Re-steal Stage."

Coming over the top of a raiser needs to be done judiciously. Adapting to your opponents' playing styles is very important. The right hands to re-raise someone all-in obviously depend on how frequently they're raising to begin with. If your foe is aggressive and constantly stealing the blinds, he's less likely to have a hand that can call a re-raise. If he's very tight, then you need to have a premium hand yourself to go up against him.

Unfortunately, most players fall somewhere in between these two extremes and judgment becomes the determining factor. Close observation and focus when you're not in a hand can help you identify these targets. The more likely your opponent is to fold, the more often you can try coming over the top.

The following two tables show a couple of example ranges that an opening raiser might have. If he comes in for an opening raise of 3BB, then you can profitably come over the top of him with the following hands, no matter how he responds.

Unexploitable Re-steals Far From the Money

Your CSI	Opponent's Range for Initial Raise		
	77+,AQ+,AJs	77+,AQ+,ATs, KTs+,QTs+,JTs	55+,AT+,KQ,KTs+, QTs+,JTs,T9s,98s
15	JJ+,AK,AQs	JJ+,AK,AJs+,KQs	88+,AQ+,AJs+,KJs+
14	JJ+,AK,AQs	TT+,AK,AJs+,KQs	88+,AQ+,AJs+, KTs+,QJs
13	JJ+,AK,AQs	TT+,AK,AJs+,KJs+	88+,AQ+,ATs+, KTs+,QJs,JTs
12	JJ+,AK,AQs	TT+,AK,AJs+,KQs	88+,AQ+,AJs+, KTs+,QJs
11	JJ+,AK,AQs	99+,AK,AJs+,KQs	77+,AQ+,ATs+, KJs+,QJs
10	JJ+,AK,AQs,KQs	99+,AQ+,AJs+, KQs	77+,AJ+,ATs+, KJs+,QJs
9	TT+,AK,AQs,KQs	99+,AQ+,AJs+	77+,AJ+,ATs+,KJs+
8	TT+,AK,AQs,KQs	99+,AQ+	66+,AJ+,KQs
7	TT+,AK,AQs	99+,AK,AQs	77+,AJ+,KQs
6	TT+,AK	99+,AK,AQs	77+,AJ+,KQs
5	99+,AK	99+,AK	77+,AJ+

Your CSI	Opponent's Range for Initial Raise	
	22+,A2+,K9o+,K6s+, Q9o+,Q6s+,J9o+,J8s+, T9o,T7s+,96s+,85s+, 74s+,63s+,53s+	Any Two Cards
15	22+,A4o+,A2s+,KJo+, K9s+,QJo,Q9s+,J9s+, T9s,98s	22+,A2+,K2+,Q5o+,Q2s+,J7o+, J3s+,T8o+,T6s+,98o,96s+,86s+, 75s+,65s
14	22+,A4o+,A2s+,KJo+, K9s+,QJo,Q9s+,J9s+, T9s,98s	22+,A2+,K2+,Q4o+,Q2s+, J7o+,J3s+,T8o+,T6s+,98o,96s+, 86s+,76s,65s
13	22+,A3o+,A2s+,KTo+, K9s+,QJo,Q9s+,J9s+, T9s,98s	22+,A2+,K2+,Q4o+,Q2s+, J7o+,J2s+,T8o+,T5s+,98o,96s+, 86s+,76s,65s
12	22+,A3o+,A2s+,KTo+, K9s+,QJo,Q9s+,JTs	22+,A2+,K2+,Q4o+,Q2s+, J7o+,J2s+,T7o+,T5s+,98o,96s+, 86s+,76s
11	22+,A3o+,A2s+,KTo+, K9s+,QTs+,JTs	22+,A2+,K2+,Q4o+,Q2s+, J7o+,J2s+,T7o+,T6s+,98o,96s+, 86s+,76s
10	22+,A4o+,A2s+,KTo+, K9s+,QTs+,JTs	22+,A2+,K2+,Q3o+,Q2s+, J7o+,J2s+,T7o+,T5s+,98o,96s+, 86s+,76s
9	22+,A4o+,A2s+,KTo+, K9s+,QJo,QTs+,JTs	22+,A2+,K2+,Q3o+,Q2s+, J6o+,J2s+,T7o+,T5s+,98o,96s+, 86s+,76s
8	33+,A3o+,A2s+,KTo+, K9s+,QJo+,QTs+,JTs	22+,A2+,K2+,Q2+,J5o+,J2s+, T7o+,T5s+,97o+,96s+,86s+
7	33+,A4o+,A2s+,KTo+, K9s+,QJo+,QTs+,JTs	22+,A2+,K2+,Q2+,J5o+,J2s+, T7o+,T5s+,98o,96s+,87s
6	33+,A3o+,A2s+,KTo+, K8s+,QJo+,Q9s+,JTs	22+,A2+,K2+,Q2+,J5o+,J2s+, T7o+,T4s+,97o+,96s+,87s
5	22+,A2+,K9o+,K7s+, QTo+,Q9s+,JTs	22+,A2+,K2+,Q2+,J4o+,J2s+, T6o+,T3s+,97o+,95s+,86s+

Playing the Move-in Stage

You've fallen below a CSI of 7 and things are looking pretty grim. There's no more playing around; every single hand is all-in or fold. Just calling the big blind is 10% or more of your stack and that's too much to waste to try and see a flop. A smaller raise other than all-in will pot-commit you and you'll be getting the correct odds to call if someone re-raises, so you might as well put maximum pressure on your opponents from the start.

You need to make a move here, so your goal is to find any reasonable hand and go all-in. If everyone folds, that's good, since you've significantly added to your stack (15% or more). If you get called, you'll either double up or be out of the tournament. You just have to pull the ripcord and do it. Otherwise, if you wait too long:

• Your fold equity may erode to the point where it's inconsequential.

• If you do double up later, you'll do so from such a low base that you'll still be low-stacked. When you take a big risk, your objective is to become comfortable chip-wise, if successful. Although "all-in moments" may be exciting to TV audiences, they're anathema to tournament pros when their tournament life is on the line.

In single-table tournaments, a lot of time is spent in the Move-in stage and good hand selection is a key winning skill. We'll spend a lot of time studying the Move-in stage in Chapters 4 and 7, since it's fairly easy to construct models when you're limited to a push-or-fold option. But here are a few key points.

• The more your CSI shrinks below 7, the more often you'll be pushing. Look for blind-stealing opportunities and take them. Those blinds are extremely valuable to you.

• The number of players behind you and their looseness will often be more important than your cards.

• Small pocket pairs and suited connectors become playable again when you're the initial raiser (first in). These hands are rarely big dogs to the range of hands your opponents may call with. So even if you're called, you still have a chance to pull through; 45s is only a 7-to-5 underdog against AK!

• Being the first into the pot is once again extremely valuable. Fold equity will factor heavily into your decisions to move in. With a relatively high CSI of around 6 or 7, you may be able to get a limper or two to fold if you push after them, but you don't have enough chips to threaten someone who raised in front of you.

For example, the blinds are 50/100 and you have 900 (CSI = 6). Someone in early or mid-position comes in for 300 or 400. If you push all-in, you don't have enough to get them to fold, unless they're very inexperienced. They're getting the right odds to call, so for most players this is an easy call.

Playing the Special Stage

The Special stage isn't where you want to be, but it has some unique characteristics, hence the term "special." Which hands to play will depend on your position and whether or not there's an ante. Hopefully, you didn't wind up with a CSI less than 2 because you were blinded away. The only reason you should ever be here is if you were all-in against another player who had a slightly smaller stack and you lost. You're down a deep hole and it's difficult to climb out, but not impossible. All of the authors have had a CSI below 2 and later came back to win the tournament. Lee won a tournament from a single 100 chip. Tysen once won a tournament when he joined the final table with less than one big blind. Anything can happen.

The thing that makes this stage *special* is that you no longer have any fold equity. Your only move is still all-in, but you're virtually certain to have at least one caller, perhaps more. Another unique thing about the Special stage is that it's no longer advantageous to be the first in anymore. In fact, the best situation for you is if several limpers are ahead of you. In that case if you win, you won't just double up, but maybe triple, quadruple, or quintuple up. An added benefit is that the other players may continue to bet each other out of the hand, but they can't push you out. The possibility of extra betting after you're all-in gives you a better chance of walking away a winner.

If you're in the big blind with a CSI of 2 or less, you should go all in every time. Don't even look at your cards; you have the proper pot odds to call with anything. In the small blind, move in with any two if there's an ante. Without an ante, you should consider folding a marginal hand in the small blind (at a full table), since you'll get to see several more hands for "free." A marginal hand will be right on the border between calling and folding for the current pot odds. Chapter 6 provides a lot more detail in determining which hands to call with, depending on the pot odds.

No ante: When you have a CSI that's less than 2, and you're under the gun, you'll need to decide which of the following situations apply:

• How should I play to give me the best chance of building my stack up beyond the Special Stage?

• How should I play to give me the best chance of surviving one more orbit?

Normally the first situation applies, meaning that you should push all-in whenever you have a +EV situation. Given such great pot odds and the fact multiple players may call, only to be pushed out later, it is +EV to push many hands. Any pair and any ace are profitable as well as any two cards that are both ten or higher. Suited semi-connectors and suited big-little (such as Q5s or K3s) also have fairly good value, since you may be called in multiple places. If it's folded to you in late position, you can push more frequently since you have fewer potential opponents. That means the quality of the hand that calls you will be lower on average.

However, if you are near the bubble of the tournament

(especially in a satellite) the second situation (survival) may take precedence. In this case you should fold more frequently. You'll have to call when the big blind hits you, but there's no need to push with a marginal hand now and risk two chances at elimination. We'll expand on this concept much more in Chapter 7.

Ante: If you're in the Special stage and there's an ante, you'll need to push all-in more frequently. The ante itself is a good portion of your stack and you can't afford to wait much longer. Always push any pair, any ace, any two cards that are both eight or higher, most suited hands, and unsuited connectors 65 or higher. Push more often if there are a lot of limpers already in the pot or if you're under the gun. If your CSI drops to 1 or below and there's an ante, push any two cards. In all these cases, use common sense. If there's heavy action in front of you, such as a raise and a re-raise, fold easily dominated hands like low aces.

I (Tysen) was reduced to the Special stage in a recent live tournament when I lost a big all-in confrontation while under the gun. The blinds were 400/800 with a 100 ante. It was 10-handed, so the CPR was 2,200. I was down to 1,000 chips (CSI = 0.45) and posted the 100 ante and 800 big blind. When the button raised, I put in my last 100 without looking, flipped over AJ, and won the hand when the button only showed K5. I was then up to 3,200 (CSI = 1.45) and the same player raised again, this time from the cut-off. I called again with 7♠5♦. Let's look and see if this was a reasonable call.

The cut-off has shown that he will aggressively raise, since I was so short-stacked. Let's give him a reasonable range of any pair, any ace, K9+, K7s+, QT+, JTs, T9s, 98s. The pot is offering 5,300-to-2,700, practically 2-to-1. It turns out that against this range, 75o wins 34.1% of the time for an expected value of:

$$(34.1\%) \text{ x } (+5,300) + (65.9\%) \text{ x } (-2,700) = +28 \text{ chips}$$

Notice that even if this calculation were slightly negative, calling would still be right. Being so short-stacked, you need to gamble when you already have a blind in the pot. Here's an opportunity to more than double up against a player who's known to take shots. I needed to take a gamble to have any hope of building myself up to a playable stack. Folding here would mean an even smaller stack that will be ground down even further by the ante in future hands.

Differences in Hand Values for Raising Versus Calling

Throughout the rest of this book, I'll frequently refer to hand ranges in terms of percentages, such as, "You should raise with your top 40% of hands," or "He'll likely call with the top 12% of hands." Which hands are those? Is it always the same in all situations? Are the best hands for raising the same as the best hands for calling?

While there's no fixed correct ordering for what hand outranks what, we'll present a general order that can be used for most situations. The best hands for each situation are unique to how tight the opponents are. Some players look at a rank order that shows how well the hand does against a random hand. That doesn't make any sense, unless you think your opponent is playing any two cards. When you're considering the relative strength of two good hands, you need to look at how well they do against other good hands, not against a random one.

When your opponents are super-tight, it can create some recommendations that look fairly strange. For example, in the next section, we'll calculate the optimal solution for pushing with a CSI of 7 when UTG (10-handed). That solution recommends pushing with A4s-A5s, but not with A9s or AJo! This is because our opponents are assumed to be (optimally) very tight, calling with only TT+ and AK (the blinds also call with AQs). Against these tight players, A4s and A5s are very mar-

Assumed Rank Order for Pushing Hands

Top 5%	AA, KK, QQ, JJ, AKs, TT, AKo, 99, AQs, AQo
Top 10%	AJs, KQs, ATs, QJs, KJs, KTs, 88, JTs, QTs, 77, 66, AJo, A9s
Top 15%	KQo, 55, K9s, T9s, J9s, Q9s, 44, A8s, ATo, 33, A7s
Top 20%	A5s, KJo, 98s, 22, A6s, A9o, A4s, A3s, T8s, QJo
Top 30%	A2s, A8o, JTo, A7o, J8s, A5o, KTo, 87s, A6o, A4o, K8s, 97s, QTo, A3o, Q8s
Top 40%	76s, A2o, T7s, 86s, K7s, K6s, K5s, K9o, J7s, 65s, T9o, K4s, 54s, Q7s, 96s, 85s, T8o, 98o, 64s, K3s, K8o
Top 50%	75s, Q6s, J6s, 87o, T6s, 74s, 95s, K2s, K7o, Q9o, T5s, K6o, K5o, J9o, Q5s, Q4s, Q3s, J8o
Top 60%	K4o, Q2s, K3o, Q8o, J7o, J5s, 97o, J4s, T4s, K2o, J3s, 43s, Q7o, Q6o, T7o
Top 70%	Q5o, 84s, J2s, T3s, Q4o, Q3o, 86o, J6o, J5o, Q2o, T2s, 94s, 93s, 96o, T6o, J4o
Top 80%	J3o, J2o, 53s, 76o, 63s, 65o, 92s, T5o, 73s, 52s, 75o, 54o, 62s, 83s, 82s, 64o
Top 90%	72s, 85o, 95o, 74o, 84o, 94o, 93o, T4o, 92o, 42s, 32s, 53o, 43o
Top 100%	63o, T3o, 52o, T2o, 73o, 42o, 32o, 62o, 83o, 82o, 72o

ginally profitable, but A9s and AJo are not. You wouldn't lose a lot of equity by folding A5s and would be correct in doing so if your opponents are not as tight as assumed. Obviously, this doesn't mean that we recommend pushing A5s in preference to AJo in most situations.

The previous table on page 79 is the rank order that we'll use for determining the top percentage of hands whenever we talk about raising. The hands are grouped in 5% or 10% buckets, but the hands are listed in their rank order, from strongest to weakest.

We'll use a different rank order for determining the top percentage of hands to call with. The reason may not be intuitive, until you consider a hand like 87s—a fairly good hand to push with, since it holds its value against strong calling hands, but not so great for calling, since it will almost always be behind. The table on the facing page is the rank order for calling.

Assumed Rank Order for Calling Hands

Top 5%	AA, KK, QQ, JJ, AKs, AKo, TT, AQs
Top 10%	99, AQo, AJs, 88, KQs, 77, ATs, AJo, 66, KJs, 55, A9s, ATo
Top 15%	KQo, 44, A8s, KTs, A5s, A7s, 33, QJs, A4s, A6s, A9o
Top 20%	A3s, KJo, A2s, 22, QTs, A8o, JTs, K9s, A7o
Top 30%	KTo, A5o, QJo, A6o, A4o, Q9s, K8s, K7s, A3o, T9s, QTo, J9s, K6s, A2o, Q8s, K9o
Top 40%	K5s, JTo, 98s, T8s, J8s, K4s, 87s, Q7s, Q9o, K3s, Q6s, K8o, 97s, 76s, K2s, Q5s, T7s, K7o, J7s, 86s, T9o, J9o
Top 50%	65s, K6o, Q4s, Q8o, 96s, 75s, Q3s, T6s, J6s, K5o, 54s, 98o, Q2s, T8o, 85s, J5s, J8o, K4o
Top 60%	64s, 87o, Q7o, J4s, 95s, Q6o, K3o, 74s, 97o, 76o, T5s, 53s, J3s, K2o, T7o, T4s
Top 70%	Q5o, 84s, J7o, 86o, J2s, 63s, 43s, 65o, T3s, Q4o, 94s, 96o, 73s, 93s, T2s, 52s, 75o, T6o
Top 80%	Q3o, 54o, J6o, 83s, 92s, 85o, 62s, 42s, 82s, J5o, Q2o, 64o, 32s, 72s, J4o, 95o
Top 90%	74o, 53o, T5o, J3o, T4o, 84o, 63o, 43o, J2o, T3o, 94o
Top 100%	73o, 52o, 93o, T2o, 83o, 92o, 42o, 62o, 82o, 32o, 72o

EQUILIBRIUM PLAYS

A Word About the Math

The next few sections of the book involve a bit of mathematics, especially equations where we calculate our expected value (EV). These equations don't use anything more than high-school-level algebra, but it really isn't essential for you to follow along. You'll still get a lot out of reading these chapters, even if you skip all the equations. The equations are there for illustration and as examples only; we obviously don't expect you to be doing complex equations at the table. But the equations often show the "why" behind many of our recommendations, and as you gain experience, that "why" will become common sense and these plays will become almost automatic.

An Introduction to Equilibrium Play

In this section we often refer to equilibrium plays for many endgame situations. An equilibrium play is the mathematically best play that can be made against an opponent who plays optimally. It assumes that our opponent is a rational thinking player who, like us, is also making optimal plays. It's often a defensive strategy based entirely on not being exploited. It has the unique characteristic that if you play the equilibrium strategy, your opponent's best response is to *also* play his equilibrium strategy. This creates a stable balance and if either player deviates from this equilibrium, they suffer in expectation.

An equilibrium play is different from an exploitive play, which tries to obtain the best possible EV from a certain opponent who *isn't* playing optimally. Many times our opponents won't play optimally, thus relying on the equilibrium play may not maximize our profits. Our aim with an exploitive play is to take advantage of our opponents' tendencies and mistakes. Clear examples of this are frequently trying to steal the blinds from overly tight players and not trying to bluff an overly loose player.

An exploitive play will always be better than an equilibrium play, but only if you're correct in your assessment of your opponent. However, it leaves you open to a counterattack if your opponent switches strategies. If you think your opponent will zig and he actually zags, you often lose a lot more than if you'd simply stuck with your original, defensive, equilibrium play. Against most pros, it's best to stick to equilibrium rather than trying to maximize.

Let's look at a real example in a heads-up game where the smaller stack has a CSI of 6. If you limit yourself to only pushing or folding, the equilibrium solution is for the SB (small blind) to push 60% of his hands and for the BB (big blind) to call with 41% of his hands. Why? The graph at the top of the facing page shows the value of pushing, assuming the BB will make the correct play of calling 41% of the time.

The maximum value, assuming he's calling 41%, is for you to push 60%. If you push more or less often, you lose money. Now turn the tables and look at the value of calling from the BB, assuming that the SB is pushing 60% as shown in the graph on the bottom of the facing page.

Again you see that, assuming your opponent is pushing 60%, you should call 41%; calling more or less often costs mon-

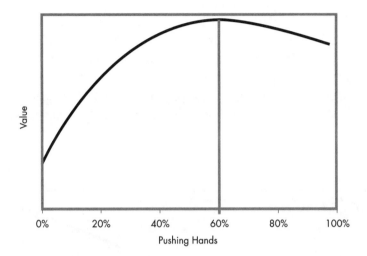

Value

0%   20%   40%   60%   80%   100%

Pushing Hands

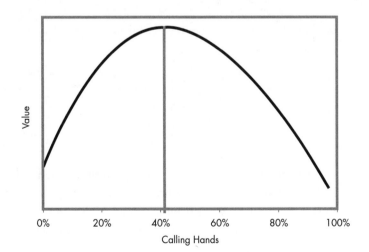

Value

0%   20%   40%   60%   80%   100%

Calling Hands

ey. This is why there's an equilibrium here—neither player has an incentive to change his play. But what if your opponent isn't making the equilibrium play?

Far from the money, the equilibrium play will make additional money even if your opponents don't use an equilibrium strategy. If they're too loose, you make more money. If they're too tight, you also make more money. In the heads-up example on the previous page, suppose your opponent didn't realize that he should be calling so often in the BB (true for many opponents). What if he only calls 20% of the time instead of 41%?

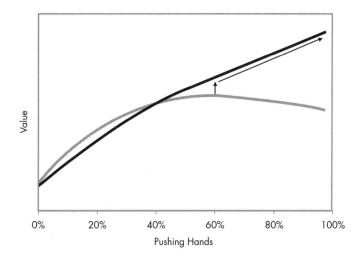

The gray line in the above graph is your original value against the equilibrium opponent; the black line is the value against this opponent who's playing too tight. You can see that even if you stick with your equilibrium 60% pushing, you make extra money against the tight player. However, you can exploit his tight play by using the exploitive play of pushing *more frequently*, even up to any two cards! Against a player who'll only call with the top 20% of hands, we can show that it's profitable to even push with 72o.

If we assume he's only calling with the top 20% of hands (22+, A7o+, A2s+, KJo+, K9s+, QTs+, JTs), with 72o we have an equity of 27.2%, *if* we're called. He has a 20.5%[4] chance of calling, so our EV is:

$$(79.6\% \times 1BB) + (20.5\% \times 27.2\% \times 9BB) - (20.5\% \times 72.8\% \times 9BB) = -0.05BB$$

The EV of folding is -0.50BB, so although we have negative EV in both cases, the EV is less negative for pushing, making it the winner.

But moving away from the equilibrium play leaves you vulnerable to a counterplay. If he really isn't as tight as you thought, you could lose a lot by pushing with weak hands. It's of paramount importance, therefore, that you have an accurate read on your competition if you're going to deviate from the equilibrium strategy. When in doubt, stick with equilibrium play.

Throughout this section we look at both equilibrium and exploitive plays. Both are useful and have their place, and it's often insightful to examine how they differ. Many times we'll start with the equilibrium play as a base case, then make adjustments from there. Taking all factors into consideration and deciding whether or not to deviate from equilibrium play will increase your profits.

Noted poker authority Sklansky has appropriately criticized other poker writers for being unable to deliver concrete advice. His point is that correct poker decisions often depend on assumptions about your opponent. But frequently they do not depend on many assumptions. Or they depend on those assumptions only to a small extent. It's the obligation of poker

---

[4] The chance is higher than 20%, because our hand (72o) has taken two cards out of the deck that he's not likely to need.

writers to clarify these situations.

One obvious solution is to restrict our analysis to situations where the best decision is robust to our assumptions. For example, suppose there's a $1,000 pot and your opponent bets your last dollar. Then you should call with almost any hand. In order to fold you need to be 99.9% certain your opponent has the better hand. And you simply can't be that confident about most real-world opponents.

Well, that obvious solution is fine for the clear-cut situations. And it's very valuable for you to know them as a "safe haven" where you can comfortably make the correct decision. In this comfort zone, you know the right answer and don't have to worry about mistakes. But poker isn't always like this. The answer frequently does depend. It depends on stack size and position. It depends on the pre-flop action. And it depends on the tendencies of your opponents. This complexity is what makes poker so fun and exciting. It's one thing to memorize a rote semi-bluffing strategy when you flop a 4-flush. But it's another to deviate from it and bluff your tight friend off the better hand. And it's darned satisfying too! But this complexity is too much to capture in a book. So what can we offer as authors?

One solution is to solve for optimal or equilibrium play. Surprisingly, this is sometimes possible. For example, with small stacks and few players, the correct strategy is to move in or fold, and we can actually calculate this. In other situations this may not be the ideal strategy, but the results are close. In contrast, the optimal or equilibrium play may not be practically computable. And even if it were, it wouldn't fit into a book. In other words, we can find a simple strategy that's approximately correct. And we'd rather be approximately correct than precisely wrong. So assuming that your opponent is a good player is a useful benchmark for analysis.

Of course, your opponents aren't always good players. Or more important, they might not believe you're a good player and consequently deviate from optimal play themselves. In these cases you can increase profits by deviating from optimal equilibrium play.

For example, optimal play frequently involves moving in. But many players will incorrectly fold to a much smaller raise. Against these players you can save money on your bluffs with smaller raises.

Alternatively, some players are suspicious "call stations." It isn't profitable to bluff these opponents. Theoretically, this would enable them to read your good hands and fold. But in practice, these call stations will call anyway. You should obviously avoid bluffs against these players and instead overplay your value hands. Ironically, these players may be more likely to call a "suspicious" large bet than a small one.

In our experience, typical opponents systematically deviate from optimal play. In particular, they're too tight when stacks are small. It takes a lot of guts to raise or call for your whole stack. In some cases, our analysis is sensitive to your opponent's calling strategy. In these cases we show how your optimal strategy depends on your opponents and make recommendations based on our assessment of typical opponents. Then you can choose to play our equilibrium strategy or modify it based on your opponents.

Equilibrium Play: Moving in Far From the Money

Our first analysis of equilibrium play is a situation that happens to all of us at one time or another. You lose a big hand early in a tournament and now your CSI is less than 7. Since you're now in the Move-in stage, your only intelligent choices are to go all-in or fold. For this analysis we're assuming that the tournament isn't far enough along for the prize structure to be a significant consideration. A safe assumption would be that these equilibrium plays are valid if there are still at least five times as many players as there are prizes to be awarded. So in a tournament that pays the top 10 finishers, you'd be safe in ignoring the prize structure as long as at least 50 players remain. If your stack is very short compared to the average, this equilibrium strategy will continue to hold beyond the "5 times" suggestion. As you get closer to the bubble, the equilibrium strategy is still similar, but starts to deviate.

Appendix 1 shows the equilibrium push or fold solution when you're moving in and far from the money[5] when the action is folded to you. A sample of the solution (when to push with CSI 6) is presented on the facing page for discussion.

This table is divided into two sections. One solution was generated with no antes and the other solution was generated with antes equal to one-quarter the small blind (a full 10-player table was assumed). There's little difference between the solutions, but the equilibrium solution generally pushes slightly more often with antes at the same CSI level.

Don't try to memorize Appendix 1—as if you could! You have two options for remembering shortcut solutions as handy guides for short-stack all-in moves. The first option is to get a feeling for how often you should be pushing from each position with the table on the top of page 92.

Combine this with our recommendations of which hands make up the top percent of pushing hands and you'll have a good idea which hands to push in short-stacked situations far from the money. Here is that ordering again on the bottom of page 92.

The second option is to use the Power Number system that's outlined next.

---

[5] The solution is simplified by the fact that it assumes there will be no overcalls. Mixed strategies *are* considered—a mixed strategy is one where you raise with certain hands only a fraction of the time. The solution presented here is a listing of all the hands where you should push at least 50% of the time. It is also assumed that all your opponents have you covered.

Pushing With CSI 6

Position	No Antes
Small Blind	22+,A2+,K2+,Q6o+,Q2s+,J8o+,J3s+,T7o+,T4s+,97o+, 95s+,87o,85s+,76o,74s+,64s+,53s+,43s (59.9%)
Button	22+,A2+,KTo+,K5s+,QTo+,Q8s+,JTo,J8s+,T7s+,97s+, 86s+,76s (32.7%)
Cut-Off	22+,A4o+,A2s+,KTo+,K9s+,QJo,Q9s+,JTo,J8s+,T8s+, 98s (27.0%)
Hijack	22+,A9o+,A2s+,KJo+,K9s+,QJo,Q9s+,J8s+,T8s+,98s (20.7%)
3 off	22+,ATo+,A7s+,A5s,KJo+,K9s+,Q9s+,J9s+,T9s (16.7%)
4 off	33+,AJo+,A8s+,KQo,K9s+,Q9s+,J9s+,T9s (13.9%)
5 off	55+,AJo+,A9s+,KQo,K9s+,QTs+,JTs,T9s (12.1%)
6 off	66+,AJo+,A9s+,KTs+,QTs+,JTs (10.1%)
7 off	77+,AQo+,ATs+,KTs+,QTs+,JTs (8.4%)

Position	Antes
Small Blind	22+,A2+,K2+,Q5o+,Q2s+,J8o+,J2s+,T7o+,T3s+,97o+, 95s+,87o,84s+,76o,74s+,63s+,53s+,43s (62.0%)
Button	22+,A2+,K9o+,K4s+,QTo+,Q7s+,JTo,J7s+,T9o,T7s+, 96s+,86s+,76s,65s (36.0%)
Cut-Off	22+,A4o+,A2s+,KTo+,K8s+,QTo+,Q8s+,JTo,J8s+,T8s+, 97s+,87s (29.1%)
Hijack	22+,A8o+,A2s+,KJo+,K9s+,QJo,Q9s+,J8s+,T8s+,98s (21.6%)
3 off	22+,ATo+,A7s+,A5s,KJo+,K9s+,Q9s+,J9s+,T9s,98s (17.0%)
4 off	44+,ATo+,A8s+,KQo,K9s+,Q9s+,J9s+,T9s (14.3%)
5 off	55+,AJo+,A9s+,KQo,K9s+,QTs+,JTs,T9s (12.1%)
6 off	66+,AJo+,A9s+,KQo,KTs+,QTs+,JTs (11.0%)
7 off	66+,AQo+,ATs+,KTs+,QTs+,JTs (8.9%)

CSI	SB	But	CO	2 off	3 off	4 off	5 off	6 off	7 off
8	53%	32%	23%	16%	13%	11%	8%	8%	8%
7	57%	32%	24%	18%	15%	12%	10%	8%	8%
6	60%	33%	27%	21%	17%	14%	12%	10%	8%
5	64%	35%	29%	23%	20%	16%	14%	12%	11%
4	68%	39%	31%	27%	22%	19%	15%	14%	13%
3	73%	43%	34%	30%	26%	23%	19%	16%	15%

Top 5%	AA, KK, QQ, JJ, AKs, TT, AKo, 99, AQs, AQo
Top 10%	AJs, KQs, ATs, KJs, QJs, 88, KTs, QTs, JTs, 77, 66, AJo, A9s
Top 15%	KQo, 55, K9s, T9s, J9s, Q9s, 44, A8s, ATo, 33, A7s
Top 20%	A5s, KJo, 98s, 22, A6s, A9o, A4s, A3s, T8s, QJo
Top 30%	A2s, A8o, A7o, J8s, JTo, A5o, KTo, A4o, A6o, 87s, K8s, QTo, A3o, 97s, Q8s
Top 40%	A2o, K7s, 76s, K6s, 86s, T7s, K5s, K9o, J7s, K4s, 96s, 65s, T9o, Q7s, 54s, K3s, K8o, Q6s, 75s, K2s, Q9o, K7o
Top 50%	85s, 98o, T8o, 64s, K6o, Q4s, J5s, 87o, 95s, J4s, 74s, T5s, K5o, 53s, J8o, Q5s, J9o, Q3s
Top 60%	Q2s, K3o, Q8o, K4o, 76o, T6s, J6s, K2o, J3s, T4s, 97o, 43s, 84s, T7o, Q7o, Q6o
Top 70%	63s, J2s, T3s, Q5o, J7o, Q4o, Q3o, 65o, 86o, 94s, T2s, J6o, J5o, Q2o, 93s
Top 80%	96o, T6o, J4o, J3o, J2o, 92s, T5o, 52s, 73s, 75o, 54o, 62s, 83s, 82s, 64o
Top 90%	72s, 85o, 95o, 74o, 84o, 94o, 93o, T2o, 92o, 42s, 32s, 53o, 43o
Top 100%	63o, T4o, 52o, T3o, 73o, 42o, 32o, 62o, 83o, 82o, 72o

Using the Equilibrium Solution in Practice: The Power Number

Since the full equilibrium solution is too difficult to memorize, we'll now present an approximation to the equilibrium solution that's a little more reasonable to remember. Use this for situations when you have a CSI between 3 and 8, are far from the money, and no one has entered the pot before you.

Take the number of opponents to your left (so on the button, this would be 2).

Multiply this by your CSI (use fractions at your discretion).

At a full table, if there's an ante bigger than one-fifth of the small blind, then subtract 5%.

• If the antes are smaller than one-fifth or if playing with 6 or fewer players, ignore the antes (i.e., don't subtract 5%).

This product is the Power Number (PN) you need in order to push all-in[6].

Examples:

• Pushing from the button with a CSI of 4.5 needs a PN of 9.

• Pushing from 3 off the button with a CSI of 6 needs a PN of 30.

• Pushing from UTG at a 9-player table (with an ante) with a CSI of 5 needs a PN of 38 (8 opps x 5 CSI = 40. Subtract 5% for ante (2) = 38).

Now that you know what PN you need, the table on page 94 shows the PN of all the different starting hands.

Use the labels at the top and left of the chart; find one card along the left and the other across the top. Pairs are found

---

[6] A similar method was first suggested by David Sklansky in *The System*.

SUITED

	A	K	Q	J	T	9	8	7	6	5	4	3	2
A	+	+	+	+	+	50	37	32	28	31	27	26	24
K	+	+	+	75	66	44	17	15	14	13	11	10	9
Q	+	48	+	75	58	38	16	11	10	8	8	8	8
J	50	31	26	+	58	39	21	12	7	7	7	7	5
T	36	19	17	22	+	43	26	15	10	9	7	5	4
9	27	12	9	9	11	+	31	17	10	9	3	3	
8	24	10	8	8	10	10	66	19	15	10	5		
7	22	9	6	5	6	7	10	58	15	10	9		
6	18	9	6	4	3	3	4	7	51	11	10	4	
5	21	9	6	4						44	11	8	
4	18	8	5	3							39	6	
3	16	8	5	3								33	
2	15	7	4	3									28

OFFSUIT

Always Push
PN 70-79
PN 60-69
PN 50-59
PN 40-49
PN 30-39
PN 20-29
PN 10-19
PN 3-9
No PN

along the diagonal of the chart. Suited cards are above and to the right of the diagonal. Offsuit cards are below and to the left of the diagonal. K9o has a PN of 12, A5s is 31, and pocket 3s are 33. Hands marked with a '+' sign can be pushed from all positions with a CSI of 8 or lower. Hands without an entry are too weak to be pushed unless your CSI is less than 3.

Again, this doesn't reflect the correct strengths of all hands in all situations; it's an average strength over many different situations. There may be times where it's preferable to push with a hand that has a lower PN than another (for example, the A5s in preference to AJo when pushing CSI 7 from 7 off the button).

When Your Opponents Don't Play Optimally

These equilibrium solutions assume that your opponents will be calling with the equilibrium calling range. Those calling ranges are specified in Appendix 2.

What if you think that your opponents might have calling ranges that are tighter or looser than optimal? Like we said before, the good news is that you make more money either way. If you want to maximize your profits against sub-optimal opponents, you should push more often against tighter opponents and push less often against loose ones. The tendencies of the blinds are the most important, since those will be the players who will most frequently call you.

Let's look at a blind-stealing situation of raising all in on the button with a CSI of 5. The equilibrium solution—again, far from the money—is to push with 22+, A2+, K9o+, K4s+, QTo+, Q8s+, JTo, J7s+, T7s+, 97s+, 86s+, 76s, 65s (35%). It assumes the SB will call with 22+, A2+, KTo+, K8s+, QJo, QTs+, JTs (26%) and the BB with 22+, A2+, K9o+, K6s+, QTo+, Q9s+, J9s+, T9s (30%). Players don't often follow the equilibrium solution and call less frequently. Looking at a large database of online hand histories, it appears that in this situation you're much more likely to be called only about 16% from the SB and 17% from the BB. If this is true, you can profitably push 94% of hands! Naturally, if your opponents observe you pushing all the time, they'll start calling you more often. But until that point, they have no idea you're pushing with such weak hands, unless someone calls and forces you to show. If you show down a weak hand and manage to win, you'll have lost much of your fold equity. This should encourage you to push less frequently than the numbers suggest.

Now look at the other extreme example of pushing UTG at a 9-player table with a CSI of 7. The equilibrium solution is to push with 66+, AQo+, ATs+, KTs+, QTs+, JTs (8.9%). It assumes that both blinds will call with 99+, AQ+ (5.1%)

and everyone else with only 99+, AKo, AQs+ (4.2%). It always seems to me that my opponents aren't capable of laying down AJo or ATs in this situation. Let's assume that your opponents are a little looser so that everyone calls with 77+, AJ+, ATs (7.5%). Against looser opponents it's best to push only with 88+, AQo+, AJs+ (5.9%).

You should push more frequently if:
• Your remaining opponents are tighter than equilibrium (especially the blinds)—most applicable when stealing from the SB or button with a CSI above 4.
• You're playing in a live tournament.
• You have a tight image.
• It has been awhile since you pushed all-in pre-flop.
• You've shown down strong hands after pushing.

You should push less frequently if:
• Your remaining opponents are looser than equilibrium (especially the blinds)—most applicable when pushing into multiple opponents when you have a CSI above 6.
• You're playing in an online tournament.
• You have a loose image.
• You have pushed all-in pre-flop several times in the last few hands.
• You've shown down some weak hands after pushing.

5

KILL PHIL:
THE NEXT GENERATION

Long Ball vs. Small Ball

Playing poker involves higher-level strategic decisions. We don't mean tactical decisions, like whether to call, raise, or fold. We mean the decision to play the game itself. A thoughtful player will decide which games to learn and whether to play cash games or tournaments, then tailor his strategy to the situation. One of those major decisions is whether to play long ball or small ball.

There are good arguments in favor of either approach. The small-ball approach plays many small pots. It's particularly good for the skilled player who can milk opponents for profits, while making big laydowns on occasion. The good small-ball player doesn't often risk his tournament life on a single hand.

In contrast, the long-ball player routinely moves in. This sounds risky—if not downright suicidal. But done properly, it can actually be safe. You see, other players are unlikely to call an all-in bet. Consequently, the good long-ball player doesn't see many showdowns. While the good small-ball player doesn't risk much in any single pot, the good long-ball practitioner plays tighter and avoids confrontations. Properly played, both strategies are low risk over a sequence of hands.

The long-ball approach is particularly good if your opponents are fearful (as in a tournament). It's also good if your opponents can outplay you. That explains the title of our previous long-ball book, *Kill Phil*. The all-in move is a tremendous equalizer against Phil Hellmuth and other players of superior skill.

Of course, when given a choice, take both. The top players use a mixture of small-ball and long-ball tactics. When the situation is appropriate, they make modest probing bets. On other occasions, they overbet the pot or simply move in. When the blinds become large relative to their stacks, all the top pros switch to long ball.

Often there are multiple ways to play a hand and you must choose between small ball and long ball. Folding or moving all-in end the hand immediately. It eliminates further strategic flexibility for all players. Lesser bets manipulate the pot size and give both players strategic flexibility.

In general, small-ball tactics are better when you benefit from uncertainty on multiple streets of play. This means neither you nor your opponents should be terribly risk-averse. In other words, you're willing to gamble and mix it up with further bets. At the same time your opponents won't be easily intimidated by all-in bets and will call them appropriately. Finally, you're capable of outplaying your opponents on further streets. For example, you have the courage to fire bluffs on multiple streets if necessary, while having the judgment to lay down hands. This tends to occur when you're a *good player* in *good position*.

On the other hand, you can't always choose to be better than your opponents and you must often play out of position. Good players avoid playing out of position. But if you make a small-ball raise and get called by a later player, then you're stuck seeing a flop. Your opponent will act last on all subsequent decisions and have the informational advantage. This is a bad spot for small raises, especially against good players.

Instead, it's an ideal opportunity for long-ball tactics on

the flop. If your opponent will call with a bad hand, then you want to extract the maximum. And if your opponent won't call, then you want to deny free cards. Often the result of long-ball tactics on the flop will be identical to the results of small ball. You'll check and fold to a bet or bet and take the pot. Occasionally, you'll get a free card with a check. And sometimes both you and your opponent will have good hands where all the money will go in anyway, even with small-ball tactics. The main difference is that long-ball tactics often extract the maximum from your good hands while still bluffing effectively. At the same time, long-ball tactics prevent you from getting outplayed when out of position.

While we can't analyze every situation, particularly coordinated flops, we can analyze some very common situations to give guidelines when out of position.

Big Pushes on the Flop

Imagine that you're in the mid-stages of a tournament with blinds of 100/200. You've just raised to 800 from the cut-off and the SB calls. The flop comes down: A♠7♥2♦.

The SB is fairly short-stacked with only 5,400 left and he pushes it all into the 1,800 pot. You have him covered, but it would be a large part of your stack to call. How strict are your calling standards to meet this bet of three times the pot? Would you call with AJ? AT? A8? Any ace?

If you think A8 is too weak to call a bet of three times the pot, consider things from your opponent's point of view. Let's say he knows you're fairly aggressive when raising from the cut-off and he correctly puts you on 22+, A2s+, A5+, K9+, QT+, J9s+, T8s+, 97s+, 86s+, 75s+, 64s+, 54s. After the flop comes down, if your calling standards are AT or better, then it's profitable for the SB to push *with any two cards*. You've set the bar too high and are letting your opponent steal from you with anything. Even if the SB pushed with something as disgusting as Q3, that push is more profitable to him than checking and folding to your continuation bet. With Q3, there's a 78.6% chance that you're folding. When you do call him, his equity is very poor: 2.6%. So his equity of pushing is:

$$(78.6\% \times 1,800) + 21.4\% \times (2.6\% \times 12,600 - 5,400) = 329$$

That means you have to call with A9 to avoid being completely run over. Even if you lower your standards to A8, it's still profitable for the SB to push with all aces, all 7s, all 2s, all wheel draws like 53, and practically any pocket pair.

Now let's look at another flop: 7♠5♥2♦. What are your calling standards now facing a triple pot bet? Can you call with 97? A5? 44? How weak are you willing to go? Did I fool you this time? Actually, even 44 isn't setting the bar low enough to make it unprofitable for your opponent to push any two. Even if you called with any set, 2-pair, overpair, any 7, any 5, 44, and even A2, that still wouldn't be calling enough. You'd need to add in hands like 33, A3, and AK to make it unprofitable.

What about paired flops? Let's take Q♠Q♥4♦. Calling with 77 or better is about the borderline for making it unprofitable for your opponent to push with any two.

What can you learn from this exercise? Am I saying that if your opponent bets three times the pot, you should call with A3 when the flop is 7-5-2? Well, yes and no. Calling with A3 is only right if you think your opponent is capable of calling the initial raise, as well as pushing post-flop with any two. If you think your opponent (and that includes just about anyone— small baller, long baller, tight, loose, pro, piker) is more selective with his actions, then calling with A3 becomes a mistake.

This is a common theme in this book: Our calling range becomes a function of our opponent's assumed pushing range. The less often we think he's pushing, the less often we should call. However, if we're the one doing the pushing and we think our opponent is tight enough, then it can be profitable to blast away. Hopefully, these examples give you a flavor of how tight your opponent has to be before you could essentially never check/fold. If you didn't like the idea of calling with A5 or 44 on a 7-5-2 flop, your opponent probably won't like it either. If that's the case and we're right about his assumed pre-flop raising hands, no matter what your cards are, pushing that flop is always better than checking and folding.

Part of the reason this works well is because the raiser had a wide range of hands with which he was making the pre-flop raise. Against a tighter opponent or an early-position raiser, it won't work as well. He'll more likely have a strong hand, like an overpair or a big ace, and you'll get caught too often.

For example, let's say the raiser is in early or mid-position and has the tighter range of 77+, AQ+, ATs+, KTs+, QTs+, JTs, and we have the A-7-2 flop. Then you can push any two when your opponent is so tight as to only call AK or better. If he'll call with AQ, you can still push sets, any ace, 7, or 2, and all wheel draws. If he'll call with AJ, it's no longer profitable to push the 2s and some of the 7s.

This type of hyper-aggressive move is probably best to be pulled out of your bag of tricks only once in a while. The first time you put in a large bet on the flop, your opponents may give you more respect and decide not to risk it. Do it two or three times and they'll start to realize that you can't be pushing only strong hands. Do it more than that and they'll know you're robbing them.

Just for fun, we took the next step and generated a pseudo-equilibrium solution for betting on the 7-5-2 flop. It's not a true optimal solution, because our model assumes there's no betting on the turn or river. This is the equivalent of saying that after the turn is revealed, if the players aren't all-in already, whoever is going to lose the hand realizes his fate and doesn't put in any more money.

For this solution, each player is allowed to check, bet a "normal" amount of two-thirds the pot, or go all-in (stacks are 3 times the starting pot). The player to act first on the flop is assumed to have a pre-flop distribution of 55-TT, A9o-AJo, A7s-A8s, KQ-KJ, KTs, QTs+, JTs. We're assuming that this player would have re-raised pre-flop with stronger hands. The player to act last has a distribution of 22+, A2s+, A5+, K9+, QT+, J9s+, T8s+, 97s+, 86s+, 75s+, 64s+, 54s.

The solution says[7] that the first player should check 100% of the time. The following key refers to the top chart on page 103:

CR Check-raise, call a jam
C-C Check and call
C-CF Check and call small raise, fold to a jam
CF Check and fold
     Not played pre-flop

When the first player checks, the second player should do one of the following, as seen in the bottom chart on page 103:

J Jam
R Raise to 3BB, call a re-raise
RF Raise to 3BB, fold to a re-raise
K Check
     Not played pre-flop

SUITED

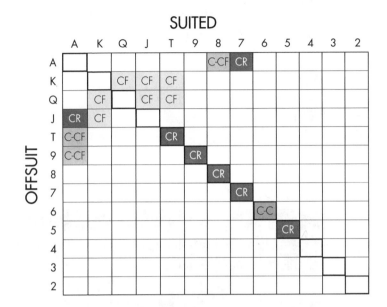

SUITED

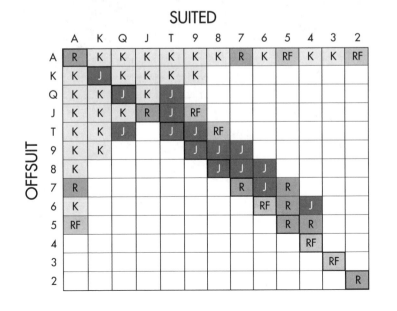

The equilibrium solution is prepared to handle normal bets and pushes from the first player, even though he doesn't do them in equilibrium. If the first player makes a normal bet, the second player should:

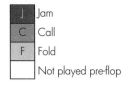

J — Jam
C — Call
F — Fold
   — Not played pre-flop

SUITED

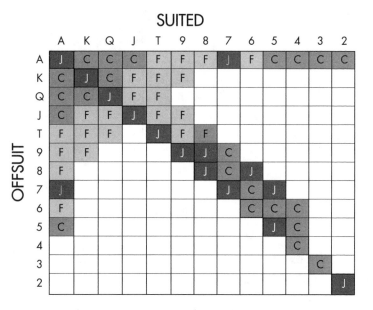

OFFSUIT	A	K	Q	J	T	9	8	7	6	5	4	3	2
A	J	C	C	C	F	F	F	J	F	C	C	C	C
K	C	J	C	F	F	F							
Q	C	C	J	F	F								
J	C	F	F	J	F	F							
T	F	F	F		J	F	F						
9	F	F				J	J	C					
8	F						J	C	J				
7	J							J	C	J			
6	F								C	C	C		
5	C									J	C		
4											C		
3												C	
2													J

If the first player pushes all-in, the second player should:

- C — Call
- F — Fold
-   — Not played pre-flop

SUITED

OFFSUIT	A	K	Q	J	T	9	8	7	6	5	4	3	2
A	C	C	F	F	F	F	F	C	F	C	C	F	F
K	C	C	F	F	F	F							
Q	F	F	C	F	F								
J	F	F	F	C	F	F							
T	F	F	F		C	F	F						
9	F	F				C	F	C					
8	F						C	C	F				
7	C							C	C	C			
6	F								F	C	F		
5	C									C	F		
4											F		
3												F	
2													C

6

PRIZE POOLS
AND EQUITIES

How the Prize Structure
Affects Your Decisions

Earlier, we ignored what the actual prizes were in order
to generate an equilibrium solution for the situation when we
were far from the money. As we get closer to the money, we
can no longer ignore how prizes are distributed. Imagine an
online tournament with a million dollars in the total prize pool.
A typical multi-table tournament will give a large percentage
of the prize to the top few finishers with progressively smaller
prizes awarded to roughly the top 10%. However, it's easy to
imagine two other extremes of payout structures:

• It could be a winner-take-all tournament where first place
becomes a millionaire, while second place gets nothing.

• The other extreme is a super-satellite tournament with
multiple prizes of the same value. A tournament might give
away $10,000 seats to the WSOP Main Event to the top 100
finishers.

All tournaments have prize structures that fall somewhere
in the spectrum between these two extremes. Some may be
closer to one end than the other. Where the tournament lies on

the spectrum will change the value of your chips as the tournament progresses.

Spectrum of Tournament Payouts

Winner-take-all or single-seat satellite	Top-heavy structure	"Normal" structure	Flattish structure	Super-satellite structure

Your chips always retain the same value in a winner-take-all tournament. If there are a million chips in the million-dollar tournament, your chips are worth $1 apiece no matter how many you have. Things aren't so clear if prizes are awarded to more than one spot. Let's say there are also a million total chips in the satellite tournament where the top 100 places get $10,000 each. Let's also say there are 101 players left, you have 2,000, and several players have smaller stacks than you. If you estimate that there's a 90% chance that you won't be the next player eliminated, your 2,000 chips are worth $9,000 to you (90% of a $10,000 seat). That's $4.50 a chip. However, if you have a monster chip stack of 50,000, they'd only be worth about $10,000 in total to you, since you can't win more than one prize. That's only $0.20 a chip. There's a non-linearity in chip value in tournaments and each chip you gain is worth less than the chip before it.

This non-linearity of chip value exists because multiple places are being paid in the tournament. If you win all the chips, you don't get the whole prize pool. Your prize EV is determined not just by your own stack, but also by everyone else's. If someone is eliminated from the tournament, your prize expectation goes up even when you don't gain any chips.

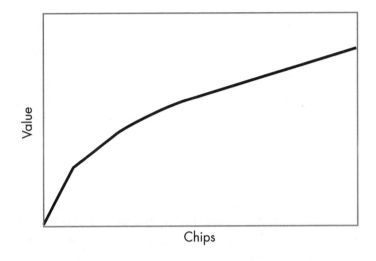

Calculating Prize-Pool EV

In order to calculate how the prize structure will affect your decisions, we need to be able to calculate our prize EV, so that we can see how different decisions will affect that EV. But in order to calculate our EV, we have to estimate our chances of finishing in each one of the prize positions.

To do this, we'll use a model called the Independent Chip Model (ICM). ICM does an excellent job of approximating equities, assuming all of the players are equally skilled[8]. An example (see chart on page 110) from a SNG will show you how to calculate equities with ICM.

---

[8] ICM has some other limitations as well. See Appendix 5 for details.

	Chips	Probability of Finishing			
		1st	2nd	3rd	4th
Player A	8,300	41.5%	30.9%	19.5%	8.0%
Player B	5,300	26.5%	29.0%	27.0%	17.5%
Player C	3,900	19.5%	23.7%	29.5%	27.4%
Player D	2,500	12.5%	16.4%	24.0%	47.1%
Totals	20,000	100%	100%	100%	100%

The probability of each player finishing in first place is equal to his fraction of the total chips in play. For example, Player B has 5,300 / 20,000 = 26.5% of the chips in play.

Calculating the chances of finishing in all the other places besides first gets a little tricky. In order for Player B to come in second, that means someone else must have come in first. Player A will be first 41.5% of the time. According to ICM, if Player A comes in first, the probability that any of the three remaining players will come in second will be equal to his fraction of the total chips among the three remaining players. So if Player A is first, there are 11,700 remaining chips among the three remaining players and the probability Player B will take second is 5,300 / 11,700 = 45.3% of the time. However, we have to repeat this process for Players C and D coming in first as well. See chart on page 111.

We have to multiply the chance of each player coming in first by Player B's chance of coming in second, given that player came in first.

To calculate the chance of coming in third, we have to iterate the process one more time. There are actually six different ways to place players in the first and second slots if Player B is to come in third: A&C, A&D, C&A, C&D, D&A, D&C.

If 1st Place is...	Player B's Fraction of Chips	Chance Player B takes 2nd	Total Probability
Player A (41.5%)	5,300/11,700	45.3%	41.5% x 45.3% = 18.8%
Player C (19.5%)	5,300/16,100	32.9%	19.5% x 32.9% = 6.4%
Player D (12.5%)	5,300/17,500	30.3%	12.5% x 30.3% = 3.8%
		Total	29.0%

We won't go through the math, but the probabilities of all six of those combinations can be calculated, then multiplied by the fraction of chips Player B has compared with the remaining chip total. That will be his chance of coming in third. And, of course, we don't have to solve for the chance of coming in fourth, since that must be 100% minus the chances of coming in all the other positions.

Now, for each player we have the probability that they will finish in each of the four positions. Most SNGs offer 50% of the prize pool to first place, 30% to second, and 20% to third. All that's needed now is to multiply the prizes by the probability that you get that prize. If the total prize pool is $100, then multiply the chance of coming in first by $50, the chance of coming in second by $30, and third by $20. Add them up and the prize EV for each of the players is:

	Chips	EV
Player A	8,300	$33.94
Player B	5,300	$27.36
Player C	3,900	$22.74
Player D	2,500	$15.96
Totals	20,000	$100.00

That was a long and tedious process using ICM to calculate EV, but it's necessary in order to make educated decisions about your play. Fortunately, a number of programs are available that will do these calculations for you. There's a free calculator to solve simple problems at chillin411.com/icmcalc.php. However, we highly recommend the analysis programs available at sitngo-analyzer.com, which offers Sit-n-Go Power Tools (SNGPT), a program that can import online hand histories for Sit-n-Go tournaments and analyze many situations using this equity model. Advantage Analysis LLC, which was instrumental in some of the all-in analysis in this book, created SNGPT. This program is simply a must-have for any serious player of SNGs. While you won't be calculating your ICM equity during play, you can import tournaments you've already played, analyze them, and do a lot of what-if thinking. In time you'll be able to get a feel for how ICM works.

Do I Really Need to Worry About This Non-Linearity?

Yes! It completely changes the whole game.

Let's revisit our first example of an equilibrium solution where we had a SB vs. BB situation with a CSI of 6. In that heads-up example, the equilibrium solution was for the SB to push 60% and for the BB to call 41%. Let's change the situation to a SNG with 50/30/20 payouts and four players left, all with equal stacks of CSI 6. Now the equilibrium solution is for the SB to push 100% and the BB to call 13%. That's right, the BB should only call 13% *even knowing for a fact* that the SB is pushing any two cards! The equilibrium solution has the SB pushing 100% for all stacks sizes bigger than a little over 2 CSI. Lower than that and the BB is calling often enough that the SB can no longer push any two.

When heads-up, any time your opponent was too tight or too loose you made extra money. That's not true with non-linear chip values. In this case, if your opponent is too loose, he hurts himself, but he hurts you too! Take a look at the chart below:

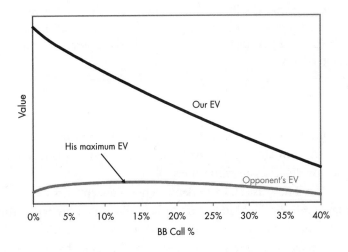

This graph shows your EV and your opponent's EV as a function of how often he decides to call. If you push 100% of the time, your opponent should maximize his own EV and only call 13%. But if he's unaware of how to properly play on the bubble, he might call more often. If he does, you lose a lot of EV. The other two players not even involved in the hand are the ones gaining from this confrontation.

If he's calling about 15% or more, then it's no longer profitable for you to push 100% and you'll have to start folding some weaker hands. Chapter 7 has many more details on how you need to adjust your pushing range as a function of his calling range.

> **KEY POINT:** When chip values are non-linear, a sub-optimal opponent always hurts his own chances. If he's too loose or confrontational, he also hurts any opponent who's involved with the hand. The players not in the hand are the ones who benefit! But if he's too tight, he actually helps the opponent who's involved and consequently hurts the others.

Is It Getting Bubbly In Here?

Once you get close to the money in a tournament, you can't rely on strict pot odds to make decisions. This is due to the non-linearity in chip values.

We'll now use ICM to define a new concept that we're going to call the "bubble factor" to help illustrate how much the tournament structure distorts normal pot-odds situations. This bubble factor is going to vary on an opponent-by-opponent basis. We're defining it as "if you go all-in against that opponent, what's the ratio of the *cost of losing* compared to the *gain from winning*?" If chips had a linear value, like in a cash game, this number would always be exactly 1. If you went all in for $500 against an opponent with equal or greater chips in a cash game, then

The cost of losing = The gain from winning = $500

But in a tournament, the cost of losing is *always* higher than the gain, so the bubble factor is never less than 1. Let's revisit our bubble situation that we talked about in the previous chapter.

	Chips	Share of the Prize Pool
Player A	8,300	33.94%
Player B	5,300	27.36%
Player C	3,900	22.74%
Player D	2,500	15.96%
Totals	20,000	100.00%

Again, put yourself in Player B's shoes. If you go all-in against the short stack (Player D), you can use ICM to calculate your equity if you win and if you lose. If you win the all-in, the chip stacks (and equities) would be:

	Chips	Share of the Prize Pool
Player A	8,300	36.11%
Player B	7,800	35.41%
Player C	3,900	28.48%
Player D	0	0%
Totals	20,000	100.00%

If you lose the all-in, then:

	Chips	Share of the Prize Pool
Player A	8,300	33.83%
Player B	2,800	17.38%
Player C	3,900	22.50%
Player D	5,000	26.29%
Totals	20,000	100.00%

Let's look at how you (Player B) fares. Winning the all-in increases your equity from 27.36% to 35.41%, a gain of 8.05%. Losing drops you down from 27.36% to 17.38%, a loss of 9.98%. So your bubble factor is:

9.98 / 8.05 = 1.24

Losing hurts 1.24 times as much as winning. You can do the same calculations going up against Players A and C and you'd get bubble factors of 2.54 and 1.54, respectively. So what does that mean? A bubble factor of 2.54 against the chip leader means that *the chips you're risking are 2.54 times as valuable as the chips you're hoping to win*. So if you think that your chances of winning against the chip leader are about 33%, then the normal pot odds of 2-to-1 are no longer enough to justify a call. You now need pot odds of *more than 5-to-1* just to make it a breakeven situation. If you're facing a big all-in move getting pot odds close to 1-to-1, you need to be a 2.54-to-1 (72%) favorite to make the call. Pre-flop this only occurs if you're dominating your opponent (for example, AK versus AQ) or if you have the better pair in a pair-versus-pair match up.

If you ever hear a poker announcer on TV say, "Well, he's about a 2-to-1 underdog, but he's getting 2-to-1 on his money, so he's got the right pot odds to call," he is, unfortunately, wrong[9].

Understanding the bubble factor is extremely important in tournaments. You can't simply rely on pot odds to make your decisions. You need to divide your pot odds by the bubble factor to get your tournament odds. When we study calling all-in bets in Chapter 7, you'll see how immensely important bubble factors become.

KEY POINT: You need to divide the actual pot odds by your bubble factor to get your *tournament pot odds*. Bubble factors are always at least 1, so you should be more risk-adverse in a tournament than in a cash game.

---

[9] Unless it's a cash game, heads-up, or a winner-take-all tournament.

Bubble Factors in SNGs

To get a rough idea of how bubble factors vary with chip position, let's calculate everyone's factor against everyone else in our SNG example in the following chart:

	Opponent			
	2,500	3,900	5,300	8,300
2,500		1.38	1.55	1.73
3,900	1.26		1.97	2.24
5,300	1.24	1.54		2.54
8,300	1.16	1.29	1.51	

The player with 3,900 has a bubble factor of 1.26 against the 2,500 player, and the 2,500 player has a bubble factor of 1.38 against the 3,900 player. Look at another example below with more extreme stacks:

	Opponent			
	700	3,500	6,300	9,500
700		1.09	1.23	1.27
3,500	1.05		2.91	3.21
6,300	1.04	1.27		3.40
9,500	1.03	1.14	1.39	

And if everyone had equal stacks:

	Opponent			
	5,000	5,000	5,000	5,000
5,000		1.88	1.88	1.88
5,000	1.88		1.88	1.88
5,000	1.88	1.88		1.88
5,000	1.88	1.88	1.88	

The bubble factor of 1.88 represents an average bubble factor found in a SNG when four players are left. But what about when more than four players are left? These bubble effects are persistent throughout the tournament, not just directly on the bubble. Let's look at a SNG with six players left:

Opponent

Player	1,400	2,000	2,600	3,300	4,300	6,400
1,400		1.13	1.15	1.16	1.19	1.24
2,000	1.13		1.22	1.24	1.28	1.35
2,600	1.12	1.19		1.32	1.30	1.47
3,300	1.12	1.19	1.28		1.49	1.61
4,300	1.11	1.18	1.26	1.38		1.79
6,400	1.09	1.15	1.21	1.30	1.47	

If we were to give all six players equal stacks, we would see that everyone's bubble factor is 1.39, again sort of an average of the bubble factors among all the players. I'll use this definition of an "average bubble factor" to show globally how bubble factors change throughout a tournament. This graph below shows how the average bubble factor changes as you progress through the SNG:

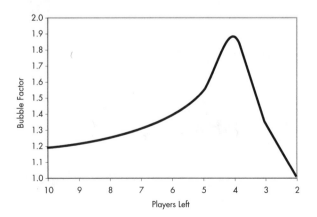

Everyone's bubble factor increases quickly as we approach the prize bubble, and it's highest when there's only one more elimination to go before the money. After the bubble breaks, the bubble factors come down again; the bubble factor is 1 when we reach heads-up. Notice that the average player's bubble factor is about 1.2, even at the very start of the SNG. Ignore this at your own risk!

How the Hell Am I Supposed to Calculate These Factors?

First, notice which circumstances give you a high bubble factor and which lower it. Here are some important observations.

• At the start of a single-table SNG, all players have a bubble factor of 1.2; when down to four players, the bubble factor climbs to 1.88 (nearly 2) if all players have equal stacks.

• If there are no short stacks at the table, everyone will be pretty close to the average bubble factor that we showed in the graph on page 118. A short stack here means relative to the other players, not necessarily relative to the blinds. There won't be much difference in factors between a given stack and a stack that covers it by a small amount.

• The closer you get to the prize bubble, the higher the average bubble factor becomes.

• The presence of small stacks widens the spread of bubble factors for all players.

• A very small stack has a bubble factor close to 1, as does everyone against that stack.

• The biggest bubble factors occur when big stacks clash. A medium stack also has a big bubble factor against anyone with more chips.

• The presence of small stacks widens the gap between stacks that are fairly close together in chips. For example, you have 6,000 chips and someone else at the table has 6,500. If there's a short stack left with only a few hundred chips, your bubble factor against the 6,500 stack is much bigger than his against yours. If the smallest stack were a heftier 4,000, for example, then your bubble factors would be much closer together.

We've also noticed a particular property of bubble factors in SNGs, which allows you to approximate them in many circumstances. It turns out that your bubble factor depends (approximately) on the percentage of the total chips that you and your opponent have, as long as the following conditions are true:

• the tournament has not reached the money;

• the other players not involved in the hand have equal stacks.

The following table and graph summarize what your bubble factor will be depending on your chip stacks:

Bubble Factors with a 50/30/20 Payout

Your Stack	Opponent's Stack										
	0%	5%	10%	15%	20%	25%	30%	35%	40%	45%	50%
0%	1.0	1.0	1.0	1.0	1.0	1.0	1.0	1.0	1.0	1.0	1.0
5%	1.0	1.1	1.1	1.1	1.2	1.2	1.2	1.2	1.3	1.3	1.4
10%	1.0	1.1	1.2	1.2	1.3	1.4	1.4	1.5	1.6	1.6	1.8
15%	1.0	1.1	1.2	1.4	1.4	1.5	1.6	1.7	1.8	2.0	2.1
20%	1.0	1.1	1.2	1.3	1.6	1.7	1.8	1.9	2.1	2.3	2.5
25%	1.0	1.1	1.1	1.3	1.5	1.9	2.0	2.1	2.3	2.6	2.9
30%	1.0	1.1	1.1	1.2	1.4	1.7	2.2	2.4	2.6	2.8	3.2
35%	1.0	1.1	1.1	1.2	1.3	1.5	1.8	2.5	2.8	3.1	3.5
40%	1.0	1.0	1.1	1.2	1.3	1.4	1.6	2.0	3.0	3.3	3.7
45%	1.0	1.0	1.1	1.2	1.2	1.3	1.5	1.6	2.0	3.5	3.9
50%	1.0	1.0	1.1	1.1	1.2	1.2	1.3	1.4	1.5	1.6	4.0

For example, five players are left in a SNG and you have 15% of the chips going against an opponent with 25%. Our approximation estimates that your bubble factor will be 1.5 if the other three stacks all have 20% each. The amazing thing is that this bubble factor is very similar to the one you'd have if there were eight players. If the other six players all had 10% stacks, we'd approximate the same bubble factor. If you were to do the lengthy calculations for these two situations, you'd get 1.46 and 1.42—pretty darn close!

Naturally, the other stacks aren't always equal; the more unequal they are, the higher your bubble factor gets. Let's take the case of 10,000 total chips, four players remaining, and you have 2,500 going against another 2,500 stack. This is how your bubble factor changes as a function of how the other 5,000 chips are split:

Their Chips	Your Bubble Factor
2500 and 2500	1.9
2000 and 3000	1.9
1500 and 3500	2.0
1000 and 4000	2.2
500 and 4500	2.6
250 and 4750	2.9
1 and 4999	3.4

Unfortunately, there's no magic shortcut for figuring out bubble factors with different chip configurations. But getting familiar with the previous charts and studying every example in this book will improve your intuition for approximating them.

Once you break the bubble in a SNG, you can look at the following two charts to figure out your real bubble factor. With only three players remaining, once you specify two stacks, the other is always fixed, so there's no guesswork:

Bubble Factors with a 50/30/20 Payout (3 Players) or
75/25 Payout (3 or more Players)

Opponent's Stack

		0%	10%	20%	30%	40%	50%
Your Stack	0%	1.0	1.0	1.0	1.0	1.0	1.0
	10%	1.0	1.0	1.1	1.1	1.1	1.2
	20%	1.0	1.0	1.1	1.2	1.2	1.3
	30%	1.0	1.0	1.1	1.3	1.4	1.5
	40%	1.0	1.0	1.1	1.2	1.5	1.8
	50%	1.0	1.0	1.1	1.2	1.3	2.0

You can also use these bubble factors as an approximation for a short-handed SNG that pays 75%/25% or 70%/30%. For short-handed tournaments, the factors should be approximately true for more than three players as well.

Bubble Factors in Super Satellites

Remember when we talked about all tournaments being on a spectrum between winner-take-all and super-satellites? In a winner-take-all tournament, everyone's bubble factor is always exactly 1 throughout the entire game. Bubble factors in large super-satellite tournaments can skyrocket. If 20, 30, or more prizes are being awarded and there's just one more elimination to go, everyone's bubble factor is insanely high, approaching infinity for big-stack clashes. The flatter the prize structure and the closer you get to a prize jump, the higher everyone's bubble factor becomes. Let's look at a graph that shows the average bubble factor in a 20 prize super-satellite on the top of the next page:

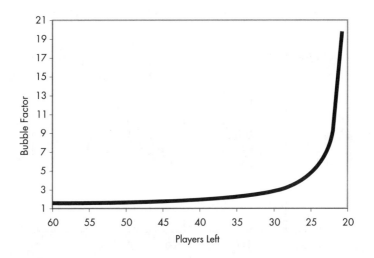

You can actually calculate the average bubble factor for any point in a super-satellite using the following formula:

(Players left -1) / (Eliminations left)

So with 15 players left in a 10-prize satellite, the average bubble factor is (15 - 1) / (5) = 2.8.

Remember that this is the *average* bubble factor around the table. Big-stack clashes have much higher numbers. When bubble factors get this high, the game no longer resembles anything close to poker. Folding pocket aces pre-flop becomes the correct play in many circumstances! More on this when we talk about specific satellite strategies.

Bubble Factors in MTTs

Let's look at average bubble factors for the entire 2006 WSOP Main Event[10] on page 124.

---

[10] We'll ignore the value of endorsements, consolatory prizes, and round-for-round effects.

Average Bubble Factors in the 2006 WSOP Main Event

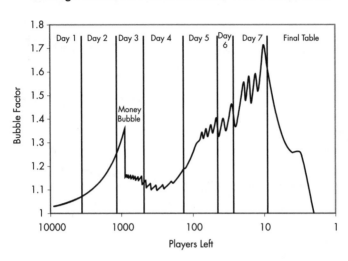

The money bubble factor at the WSOP is much smaller compared to a SNG (1.36 vs. 1.88). After the money bubble breaks, the bubble factor drops dramatically, then rises as the final table approaches. The saw-tooth shape of the graph is the effect of the mini-prize bubbles when a new pay level is reached. These effects are safely ignored at the lower pay levels (not much value in trying to survive a pay jump from $39K to $43K). But the bubble factors steadily increase and the saw-tooth becomes bigger as each step becomes a bigger pay jump. This continues until you reach the final-table bubble. Final-table play provides a steady decrease in bubble factors as the table becomes more short-handed, until it reaches 1 when heads-up.

A similar profile can be seen in the PokerStars Sunday Millions tournament that has a slightly flatter payout structure and pays 15% of the field:

Average Bubble Factors in the PokerStars Sunday Millions

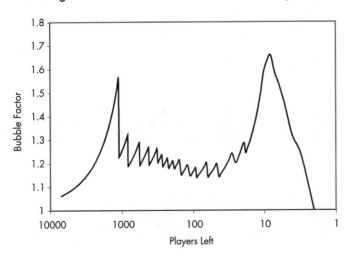

The bubble factor at the money bubble is a little higher (1.55) and rapidly increases once it gets down to two tables. Every tournament has a unique structure.

This year during the 2007 WSOP ME, a flatter payout structure was introduced, guaranteeing over $20,000 for making the money. Contrasting this payout structure to the 2006 ME shows some interesting differences. See the top chart on page 126.

The bubble factor at the money bubble in 2007 is much more significant, almost 1.6, but there was almost no premium for making the final table. Contrast this to the 2006 tournament where making the money was no big deal, but the bubble to make the final table was huge. In 2007, the biggest relative jumps in prize money are around 7th to 4th place, making those the most strategically interesting times in terms of non-linear chip values.

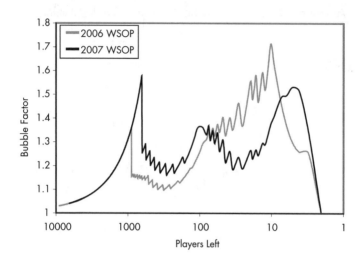

So is the WSOP an unusual tournament since it's so big? Let's look at a smaller MTT that pays only the last 9 players:

Place	Prize
1st	30%
2nd	20%
3rd	12%
4th	10%
5th	8%
6th	6.5%
7th	5.5%
8th	4.5%
9th	3.5%

Bubble factors for a typical distribution of chips
(10 players remaining):

Opponent

	21,500	36,800	51,100	62,400	77,700
21,500		1.41	1.50	1.53	1.57
36,800	1.28		1.87	1.93	1.97
51,100	1.24	1.51		2.09	2.13
62,400	1.17	1.38	1.69		2.19
77,700	1.17	1.29	1.47	1.69	
94,100	1.13	1.23	1.36	1.49	1.76
111,500	1.08	1.17	1.25	1.35	1.52
136,000	1.07	1.13	1.19	1.26	1.36
170,800	1.08	1.11	1.16	1.19	1.26
238,100	1.06	1.07	1.12	1.13	1.17

Player

Opponent

	94,100	111,500	136,000	170,800	238,100
21,500	1.59	1.61	1.62	1.62	1.64
36,800	2.01	2.02	2.04	2.08	2.09
51,100	2.16	2.20	2.23	2.26	2.30
62,400	2.23	2.26	2.31	2.34	2.39
77,700	2.30	2.33	2.38	2.42	2.48
94,100		2.37	2.43	2.47	2.55
111,500	1.79		2.44	2.50	2.57
136,000	1.50	1.74		2.52	2.61
170,800	1.34	1.46	1.69		2.66
238,100	1.22	1.27	1.36	1.56	

Player

The average bubble factor here at the money bubble is 2.05. That's slightly higher than our SNG bubble. The 2006 WSOP money bubble is much smaller, since such a small portion of the prize pool is awarded at the bubble. A $14,597 prize isn't anything compared to a shot at $12 million. For a smaller tournament, just making the bubble is significant and the prize pool is fairly flat thereafter.

Let's take one final look at this smaller MTT and see how bubble factors change approaching the bubble as well as after the bubble breaks:

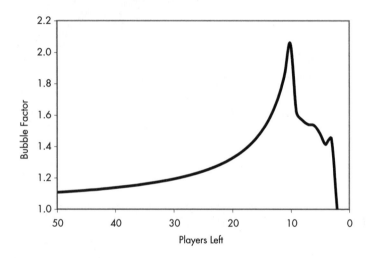

The actual bubble factors after the bubble bursts are highly dependent on the prize for each place. Although there's some wobbling around, it's important to note that it stays relatively high (around 1.5) until it's heads-up. We examine final-table structures in a little more detail in Chapter 7 when we talk about MTT final-table strategy.

Bubble Factors: Putting It All Together

So now you know how to approximate bubble factors, but what are you supposed to do with these numbers? It's a good idea to study the examples we give throughout this book to get comfortable with how high your bubble factor will be in certain situations. For example, there's a lot of practical value in knowing that the bubble factor is high in big-stack versus big-stack and medium-stack versus bigger-stack clashes. The bigger the stack you confront, the higher your bubble factor. Picking on stacks shorter than yours is supported by the math. As you're playing any tournament, you can start approximating your own bubble factors using the method we outlined.

You should also note what your opponents' bubble factors are against you. If they're aware of this effect of tournament structure, then you can put yourself in their shoes and adjust accordingly. Opponents who know they have high bubble factors are much more likely to fold, so you'll have a lot of fold equity against them. Examining everyone's bubble factors will give you guidance as to how you should deviate from how you play far from the money, where everyone's bubble factor is very close to 1. This 2x2 matrix is a summary of some of the playing adjustments you should make based on the bubble factor:

Bully on the Playground	Game of Chicken
Your Bubble Factor is Low His Bubble Factor is High (Big Stack vs. Medium Stack)	Your Bubble Factor is High His Bubble Factor is High (Big Stack vs. Big Stack or Satellite Situations)
Aggression, aggression, aggression	Keep the pot small or be the first to push all-in
Cash Game	Pick Your Spot
Your Bubble Factor is Low His Bubble Factor is Low (Small Stack vs. Small Stack or Far From the Money)	Your Bubble Factor is High His Bubble Factor is Low (Medium Stack vs. Big Stack)
Play normal poker	Don't bluff and play your good hands hard and fast

Both of your bubble factors are low. This will be fairly close to a cash game in strategy. Since chip values are fairly linear, normal pot odds can dictate many of your decisions. Just play normal poker. If in the Move-in stage, you can use the equilibrium plays discussed for far from the money.

Both of your bubble factors are high. Now you essentially have a game of chicken. Neither of you wants a confrontation, as there's not much to gain and everything to lose. So you have two options: either avoid a confrontation (fold or just keep the pot small) or show that you're 100% committed (be the first to go all-in). *If* your opponent understands bubble effects, he should back down if you push first. There's a "right of first bluff" in chicken situations and it actually gives an advantage to those in earlier positions.

This is most explicit near the bubble of a satellite that offers multiple equivalent prizes. In satellites everyone, not just the chip leaders, has a high bubble factor. So the best strategy is usually to either fold pre-flop or push all-in, forcing everyone else to fold. Making a raise smaller than all-in is the worst choice. This gives someone else the initiative, allowing him to be the one to push first. If he comes over the top of you, you'll have to let the hand go, sometimes even if you have pocket aces.

Yes, it's sometimes right to fold pocket aces pre-flop, but only in satellite tournaments. Here's an example of why. Let's say you're in a satellite tournament that awards a seat into a larger tournament to the top five winners. There are six people left in the tournament. You're the chip leader and are in the cutoff position. The stacks are:

	Chips
Player A	3,000
Player B	4,000
You	16,000
Button	12,750
Small Blind	6,500
Big Blind	7,750

The blinds are 200/400 and you're dealt a nice pair of pocket aces. Players A and B both fold and you raise to 1,200 (a mistake as we'll soon see). The button pushes all in and both of the blinds fold. Can you call with your aces? To answer this, you need to figure out your EV of folding, winning an all-in, and losing an all-in. Using ICM, you can calculate that by folding, you're left with 14,800 chips and a 97.5% chance of getting a seat. If you call and win with your aces, the tournament is over and you have a 100% chance of getting a seat. If you call and lose, you're down to 3,250 chips and a 71% chance of winning a seat. This means you need to win more than 91% of the time just to break even!

(97.5% - 71%) / (100% - 71%) = 91.4%

Even if your opponent went all in without looking at his hand, you'd only be 85.2% to win. And if your opponent flashed a 72 offsuit, you'd only win 88.2%. Aces simply don't win often enough to call. You can sit tight and wait for your seat. Losing that all-in hurts your chances of winning by a lot and winning the all-in doesn't help much. You have enough chips; you don't need to take the risk to try and get more. Your bubble factor is more than 10. His was almost 40! But you made the mistake of coming into the hand to begin with for less than all-in, giving him the opportunity to put you to the last guess. And this is a guess with only one right answer. Fold!

Your bubble factor is low, but his is high. Now your opponent can't afford to lose chips, but they aren't worth as much to you. This is the time to steal pots with reckless abandon. Your fold equity here is extremely high, so raise much more often than you would when far from the money. Near the bubble of any major tournament, pro players take advantage of their opponents' tight play. As the prize bubble nears, many inexperienced players act as though their bubble factor is a lot higher than it really is. More on this when we talk about specific bubble strategies for multi-table tournaments.

Your bubble factor is high, but his is low. Now you have to be cautious. Your opponent is likely to be fairly loose, so you should stop bluffing or making wild steal attempts. You can't afford to bluff away your chips, since they're too valuable to you and he's more likely to call. However, if you do have a good hand, you should push it more aggressively than against other players, since he'll be more likely to pay you off. There can be extreme cases, such as satellite situations, where your bubble factor is so high that you can't even be aggressive with your best hands. You should simply fold 100% of the time.

Quantifying bubble factors allows us to dispel a couple of big-stack myths as well.

Big-Stack Myth #1: As the Big Stack, You Should Attack the Small Stacks

It's actually much better to attack the medium stacks, as long as they aren't too big compared to yours. The medium stacks have a much higher bubble factor against you, and yours is about the same against the small or medium stacks. The medium stacks will be afraid of you, but the small stacks might be desperate enough to take a stand.

As an example, let's look at a SNG where the last four players have 1,000, 2,000, 3,000, and 4,000 chips. In the graph on page 133, compare how the medium (3,000) stack has a much more concave equity curve than the small (1,000) stack when they go up against the big (4,000) stack.

The medium stack has a lot more to lose and not as much to gain. He'll be much more likely to avoid a fight with the chip leader compared to the small stack.

How the Small (1,000) and the Medium (3,000) Stacks
Change Value Against the Big (4,000) Stack

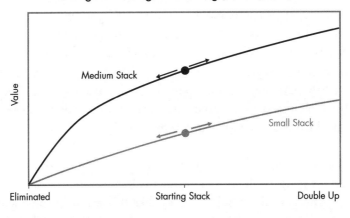

Big-Stack Myth #2: As the Big Stack, You Should Call Liberally to Knock Out Players

Dan Harrington, in his excellent book *Harrington on Hold 'em Volume II*, even takes this to the extreme by using what he calls the "10-to-1 Rule". He says, "If I have at least 10 times as many chips as another player, I will cheerfully put them all-in with any two cards." He then cites an example where he made a call of a 3.7BB all-in button raise with J3o, simply because he had more than 10 times as many chips as the button.

Actually, this 10-to-1 rule doesn't make sense to us. No matter how the stacks are arranged, your bubble factor can never be less than 1. That means that if you wouldn't make the call in a cash game, then you shouldn't make the call in a tournament[11]. Super-loose calls will just double up your opponents too frequently. Harrington says it's because you want to

---

[11] Tournaments are different, though, due to escalating blinds. Calling ranges are thus highly dependent on betting ranges. But it's a strict cash-game pot-odds decision.

try and eliminate players. But as the big stack, you don't care if you eliminate players. When you bust a player, you increase everyone else's equity more than yours. To you, they're simply chips. True, it doesn't hurt you that much to call, but it doesn't *help* you that much either. Many times it can be right to call, because the tiny stack is pushing a wide range of hands. But we believe it's correct to let pot odds, combined with the likely betting range of your opponent, dictate your decisions. There's no added bonus for knocking someone out.

Ed Miller also echoes this sentiment in *Getting Started in Hold'em*, saying, "Your job is to win chips, not eliminate players. (Many people will tell you otherwise, but they are wrong.)"

Thinking about bubble factors like this will help you make more intelligent decisions in tournaments. We'll use bubble factors throughout the rest of this book to guide our decisions. However, your opponents may not be as aware of these effects and that can make a big difference. An opponent who isn't aware of bubble factors will play as if his bubble factor were closer to 1 than it actually is. Your bubble factor remains unchanged, so you have to be more cautious around an ignorant player. The following guidelines apply:

• Don't steal as much with weaker hands.

• Don't play at all near a satellite bubble in most circumstances.

• Don't try to play chicken against someone who doesn't understand the rules of the game. Look for players who call with weak hands in high-bubble-factor situations. These are the ignorant players that you need to avoid.

Calling All-In Raises

If a short stack raises all-in and you're faced with a decision to call, five factors influence your decision:

• your cards;

• the assumed hand range of the raiser;

Prize Pools and Equities • 135

• the tournament odds you're getting (pot odds divided by your bubble factor);
  • the possibility of overcalls;
  • in live tournaments, any tells you might have on your opponent.

Possible overcalls can complicate matters, depending on how likely it is that someone will overcall behind you. You're probably safe ignoring overcalls if no one had previously come in before the raiser and the raise was CSI 4 or higher. This isn't to say that overcalls never happen, but rather that the probability is small enough that they won't significantly affect your decision to call. You can try to discourage overcalls by raising again yourself, but this commits more of your stack. If overcalls seem like a real possibility, then it's prudent to be more conservative with your calls.

This following four-page table shows the tournament odds (pot odds divided by bubble factor) you need to call with the top 20% of calling hands[12] versus multiple possible hand strengths for the raiser:

---

[12] Just as there is no single correct sort order for pushing hands, there is no set order for calling hands. These are our best recommendations to cover most common situations. Note that the rank order is different between calling and pushing.

Tournament Odds Needed to Call Opponent's All-in Push

Your Hand		TT+, AK	99+, AQ+	Top 8%	Top 10%	Top 15%
	AA	0.2	0.2	0.2	0.2	0.2
	KK	0.5	0.4	0.4	0.4	0.3
	QQ	0.9	0.7	0.6	0.5	0.4
Top 5%	JJ	1.3	1.0	0.8	0.7	0.6
	AKs	1.3	1.0	0.8	0.8	0.7
	AKo	1.5	1.1	0.9	0.9	0.7
	TT	1.9	1.3	1.0	0.9	0.7
	AQs	1.9	1.6	1.2	1.1	0.8
	99	2.2	1.7	1.3	1.1	0.9
	AQo	2.3	1.8	1.3	1.2	0.9
	AJs	2.1	2.0	1.4	1.3	1.0
	88	2.2	1.8	1.5	1.2	1.0
	KQs	2.1	2.0	1.6	1.3	1.2
	77	2.2	1.8	1.6	1.4	1.1
Top 10%	ATs	2.3	2.1	1.6	1.4	1.1
	AJo	2.5	2.4	1.7	1.4	1.1
	66	2.2	1.8	1.6	1.6	1.2
	KJs	2.3	1.9	1.7	1.4	1.3
	55	2.2	1.8	1.7	1.7	1.3
	A9s	2.4	2.3	1.8	1.6	1.3
	ATo	2.8	2.5	1.9	1.6	1.3

Opponent's Pushing Range

Tournament Odds Needed to Call Opponent's All-in Push

Your Hand		Opponent's Pushing Range			
		Top 20%	Top 25%	Top 50%	Any Two
Top 5%	AA	0.2	0.2	0.2	0.2
	KK	0.3	0.3	0.3	0.2
	QQ	0.4	0.4	0.4	0.3
	JJ	0.5	0.5	0.4	0.3
	AKs	0.6	0.6	0.5	0.5
	AKo	0.7	0.6	0.6	0.5
	TT	0.6	0.6	0.5	0.3
	AQs	0.7	0.7	0.6	0.5
Top 10%	99	0.8	0.7	0.5	0.4
	AQo	0.8	0.7	0.6	0.6
	AJs	0.8	0.7	0.6	0.5
	88	0.9	0.8	0.6	0.4
	KQs	1.1	1.0	0.8	0.6
	77	0.9	0.9	0.7	0.5
	ATs	1.0	0.8	0.6	0.5
	AJo	0.9	0.8	0.7	0.6
	66	1.0	0.9	0.8	0.6
	KJs	1.3	1.1	0.8	0.6
	55	1.1	1.0	0.9	0.7
	A9s	1.1	1.0	0.7	0.6
	ATo	1.1	0.9	0.7	0.6

Tournament Odds Needed to Call Opponent's All-in Push

Your Hand		Opponent's Pushing Range				
		TT+, AK	99+, AQ+	Top 8%	Top 10%	Top 15%
Top 15%	KQo	2.5	2.4	1.8	1.5	1.3
	44	2.2	1.9	1.7	1.7	1.4
	A8s	2.4	2.3	1.9	1.6	1.4
	KTs	2.6	2.0	1.8	1.5	1.4
	A5s	2.2	2.2	1.8	1.7	1.4
	A7s	2.3	2.3	1.9	1.7	1.4
	33	2.3	1.9	1.7	1.8	1.5
	QJs	2.1	2.0	1.8	1.5	1.4
Top 20%	A4s	2.3	2.2	1.8	1.7	1.5
	A6s	2.4	2.3	1.9	1.7	1.5
	A9o	2.9	2.9	2.2	1.8	1.5
	A3s	2.3	2.2	1.9	1.7	1.5
	KJo	2.8	2.2	2.0	1.6	1.5
	A2s	2.3	2.3	1.9	1.7	1.5
	22	2.3	1.9	1.8	1.8	1.6
	QTs	2.3	2.1	2.0	1.7	1.5
	A8o	2.9	2.8	2.3	1.9	1.6
	JTs	2.4	2.0	1.9	1.7	1.5
	K9s	2.7	2.3	2.0	1.7	1.5
	A7o	2.8	2.8	2.3	1.9	1.7

Tournament Odds Needed to Call Opponent's All-in Push

Your Hand		Opponent's Pushing Range			
		Top 20%	Top 25%	Top 50%	Any Two
Top 15%	KQo	1.2	1.2	0.8	0.6
	44	1.2	1.1	1.0	0.8
	A8s	1.2	1.1	0.8	0.6
	KTs	1.3	1.2	0.8	0.6
	A5s	1.3	1.2	0.9	0.7
	A7s	1.3	1.2	0.8	0.6
	33	1.3	1.2	1.1	0.9
	QJs	1.3	1.2	1.0	0.7
Top 20%	A4s	1.4	1.3	0.9	0.7
	A6s	1.3	1.2	0.9	0.7
	A9o	1.3	1.1	0.8	0.6
	A3s	1.4	1.3	1.0	0.7
	KJo	1.4	1.3	0.9	0.7
	A2s	1.4	1.3	1.0	0.7
	22	1.4	1.3	1.1	1.0
	QTs	1.4	1.3	1.0	0.7
	A8o	1.4	1.2	0.8	0.7
	JTs	1.4	1.4	1.1	0.7
	K9s	1.5	1.4	0.9	0.7
	A7o	1.5	1.3	0.9	0.7

For example, you have pocket kings against an opponent you think is raising with the top 10% of his hands. Your pot odds are 1.6-to-1 and you need at least 0.4-to-1 tournament odds to call. This means you should fold if your bubble factor is more than 4 and call if it's less.

Note that pocket aces need about 0.2-to-1 tournament odds to call, no matter how often he pushes. This means that if your bubble factor is more than 5 times your pot odds, you should fold aces. If your bubble factor is 10, you need 2-to-1 pot odds to call with aces.

Some general rules for calling can help guide your decisions for all pushing and calling ranges. The following slightly smoothed graph shows the relationships between how often your opponent pushes and how often you can call:

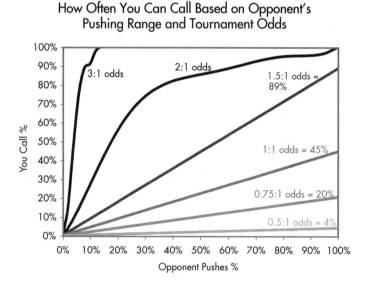

How Often You Can Call Based on Opponent's Pushing Range and Tournament Odds

When your tournament odds are 1.5-to-1 or less, the number of hands that you can call with is surprisingly close to a linear fraction of the number of hands your opponent pushes with. For example, given tournament odds of 1-to-1, you can call 45% as often as your opponent pushes; if your opponent pushes 80% of his hands, you can call with the top 36%. If he pushes 20%, you can call with 9%.

With higher tournament odds, the relationship becomes highly non-linear, as many weaker suited hands can call when given good odds. With 2-to-1 tournament odds, it's correct to call with any 2 cards, if your opponent is likely to be pushing any 2. Given 3-to-1 odds, you can call with any two cards, so long as your opponent is pushing 12% or more.

Example: You're on the bubble of a SNG with the following chip stacks:

	Chips
Cut-off	3,000
Button	4,000
Small Blind	8,000
Big Blind (You)	5,000

Blinds are 300/600, the cut-off folds, the button pushes all-in, and the small blind folds. You have pocket 5s. You're getting 1.44-to-1 pot odds. Recall from earlier in this chapter that we estimate our bubble factor as being 1.5 when we have 25% of the chips and our opponent has 20%. That holds true when the other two players split the remaining chips evenly; since they're slightly uneven, the real bubble factor is slightly higher (about 1.6). Your tournament odds are 0.9-to-1, so looking at the table on page 137, you can call as long as you think the button is pushing 50% or more. Most players aren't pushing this often, so unless you've noticed that this player is very aggressive, folding the pocket 5s is correct.

But notice how sensitive the correct answer is to the tournament odds. If the tournament odds were just 1-1, then calling would be correct if he's pushing the top 25% or more, which could easily be the case. This just means that it's a close call either way, like many decisions in poker. Fortunately, a close decision means that the wrong answer won't be that bad of a choice.

Calling with Pocket Deuces

Many players are loath to call with pocket deuces in almost any situation. The logic is, "Why would I call when I'm at best a small favorite and at worst a big dog?" Based on your CSI, there are times, however, when the pot odds are high and/or your opponent's range is wide, making calling correct. To give you a sense of when it's right to call with a tiny pair, take a look at this graph that shows when you can call a push when in the BB:

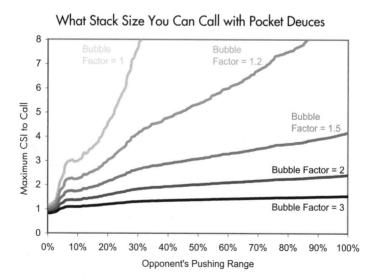

What Stack Size You Can Call with Pocket Deuces

When the bubble factor is 1, even if your opponent is only pushing his top 10% of hands, you can call as long as your (or his) CSI is 3 or less. You can even call an 8 CSI push, if he's pushing at least 30% of his hands. The reason for the S-curve of the graph around 10% is because there's a concentration of suited semi-connectors and mid-pocket pairs around the tenth percentile that do well against 22.

7

SPECIFIC STRATEGIES FOR DIFFERENT TOURNAMENT TYPES

INTRODUCTION

Cash-game strategy makes decisions based on the expected win or loss. If you lose, you can reach into your pocket for more cash and continue playing. Conversely, your opponents can also reload, so they're not inordinately intimidated by large confrontations.

But tournaments are different. Due to distinct payoffs to different tournament spots, you should alter your play. Even more important, your opponents will modify their play. This creates completely different strategy dynamics at the final stages.

It has long been recognized that tournament situations are different, because the value of chips depends nonlinearly on stack size (see Malmuth's *Gambling Theory and Other Topics* and Sklansky's *Tournament Poker for Advanced Players*). The old saying "a chip and a chair" emphasizes that a single chip gives you a chance to win a tournament. More important, a single chip gives you a chance to cash in the money. The last few chips in a small stack have the potential to win a prize and have disproportionate value. The traditional analyses by Malmuth, Sklansky, and Harrington and Robertie emphasize stack sizes.

In contrast Snyder raised a controversy in his book *The Tournament Formula* by considering the "speed" of a tournament. In principle, the pace of a tournament shouldn't affect the play of hands. But in practice, the small Vegas tournaments Snyder described do indeed play differently than slower tournaments. And anything that affects your opponents should impact your play.

So who's right? In a sense, both groups are. Certainly, all poker decisions should be made based on the current situation. Usually, the prime consideration is stack size, where the traditional analysis holds. If I have a stack of 3,500, with blinds of 100/200, I'm not going to decide to suddenly push all in with my pockets fives just because the structure is fast and the blinds are doubling in a few hands.

But the tournament structure exerts a strong effect on the value of those stacks. Snyder's contribution was to emphasize how the structure of the tournament changes the prize value and behavior of those stacks. When bubble factors are high for most of the tournament, players are quite rationally risk-averse. Snyder considers fast tournament structures that quickly reach the bubble and spend much of their time in the end stages. Paradoxically, the correct strategy in such conservative risk-averse situations is to become hyper-aggressive. But the correct play depends critically on the prize structure, the stack sizes, and the order of those stacks. This section analyzes important end-game situations and gives a rigorous treatment of these issues.

SPECIFIC STRATEGIES FOR SNGs

How I Learned to Stop Worrying and Love the Bubble

• Once the blinds are high enough to be worth stealing (>5% of starting stacks), you should frequently raise from late position, if everyone before you has folded.

• Observe your opponents and see who's being aggressive (playing for first) on the bubble and who's just trying to squeak into the money. This will let you know from whom you should steal.

• Respect your opponents' raises until they give you reason to believe they raise with poor hands. With high bubble factors, you can't call many raises and most players don't raise with mediocre hands.

• It pays to know the CSI of every player at the table.

Proper SNG play near the bubble depends on the skill level of your opponents. In all forms of poker, you'll find more skillful players as the buy-in escalates. This is especially true of online SNGs; MTTs have a much weaker correlation between buy-in and playing skill. Although this correlation is higher for SNGs, you still find good players at low levels and players making fundamental mistakes at the higher levels.

Low Buy-ins: There are always exceptions, but most players in the smallest-buy-in games call too frequently, aren't sufficiently aggressive, and have no concept of position or CSI. Post-flop play is particularly bad—players call large bets with poor draws and make bets that are too small to protect their hand. Some players don't adjust enough on the bubble, so don't be surprised when they call your all-in with a weak ace. Others simply play too tight to try and ease into third place, often folding as the small stack even though they're presented with good odds.

Medium Buy-ins: In these games you'll find many more players who've learned that aggression on the bubble is important and will frequently push all-in when their stack drops below 10BB. Several of them have learned about position and frequently steal blinds. Most know something about bubble effects and tighten up around the bubble. But usually, this is just a general tightening up; many don't realize that big stacks should avoid each other or that you should be extremely tight when the short stack is very short.

High Buy-ins: Most players in these games are very aggressive, make blind stealing an art form, and have a solid understanding of ICM (whether or not they actually know the math). You can still find players who play quite poorly here; I (Tysen) have seen some quite puzzling plays, sometimes with buy-ins over $100:

• A player folded to a raise when he had 80 chips after posting 200 in the big blind.

• A player with 900 chips limped for 400, then folded to a raise behind him.

• A player bet and then called a 1.5-times-pot all-in check-raise on a 9♠6♥4♥ flop when he had 6♣3♣.

• A player went all-in every hand for the first six hands of a tournament. No one called him until the sixth hand, when someone called with Q7o.

But poor players become more rare as you move up in buy-ins. Since SNGs are so fast to play, at the higher levels poor players lose money quickly.

Bubble Play in SNGs

Bubble play in a SNG is what separates the men from the boys. When four players are left, bubble factors are at their highest and those who understand how they work will, over time, walk away with most of the money. Bubble play can be very exciting and you need to reach a state of mind where you no longer fear the bubble, but embrace it as a way to instill fear in others.

Observation of your opponent's behavior on the bubble is also critical to your success. The higher your bubble factor, the more important it is to know your opponent's calling ranges.

Let's look at the specific example of pushing from the SB with a CSI of 6. You can determine your most profitable percent of hands to push as a function of how often you think the BB will call. The less often he calls, the more often you push.

The bubble factor makes a huge difference—take a look at this graph:

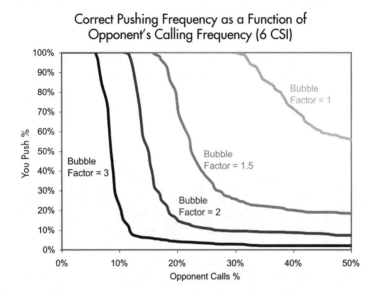

Correct Pushing Frequency as a Function of
Opponent's Calling Frequency (6 CSI)

If you estimate the chance your opponent will call along the bottom of this chart, you can see what your best push percentage is along the left, as a function of the bubble factor. You can see that as the bubble factor increases, your exploitive response becomes hypersensitive to how loose your opponent is. For example, with a bubble factor of 3, you should push 100% of the time if he'll call less than 6%, but you should push only 7% if he'll call 13%. The correct response looks like a cliff—if you think your opponent might be a little loose, you simply can't push as often.

Equilibrium Steals From the Button on the Bubble

To get a feel for how your frequency of steals should depend on the stacks around the table, let's look at a few different situations involving pushing from the button with four players left in a 50/30/20-payout SNG. The blinds are 150/300 for these examples, and we'll examine situations covering all four sections of our 2x2 bubble factor matrix on page 128. All of these situations show the equilibrium percentage of hands to push from the button, assuming the cut-off has folded[13]. The equilibrium calling frequencies are also shown here.

Bully on the Playground
Your Bubble Factor is Low, Theirs is High (Blinds 150/300)

Stack Sizes				Equilibrium Push%	Equilibrium Call %	
Cut-off	Button	SB	BB	Button	SB	BB
1000	4000	2000	3000	100	4	3
1000	4000	3000	2000	100	3	8
4000	3000	1000	2000	74	37	7
4000	3000	2000	1000	72	3	52

Above are four different situations involving stacks of 1,000, 2,000, 3,000, and 4,000 where the button can really push around the blinds. The most obvious situation is when the big stack is pushing against the medium stacks after the small stack has folded. Also note that after the big stack has folded, the next biggest stack can take on the role of the bully.

The reason that the big-stack button can push 100% of the time is because the blinds can rarely call. Their bubble factors against the button (2.36 for the 2,000 stack and 2.68 for the 3,000) are so high that they can only call with premium hands, even though they know for a fact that the button is pushing any two.

---

[13] The possibility of overcalls is ignored here, but we'll talk about them later.

The 3,000 stack gets to play bully when the big stack folds. Even though the short stack can call relatively frequently, it's still correct for the button to push many hands, since the short stack doesn't put that much of a dent into his stack. Note that the 2,000 stack can rarely call as long as the small stack is still alive. His bubble factor against the 3,000 stack is 2.19.

Pick Your Spot
Your Bubble Factor is High, Theirs is Low (Blinds 150/300)

Stack Sizes				Equilibrium Push%	Equilibrium Call %	
Cut-off	Button	SB	BB	Button	SB	BB
1000	2000	3000	4000	24	7	11
1000	2000	4000	3000	29	10	9

Here, the 2,000 stack needs to tread lightly, since he's pushing into the two bigger stacks. Even though he can take the blinds without a fight about 80% of the time, the other 20% of the time is devastating to him. He just can't take that risk without at least a semi-decent hand. Some people say that in these situations, they'd rather push with 64s than A2o. Their reasoning is when they're called, they'll have two live cards. That's true, but only half of the equation. When you push with a weak ace, you'll be in more trouble when you're called, but you'll be *called less often*. That ace in your hand makes it less likely that someone else has one. In most cases, that's more important than avoiding domination.

Cash Game/Game of Chicken—Both Your Bubble Factors Are Similar

Okay, we know that when one side has a higher bubble factor than the other, they have to be more careful. But what about when they're similar? If you're pushing on the button with high bubble factors all around, you don't want to be called, but they don't want to call either. So who wins? The right of first bluff wins out.

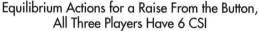

Equilibrium Actions for a Raise From the Button,
All Three Players Have 6 CSI

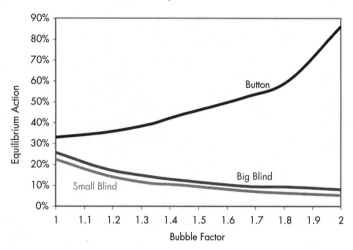

In this situation, we're looking at all three players having the same-sized stacks (6 CSI) and thus the same bubble factors. We can change the remaining number of players and/or the prize structure to vary the bubble factor and observe what happens. As the bubble factor gets higher, the blinds are forced to call much less frequently. And although it becomes more painful for the button to be called, he pushes more often, because he has the right of first bluff.

Exploitive Steals From the Button on the Bubble

Now, the reason we all play poker is that our opponents do not play optimally. Highly skilled opponents may play close to optimally, but the players you'll find in low-buy-in SNGs are far from perfect. Based on a large database of online hand histories, I've made a simple model of how low-buy-in SNG players behave on the bubble. I use this model of how often the typical low-buy-in player calls in these circumstances to look at *exploitive* pushing frequencies from the button. The "Average Call %" frequencies are how the average player behaves; some are tighter and others looser.

Bully on the Playground
Your Bubble Factor is Low, Theirs is High (Blinds 150/300)

Stack Sizes				Equilibrium Push%	Exploitive Push %	Average Call %	
Cut-off	Button	SB	BB	Button	Button	SB	BB
1000	4000	2000	3000	100	96	9	8
1000	4000	3000	2000	100	94	8	11
4000	3000	1000	2000	74	100	12	11
4000	3000	2000	1000	72	100	9	24

Pick Your Spot
Your Bubble Factor is High, Theirs is Low (Blinds 150/300)

Stack Sizes				Equilibrium Push%	Exploitive Push %	Average Call %	
Cut-off	Button	SB	BB	Button	Button	SB	BB
1000	2000	3000	4000	24	15	9	12
1000	2000	4000	3000	29	25	9	11

We've observed that real opponents respond more to their own stack size rather than their bubble factor. They're more likely to call when the raise is only a fraction of their stack. Small stacks tend not to call as often as they should. In addition, players don't respond to bubble factors as strongly as they should; they call too often with high bubble factors and not enough when the factors are low.

As a result, we've found that the best play is often to push more often when there are short stacks in the blinds, as they don't call as often as they should. In addition, large stacks may call too frequently, especially against other large or medium stacks. Therefore, you need to push less often when the big stacks are in the blinds. Compare the following chart, showing the exploitive pushes, to the previous one.

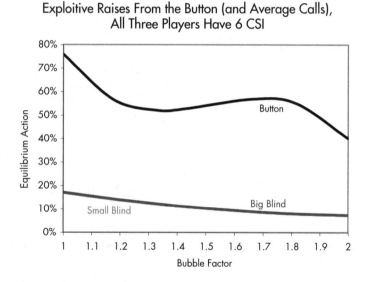

Exploitive Raises From the Button (and Average Calls),
All Three Players Have 6 CSI

For exploitive steals, we see that the model predicts that the SB and the BB will call with practically the same frequency when all three players have 6 CSI. You can also see that the blinds don't call frequently enough with low bubble factors, but call too often with high ones. The perfectly exploitive push percentage from the button follows a somewhat strange pattern, simply because of the competing forces at work. At first the increasing bubble factor takes precedence, but then as the blinds start calling less frequently, it becomes correct to push more. Finally, bubble factors win out again, because the blinds are calling too often—they're not adjusting to the bubble factors as much as they should.

KEY POINTS:
• In most circumstances, push more often than equilibrium play suggests. Your opponents are tighter than equilibrium. They aren't used to opponents pushing with such wide ranges, so their tighter calling range is "more correct" against the foes they typically encounter. Take advantage of this and jam jam jam!
• Medium stacks shouldn't be overly aggressive when the big stack is in the BB. They should push frequently when the small stack is in the BB or when the big stack has folded.
• As the big stack (or as the next biggest stack after the big stack folds), you can usually push any two cards until your opponents catch on and loosen up their calling ranges.

Naturally, you still need to pay attention to your opponents' tendencies, since they could be tighter or looser than these averages. Also, their calling ranges can adjust as they witness your behavior. If your opponents see you pushing every time it's folded to you, they'll start to notice. All but the densest opponents will loosen up, at least slightly. Therefore, you should consider folding your absolute worst hands, even though they're slightly +EV, in order to preserve fold equity on future hands. The reason you can push so often in this situation is because you have very high fold equity. But what do you think will happen to that equity when you get called and you show down 92o? So, consider folding terrible hands just to show your opponents that you do occasionally fold.

Considering Overcalls

If two players are all-in, it's rare for anyone else to want to join the party. This is for a good reason—often the third player gains equity by just sitting out and letting the other two battle. But overcalls do happen, usually when one of the stacks is very short. How does that affect our equilibriums? The short answer is "not very much," except in a couple key circumstances.

Let's look at our old situations and see the new equilibrium actions allowing overcalls and compare those numbers to without overcalls (in parentheses).

Equilibrium Actions With Overcalls (Without Overcalls) Blinds 150/300

Stack Sizes				Equilibrium Push%	Equilibrium Call %		
Cut-off	Button	SB	BB	Button	SB	BB	BB Overcall
1000	4000	2000	3000	100 (100)	4 (4)	3 (8)	1
1000	4000	3000	2000	100 (100)	3 (3)	8 (8)	1
4000	3000	1000	2000	84 (74)	26 (37)	8 (7)	28
4000	3000	2000	1000	72 (72)	3 (3)	52 (52)	1

Stack Sizes				Equilibrium Push%	Equilibrium Call %		
Cut-off	Button	SB	BB	Button	SB	BB	BB Overcall
1000	2000	3000	4000	24 (24)	7 (7)	11 (11)	3
1000	2000	4000	3000	29 (29)	10 (10)	9 (9)	0

You can see in almost all of these cases an overcall is extremely rare; usually KK+ or QQ+ is needed, but sometimes not even AA should be called. In all of those cases, allowing an overcall was not enough to change the previous actions. However, there is one specific case where it is significant:

If a big stack is pushing a wide range and the smallest stack goes all-in, the *second smallest* stack can overcall more frequently than if the smallest stack folds.

This is because the second shortest stack only gets hurt if, specifically, the small stack wins the main pot and the big stack wins the side pot. If the big stack wins the whole thing, the second stack will still take home the third-place prize. We'll see another example of this in Chapter 9 when we look at a professional SNG.

The strong chance of the big blind overcalling actually makes the small blind tighter in equilibrium. The button actually pushes more often, since the tighter small blind has a bigger impact than the chance of an overcall.

The possibility of overcalls is always important when we look at what the small stack should do on the button. Let's look at a few different cases where the 1,000 stack is on the button.

Equilibrium Actions With Overcalls (Blinds 150/300)

Stack Sizes				Equilibrium Push%	Equilibrium Call %		
Cut-off	Button	SB	BB	Button	SB	BB	BB Overcall
3000	1000	2000	4000	25	22	48	7
2000	1000	3000	4000	25	20	47	5
2000	1000	4000	3000	28	26	47	4
4000	1000	2000	3000	28	23	47	8
3000	1000	4000	2000	32	29	46	7
4000	1000	3000	2000	32	29	47	8

The small stack always pushes around 25%-30% and is not greatly influenced by the sizes of the other stacks. This is because the bubble factors are all fairly low and similar from stack to stack. The big blind can overcall more often than most people's first impression. As a reference, 7% is about 77+, AJo+, ATs+, KQs. Those are some weak hands, considering that the small blind is actually pushing instead of flat-calling the small stack. If we allow the possibility of flat calls, this complicated problem gets even more complicated. We would have to consider steals by the big blind by overpushing and trap calls from the small blind. That's beyond the scope of this book.

How Often Do Real Players Raise?

Obviously, it can vary quite a bit from player to player and depends a lot on the stack sizes. But by studying a large database of hand histories, we can see how often low-buy-in SNG players try to open-raise from late positions. This at least gives you a ballpark figure as to how these players typically play.

We've noticed that the only things that really affect how often a low-level player raises is their stack size, their position, and the number of players remaining. The stack sizes of their opponents have almost no effect on most players' decision to raise at low levels of play.

Raise Frequency of Low-Level Players

CSI	Small Blind			Button			Cut-off (1 off the Button)			Hijack (2 off)	
	4 Players	5 Players	6 Players	4 Players	5 Players	6 Players	4 Players	5 Players	6 Players	5 Players	6 Players
1	57%	62%	61%	31%	34%	36%	33%	32%	32%	34%	29%
2	42%	48%	43%	29%	32%	33%	25%	25%	28%	24%	21%
3	37%	42%	42%	26%	29%	32%	19%	23%	24%	19%	20%
4	32%	36%	38%	23%	25%	26%	16%	20%	19%	16%	16%
5	32%	35%	33%	22%	25%	24%	16%	18%	19%	14%	15%
6	31%	33%	30%	22%	22%	21%	16%	18%	16%	13%	13%
7	30%	31%	30%	22%	21%	20%	17%	16%	17%	13%	13%
8	29%	29%	30%	22%	23%	22%	16%	16%	16%	12%	14%
9+	32%	28%	25%	23%	22%	20%	18%	18%	16%	14%	12%

Naturally some players will steal more often and others less often, but this is the average rate that low-buy-in players raise when the action is folded to them.

Advanced SNG Tactic: Keeping the Small Stack Alive

By now it should be clear that the big stack on the bubble of a SNG enjoys a lot of fold equity and can push the other stacks around. If you're the big stack and the medium stacks at your table seem to understand bubble factors and are playing tightly against you, try the advanced play of keeping the small stack alive.

When you have a marginal +EV situation against the small stack, consider folding, even though you have a small advantage! When you keep the small stack alive, you can continue to dominate the other two players. If you bust the small stack, the bubble is over and you've lost some of your strength.

Obviously, don't fold strong hands that are very +EV, only the marginal ones. The object is to give up a little EV against the short stack in exchange for a larger gain in future hands.

SPECIFIC STRATEGIES FOR MULTI-TABLE TOURNAMENTS

Predators vs. Prey

• As the bubble of a MTT approaches, players will tend to divide themselves into two camps: those hoping to just make it to the money and those who have their sights set on the top prize and are willing to take gambles to get there. Players just hoping to make the money generally play very tightly and wait for other small stacks to bust. A good tactic is to target these players and frequently raise from any position to take their blinds.

• The larger the buy-in for the tournament, the more likely players are to shift into survival mode. Therefore, the approach to the bubble lasts a lot longer in a $10,000 live event than a $10 MTT online. Inexperienced players often underestimate how long it takes to burst the bubble and lose a lot more in blinds and antes than they anticipate, while trying to wait it out.

• Bubble factors for large MTTs aren't as big as most people suspect, so most of your opponents will play too tightly. Take advantage of this by increasing your aggression as the bubble approaches. Learn which of your opponents will step down from a fight. We saw from the examination of the 2006 WSOP Main Event structure that the average bubble factor at the money bubble is quite small, only 1.36. The bubble is the time to accumulate chips in order to fight for a top prize, not a time for squeaking into the money. Virtually all of the top tournament players go into hyper-drive and significantly add to their stacks at bubble time.

• Large stacks should avoid confrontations with each other and look to pick on the medium stacks. Short stacks might be desperate enough to put their chips in, but medium stacks are the most likely to try and wait out the bubble.

The play approaching the bubble of a MTT isn't that different from that of a SNG; the only real differences are:
• You're more likely still playing at a full table.
• The bubble factors could be different.

The bubble factors approaching the money bubble could be higher or lower than for a SNG, but most players will act as though it's always *much* higher. As we saw on page 124, the average bubble factor for a very large MTT (like the 2006 WSOP) is much smaller than a SNG, where the average bubble factor is 1.88. However, we also saw that a smaller MTT can have average bubble factors of more than 2.

As the money bubble approaches, especially in a major tournament, players begin to have different agendas. Some players don't want to take any risks until the bubble breaks. "There'll be plenty of time to gamble after the bubble," they say to themselves. If a player is inexperienced, especially if this is the biggest tournament he's ever played, he's more likely to adopt this attitude.

Others realize that players are too tight on the bubble and start becoming hyper-aggressive. If the players at your table are tight enough, it can be profitable to raise every single hand from any position, no matter what cards you hold. Often you hear stories being told of someone raising every single hand. "I can't believe it. He raised like twenty hands in a row and was never called!" Well, think about it: If everyone always folds every time you raise, wouldn't you raise every hand?

Every time you raise and are unchallenged, you gain 1 CSI. Raising 20 times unchallenged during the bubble period just added 20 CSI to your stack. If someone comes over the top of you, you'll lose about 2 CSI, but that's assuming you throw the hand away.

KEY POINT: If your bubble factor is 1.5, you can raise with 72o if you think you can take the blinds at least 75% of the time.

Seventy-five percent of the time you'll win 1 CSI and 25% of the time you'll lose 2 CSI (worth about 3 because of the bubble factor). That's a wash. If your table is playing scared, there should be many opportunities that offer more than a 75% chance of success. Plus, if you have a hand that has some playing value, you can afford to accept less than a 75% chance. What should you do?

• Try to become the table captain. The effectiveness of these tactics depends on the table composition. It won't be as effective if you're called frequently (online or if there are very short stacks). It's most effective in a major live event where the prize money is significant and no one at the table is very short.

• Fold and fear equity are your friends. Don't lose them. If you raise to 6,000 with 93o from mid-position and the super-short BB goes all in for 4,000 more, what are you going to do? Call and show what you've been raising with? Yuck. Fold despite the great odds and show the table you're a coward? Yuck. Better not to raise with complete junk and wait until a medium stack is in the blind.

• Defend your blinds liberally, especially if someone else has emerged as the table captain. Don't be just another victim. If you fight back and gain some fear equity for yourself, others won't be as likely to pick on you. The captain will see that he has seven others he can pick on for easy money—he can afford to give you a rest.

Re-stealing is a tricky topic because of the bubble factors involved. I presented some equilibrium re-steals in Chapter 3 when the bubble factors are 1, but when the bubble factors are higher, you really need to know your opponent. You need to approximate how often he's making his initial raise and how often he'll call a re-raise. Opportunities for re-stealing come up all the time, both in SNGs and MTTs, especially when your CSI is in the "re-steal" stage of 7 to 12. If your opponent folds often enough, you may be able to steal with any two. But you really have to know who'll cave in.

Let's assume that you're contemplating re-stealing with some low suited cards; it could be 87s, 74s, or even 42s. If you're called, let's say you have 33% equity[14].

If someone raises to 3BB, you can use the following graph to see how often he needs to fold to a re-steal for it to be profitable for you to come over the top.

Re-stealing With Low Suited Cards (33% Equity if Called)

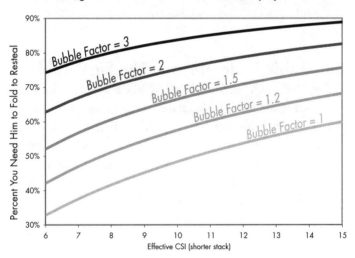

The higher your bubble factor, the more careful you need to be. However, if his bubble factor is high as well, he should

---

[14] Your actual cards and his calling range could result in an equity higher or lower than this.

fold more often as well (if he understands bubble play). So the best times to re-steal are the same situations as stealing; we want to be a big stack against a medium stack. Our bubble factor is low and his is high—he'll fold often enough to make stealing right. Obviously, our fold equity is crucial; if either one of us has a short stack, he's much less likely to fold. In those cases we should give up the idea of re-stealing and just re-raise for value.

For example, your CSI is 10; your opponent has you covered and raises to 3BB with 22+, ATo+, A2s+, KJo+, K9s+, Q9s+, J9s+, T8s+, 97s+, 86s+, 76s, 65s (20%). If your bubble factor is 1.2, you need him to fold 57% of the time for you to re-steal. That means if his calling range is tighter than 55+, AJo+, ATs+, KJs+, go for it. A bubble factor of 1.5 needs 77+, AQo+, ATs+, KQs, and a bubble factor of 2 needs 99+, AQ+.

Multi-Table Tournaments: The Final Table

Play during the final table of an MTT is very similar to a SNG, except for the bubble factors. Final-table payout structures can vary from top-heavy to fairly flat, but most have structures that keep the average bubble factor fairly constant at around 1.4-1.5. This is a good average number to use for your bubble factor in a MTT. Let's look at five example final-table payouts and the bubble factors that result:

Place	2006 WSOP ME	2007 WSOP ME	Poker Stars $50 10-Table	2006 Aussie Millions	2007 Aussie Millions
1	$12,000,000	$8,250,000	$1,350.00	$972,822	$1,200,000
2	$6,102,499	$4,840,981	$900.00	$517,792	$800,000
3	$4,123,310	$3,048,025	$540.00	$282,432	$560,000
4	$3,628,513	$1,852,721	$450.00	$203,979	$400,000
5	$3,216,182	$1,255,069	$360.00	$156,907	$320,000
6	$2,803,851	$956,243	$292.50	$125,525	$240,000
7	$2,391,520	$705,229	$247.50	$94,144	$176,000
8	$1,979,189	$585,699	$202.50	$62,763	$124,000
9	$1,566,858	$525,934	$157.50	$62,763	$124,000

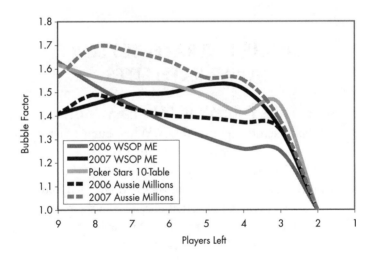

The 2006 WSOP bubble factors start high, since each place is a significant percentage improvement for eighth and seventh places; they quickly come down with fewer players, since the structure is fairly top-heavy. In contrast to the other tournaments, the 2007 WSOP bubble factors slowly get more significant as the final table is reduced from 9 to 4 players. Each pay jump after seventh place becomes very significant. However, if you add in the value of additional perks for being the world champion and endorsements (likely worth more than $1 million), both WSOP structures becomes a bit more top-heavy, lowering all the bubble factors.

The bubble factors of the other three tournaments stay higher longer, since the pay steps at the lower levels are not as significant. The top three spots have most of the money, but it isn't as concentrated in first place as is the 2006 WSOP. The 2007 Aussie Millions has the highest bubble factors most of the time, since the pay structure is fairly flat. First place is only 1.5x that of second place and the steps below that are fairly shallow as well. Tighter play will be more rewarded in these tournaments due to the flatter payouts.

SPECIFIC STRATEGIES FOR SUPER SATELLITES

How to Fold Your Way Into Easy Money

• Bubble factors are everything. When bubble factors are high, the proper play depends on whether your opponents understand bubble factors. If they do, either fold or be the first to go all-in. If they don't know what they're doing, just fold.

• It's not your job to bust other players—let them bust each other. Many players don't understand the right strategy to use in super satellites, so it becomes even more critical to just keep folding and let others duke it out.

• If the blinds are so high that there are multiple players in the Special Stage, ICM is no longer useful. Instead, you need to look at who has to post his blind first.

Here's one example of a smaller satellite tournament that awarded two seats involving a well-known pro. The blinds were 400-800 with a 100 ante.

	Chips	CSI
Button	19,000	15
Small Blind	30,000	23
Big Blind (Pro)	49,000	38

The button folded, the SB called, and the pro checked with A♦7♦. The pro's bubble factor against the SB is 1.85 and his is 3.11 against the pro. Normally, raising pre-flop with A7s is correct, since he's in position and it's blind vs. blind. However, with the fairly high bubble factors, checking behind is likely best as it helps keep the pot small. The flop comes up 7♥7♣3♥ and the SB pushes all in for 29,100 into a 1,900 pot. Should the pro call or fold?

The SB just bet more than 15x the pot, *a very poor bet no matter what he has*. The SB can't be certain that the pro will be so tight as to fold trips here. So he shouldn't be doing this as a bluff, hoping to steal. What he's stealing is worthless compared to what he's risking. On the other side, with a monster hand he can make more by betting a smaller amount.

The pro's bubble factor against the SB is 1.85. He's getting 1.07-to-1 pot odds and tournament odds of 0.58-to-1. The pro needs to be 63.4% sure of winning to make the call. Look at his equity against some possible hands:

K3	99.6%
88	91.4
7♠ T♠	79.6
K♥ Q♥	74.8
A♥ 8♥	71.5
4♥ 5♥	65.3
33	22.9
73	19.8

The pro could easily be ahead more than 63.4% overall; it depends on how often the SB might push with a draw, worse trips, or just two pair. The pro might justify a call based on the numbers. However, we don't think the numbers matter much for this problem *because of how the SB is playing.* We think folding is right. We may be giving up a small +EV situation now in exchange for a bigger +EV situation later. In this case it isn't because we're waiting to be a bigger favorite later to make the call, it's because our opponent has shown that he's reckless. The blinds are so small that we can just fold into the money. If he's willing to risk it all on such an overbet, sooner or later our opponents will run into each other and destroy themselves. We don't have to play a hand. The two larger stacks should avoid each other and simply try to knock out the smallest stack. They have little to gain and everything to lose.

Here's another satellite example, this time an online qualifier for a $215 seat. Top 21 players get $215, 22nd gets $145, 23rd gets nothing. There are 23 players left and you're the shortest stack with 5,400. The blinds are 4,000/8,000. The next smallest stack is forced all-in in his BB this hand and has 5,740 chips. There are short stacks at the other tables too, but none of them will be forced all-in for at least 3-4 hands. You're dealt pocket queens on the button. Here are all the chip stacks at your table:

	Chips
Player A	42,482
Player B	59,213
Player C	10,590
Player D	6,260
Button (you)	5,400
Small Blind	27,363
Big Blind	5,740

Everyone folds to you on the button. *Do you play your pocket queens?*

No! You should fold. The BB is all-in and the SB will almost certainly call the extra $1,740, although it probably makes little difference to him. He's practically guaranteed a seat no matter what he does, but by calling he has a chance to end the tournament now by knocking out both of you. If you push, you'll win the hand 65%-80% of the time, depending on how frisky the SB feels. However, by folding, there's a 50/50 chance the BB will be eliminated this hand.

In addition, Players C and D will be hitting the blinds before you. This is a very important consideration. Each time one of them is forced in, there's a good chance he'll be out. Plus, some of the small stacks at other tables may be eliminated as well. Considering all of this, it's probable that you'll do better by folding and hoping that others are eliminated. It's not worth trying to triple up to survive another round. This isn't poker anymore … it's a satellite!

Notice that we didn't try to use bubble factors in this solution. That's because the blinds are so high that the dominating factor is when the blinds are going to hit you. A prize-EV model, based on chip counts, no longer applies.

What about if you had aces in the previous example? That's much closer, but probably still a fold. We can make a very back-of-the-envelope estimate of our equity by saying that four players will have a 50/50 chance of elimination in the next five hands. That means there's a 6% chance that none of them are eliminated, a 25% chance that exactly one is gone, and a 69% chance you get a seat. That's approximately $184 in equity. Our actual equity is a little better, since this assumes that we'd lose after these five hands. We need at least an 86% chance of winning ($184/$215) to justify pushing under these assumptions. Pocket aces don't cut it.

One more hypothetical example: 10 people left in a final table satellite that awards eight seats. Everyone has around

20,000 chips and the blinds are 2,000/4,000. You're in mid-position with AKo. You estimate that your opponents will call you with TT+ and AQ+. Do you push? If you fold, everyone has the same stacks, so your chance of getting a seat should be 8 out of 10: 80%. If there are six people behind you and you push, that means there's a 79.9% chance you'll not be called, giving you an 87.7% chance of a seat. If you're called, you have a 49.2% chance of winning, giving you about a 98.6% chance of getting a seat. If you lose the all-in you're out. The EV of pushing is:

$$(79.9\%) \ (87.7\%) + (20.1\%) \ (49.2\%) \ (98.6\%) = 79.8\%$$

This is less than the EV of folding. Pushing would only be profitable if you could be sure your opponents were tighter than this.

The ironic thing about high-bubble-factor situations like this is that if your opponents were all game-theory experts, you could profitably push 72o, but since they're not, you can't even push AKo. That's because we assumed that our opponents would call with hands much weaker than optimal. If your opponents all understood the situation perfectly, they could only call with KK+ (plus QQ from the SB and TT+ from the BB). Against opponents this tight, it's profitable to push any hand. The game of chicken rears its ugly head again.

Another reason for folding against poor players is a common theme in our satellite advice—your opponents often get into conflicts and bust each other. You can often just fold into the money. Unless you know your opponents personally, *don't underestimate their ignorance of correct satellite play*. Plays like the following happen all the time in low buy-in games:

Satellite that pays 6	Blinds 200/400
Position	Chips
UTG	5,303
Mid-position	12,050
Hijack	14,545
CO	9,215
Button	2,875
SB	6,677
BB	12,335

On this hand, everyone folded to the SB, who made an 11-CSI push with AJo. The BB called with A2s. Note that even if the SB were to push 100% of the time, the BB should only call with JJ or better. A2s is nowhere close to strong enough to call. If the SB knew that the BB would call with hands as weak as A2s, that means AJo isn't strong enough to push from the SB. In fact, if your opponent is tight enough to only call with TT+, AK, and AQs, that's still too often for you to push with AJo!

One option for the SB is to just call, which helps to keep the pot as small as possible. However, we would recommend folding in the SB against a weak opponent, since there are very few flops on which you would be confident enough to risk chips. At least in this example, the SB didn't make a standard raise, say to 1200. That would have been the worst choice. For this hand:

Folding > Calling > Pushing > Raising to 1,200.

8

SHORT-HANDED AND HEADS-UP PLAY

SHORT-HANDED PLAY WITH DEEPER STACKS

• Keep an eye on all the stack sizes. Avoid big-stack versus big-stack confrontations. Big stacks should push around the small and medium stacks. The final table is similar to a SNG, except that the bubble factors are generally lower, meaning that the big stacks don't have quite as much bullying power.

• Make frequent attempts to steal the blinds and antes. You'll frequently find yourself in late position and in a prime spot to raise. Make a standard raise, not a push. Aggressive players are winning players.

• Raise with hands that have more "playability," such as suited connectors, since you might have to play after the flop.

• Call liberally from the blinds, especially if there's an ante. Let's say the blinds are 10,000/20,000 with a 2,000 ante; six players are left and you're facing a 3BB raise in the BB. You're getting 2.55-to-1 on your call. These are great odds to call and see the flop with a lot of hands, especially if the raiser is aggressive.

• Short-handed play is the best time to re-steal, especially if your CSI is in the 7-to-12 range. Players will frequently be stealing from late position and if you re-raise from the blinds, you can frequently take down a larger pot. While a successful steal adds 1 CSI to your stack, a successful re-steal adds about 3 CSI, compared to folding. If stacks are deeper than 12 CSI, you probably shouldn't go all-in, and since you'll be out of position on the flop, it makes re-stealing less attractive.

When your CSI is above 7 or 8, you won't be in jam-or-fold mode and when you're short-handed, you'll find yourself in position to raise and steal the blinds, but it won't be an all-in move. Since you may have some post-flop play, it's preferable to raise with different hands than you would when pushing. You should shift your selection of hands toward suited semi-connectors and away from offsuit big-little hands, such as A5o and K8o. So, while an aggressive short-stack might push all-in from the cut-off with 22+, A2+, K8o+, K3s+, QTo+, Q8s+, JTo, J8s+, T8s+, 98s, and 87s, a bigger stack might make an aggressive 3-4BB raise with 22+, A7o+, A2s+, KTo+, K6s+, QTo+, Q8s+, JTo, J8s+, T9o, T8s+, 98o, 96s+, 87o, 86s+, 76s, and 65s.

These hands are easier to play post-flop, since you're less likely to run into a situation where you're dominated. Raising with this wide range of hands has plenty of deception value for post-flop play. You can put in a continuation bet of about two-thirds the pot on any flop, since from your opponent's point of view, you could have a real hand, no matter what comes out.

Example 1: Five players remain in an online MTT. You're in the BB with 2.8 million chips, which is about an average stack. Blinds are 50,000/100,000 with a 10,000 ante, giving you a CSI of 14. The cut-off, an aggressive player who has you covered by a small amount, raises to 300,000. It's folded to you and you look down at K♦ 6♦. *Your action?*

• You should call. K6s is much too weak for a re-steal, even against an aggressive player. However, you're getting 2.5-to-1 pot odds to call. Your bubble factor will depend on the prize structure, but is probably around 1.5, giving you tournament odds of 1.7-to-1 and requiring a breakeven equity of 37.5%. If your opponent is raising with exactly the aggressive example range on the previous page, K6s has a 44% equity, more than enough to see the flop, despite the positional disadvantage.

The flop comes T♦7♠5♦. The pot contains 700,000. *Your action?*

• This is a fairly good flop for you and you're actually a slight favorite (52%) over his entire assumed range. You have 2.5 million left, a very good size to try a semi-bluff check-raise. Assuming he puts in a continuation bet of about 400,000 almost all the time, you have slightly more than a pot-sized reraise if you push all-in after him. It will be very difficult for him to call without top pair or better, giving you a great opportunity to significantly add to your stack, while also acquiring some fear equity. After this move, your opponents may show you some respect!

Example 2: Final 4 of a major live tournament. You're the chip leader with the following chip stacks:

Position	Chips
Cut-off	480,000
Button (You)	2,660,000
Small Blind	720,000
Big Blind	1,210,000

Blinds are 10,000/20,000 with a 2,000 ante. You have been using your chip lead as a weapon and playing very aggressively for the last several rounds. The cut-off, a fairly tight player, raises to 70,000. You have 5♥5♠. *Your action?*

• You should fold. Flat-calling violates the Rule of 5 and 10, since the raise is 15% of his stack. Unless you hit a set on the flop, you won't know if you're ahead or behind—and his stack is too short to call for set value. Being in position isn't enough. You also have to worry about one of the blinds making a squeeze play if you call. Re-raising probably isn't a good option either, as the cut-off is fairly tight and you have a reputation for aggressive play. This cuts down your fold equity. One final reason is that the short stack is the most likely player to contest you; the larger stacks have bigger bubble factors against you and are less likely to want to fight.

HEADS-UP PLAY

Heads-up play for some players is a thrilling challenge; for others it's a complete mystery. Once play is down to two players, there's only one person to outwit, but he'll be doing his best to outwit you as well. Because of this, the proper heads-up play is extremely opponent dependent, especially if the stacks are deep.

Before we get into the strategy, here are some lessons that even pros forget.

The prize structure is irrelevant. Once you're heads-up, it doesn't matter what the prizes are for first and second place. First could be a million dollars and second nothing. First could be $20,000 and second $10,000. It doesn't matter even if first and second pay the same, except for a plastic trophy and bragging rights; the correct heads-up strategy is the same in all cases. You can see this is the case by simply rewarding both players the second-place prize, then having the eventual winner earn the additional difference. When heads-up, bubble factors are always exactly 1.

The size of the bigger stack is irrelevant. In determining the proper strategy, the only relevant stack size is the smaller stack.

It's as if the additional chips in the bigger stack aren't there, since they won't come into play. If your opponent has 10BB remaining, your strategy should be the same whether you have 10BB, 30BB, or 100BB. The "effective stack size" is 10BB in all cases. *It doesn't matter if you're ahead or behind.* Your strategy with 10BB vs. an opponent with 30BB should be the same as your strategy with 30BB vs. someone with 10BB. This is a corollary to the above point, as you're both playing with only 10BB this hand.

Think about it this way: If you're the short stack with 10BB and you feel that you have a 25% chance of winning the tournament (because you have 25% of the chips), you should be willing to take a 50/50 shot at doubling up to 20BB or busting out. With 20BB, you should have a 50% chance of winning, so a 50/50 shot at 20BB is neutral in EV terms.

As the big stack with 30BB, if you have a 75% chance of winning the tournament, you should be willing to take a 50/50 shot at busting your opponent. Half the time you'll win, but half the time you'll be down to 20BB. Again EV neutral.

The only time this doesn't apply is if you think there's a big skill gap between the players and both stacks are deep enough so that skill becomes a factor. In five minutes, I could teach my grandmother how to have about a 50/50 shot against Phil Ivey … so long as both of them have 12BB or less. Give them both 50BB and Phil would run over her. If you think you have a skill advantage over your opponent and stacks are deep enough, that means as the short stack you should have more than a 50% chance of doubling up before going broke. Therefore, you should be more conservative with wild gambles than a weak player in all situations, but you should be even more conservative when you're the shorter stack—your survival is worth more.

We'll begin our heads-up strategy by first looking at the easier subject of how to play in the Move-in Stage. Later, we'll discuss heads-up play with deeper stacks.

Heads-Up For the Move-in Stage

The following two charts show the equilibrium solutions[15] for jam-or-fold when the shorter stack has a CSI of 8 or less. In both charts, the shade of the cell represents the largest CSI that the hand is pushed in equilibrium. Therefore, if you want to follow the equilibrium solution, you should push if your stack size is the CSI given or smaller. For example, J7o pushes in the SB with a CSI of 5 or less. J7o calls an all-in with a CSI of 4 or less.

CSI
8
7
6
5
4
3
2
1
<1

Following this equilibrium strategy will guarantee that you cannot be exploited, as long as your opponent follows the jam-or-fold strategy as well. But as we know, not only do our opponents play sub-optimally, but they won't always strictly jam-or-fold once under 7 CSI.

We'll return once again to our observed online hand histories from low-level SNG's to see how frequently these players do various actions. It turns out that these players behave differently depending on if they're the big or short stack. The chart on page 180 shows the actions taken by the SB both when he is the short stack and big stack:

---

[15] Again, mixed solutions *are* considered for equilibrium, and the table shows the hands that push more than 50% of the time. Some hands are not in the equilibrium solution for all stack sizes below the one given, but this occasional difference will have no material impact on profitability.

EQUILIBRIUM RAISING STRATEGY (ALL-IN OR FOLD)

SUITED

OFFSUIT \ SUITED	A	K	Q	J	T	9	8	7	6	5	4	3	2
A	8	8	8	8	8	8	8	8	8	8	8	8	8
K	8	8	8	8	8	8	8	8	8	8	8	8	8
Q	8	8	8	8	8	8	8	8	8	8	8	8	8
J	8	8	8	8	8	8	8	8	8	8	8	7	5
T	8	8	8	8	8	8	8	8	8	8	7	5	4
9	8	8	8	8	8	8	8	8	8	8	3	3	2
8	8	8	8	8	8	8	8	8	8	8	5	1	1
7	8	8	6	5	6	7	8	8	8	8	8	1	1
6	8	8	6	4	3	3	4	7	8	8	8	1	1
5	8	8	5	4	2	2	2	1	1	8	8	8	1
4	8	8	5	3	2	1	1	1	1	1	8	6	1
3	8	8	5	3	2	1	1	1	1	1	1	8	1
2	8	7	4	3	2	1	1	1	1	1	<1	<1	8

EQUILIBRIUM CALLING STRATEGY (ALL-IN OR FOLD)

SUITED

OFFSUIT \ SUITED	A	K	Q	J	T	9	8	7	6	5	4	3	2
A	8	8	8	8	8	8	8	8	8	8	8	8	8
K	8	8	8	8	8	8	8	8	8	8	8	7	7
Q	8	8	8	8	8	8	8	7	6	5	5	5	4
J	8	8	8	8	8	8	7	5	4	4	4	3	3
T	8	8	8	7	8	7	6	4	4	3	3	3	3
9	8	8	7	6	5	8	5	4	3	3	2	2	2
8	8	8	6	5	4	4	8	4	3	3	2	2	2
7	8	8	5	4	3	3	3	8	3	3	2	2	2
6	8	7	4	3	3	2	2	2	8	3	2	2	2
5	8	6	4	3	2	2	2	2	2	8	3	2	2
4	8	6	4	3	2	2	2	2	2	2	8	2	2
3	8	5	3	2	2	2	1	2	2	2	2	8	2
2	8	5	3	2	2	2	1	1	1	1	1	1	8

Observed Actions of Low-level Players When Heads-up

	Short on SB				Big on SB			
CSI of short	Push	Raise	Limp	Fold	Push	Raise	Limp	Fold
1	74%		6%	20%	52%		36%	13%
2	55%		16%	29%	50%		26%	24%
3	49%		23%	28%	46%		29%	25%
4	31%	13%	26%	30%	24%	20%	31%	25%
5	24%	18%	31%	28%	18%	23%	34%	24%
6	20%	20%	32%	28%	14%	26%	36%	24%
7	16%	23%	35%	26%	12%	27%	36%	25%
8	14%	26%	39%	21%	11%	29%	39%	21%

So on the SB with a CSI of 1, the average low-level player will push 74% of the time, limp 6%, and fold 20%. For this chart we defined any raise that is 40% or more of the short stack as a push, even if the actual raise was less than all-in. Therefore, for someone with a CSI of 6 (9BB), a "raise" is any bet between 2BB and 3.6BB and a "push" is any bet over 3.6BB.

From these data it appears that a short stack on the SB tends to push more aggressively, but folds more often as well. The big stack is more likely to limp or raise compared to the short stack at the same effective stack size. It should also be apparent that players don't push nearly as often as the equilibrium solution, which pushes 60%-80% of the time from the SB. Since most players aren't pushing this much from the SB, your calling strategy should be much tighter than the equilibrium solution.

Most players are tighter than equilibrium for calling an all-in when in the BB. This is probably correct, given that players aren't pushing all-in as frequently as they should. You can take advantage of this tight play *by pushing even more than equilibrium.* When looking at how often low-level players call all-ins, there isn't a significant difference in behavior between a short stack and a big stack. All that matters is the CSI of the smaller stack.

The following table shows how often the average low-level player calls an all-in, and what is the right exploitive percentage of hands to push, if they're calling that often.

CSI of Short	Call	Exploitive Push
1	80%	100%
2	54%	100%
3	42%	100%
4	37%	100%
5	34%	100%
6	33%	90%
7	32%	74%
8	32%	60%

Hyper-aggression is the key to short-stacked heads-up play. You can hardly go wrong by pushing every hand. Most players don't adjust enough to punish you; some won't adjust at all. You should have the cardinal rule of short-stacked heads-up play etched onto your brain: *Pushing too often is always better than not pushing enough.*

What About Raises Smaller Than All-In?

Those players not used to the jam-or-fold mentality might find it tough to put all their chips in with 10 or 12BB. Why not try adding in the possibility of smaller raises? Why not limp? It turns out that if you solve the equilibrium problem for 12BB and allow the additional possibility of jam, raise to 3BB,

---

[16] JJ+, K7s, K6s, K3o, K2o, Q9s, Q8s, Q8o, Q7o are raised to 3BB at least 50% of the time. The offsuit hands are folded if the BB pushes over the raise.

or fold, the equilibrium chooses to make the smaller raise only 7% of the time[16] and improves the EV by a measly 0.002BB! Adding the ability to limp makes a bigger difference; the equilibrium solution limps 39% of the time[17], but the EV is only improved by 0.04BB. Unfortunately, these models can't take into account post-flop play; it's as if once the flop is dealt, whoever is going to lose the hand realizes it and doesn't put in any more money. So while these aren't perfect models of reality, they do show that there's not a major EV loss by restricting yourself to jam or fold.

> **KEY POINT:** If you have 12BB or less, it's close to optimal to use a push-or-fold strategy rather than making a 3BB raise or limping.

Let's look at one more equilibrium solution and allow a lot more options. In this game, the effective stack size is a CSI of 10 (15BB) and the SB has the option of folding, limping, raising to 3BB or jamming. The BB can also raise to 3BB or jam if the SB limps and can jam if the SB raises to 3BB. There is no post-flop betting. The following charts show the most probable action for each hand. Here is the solution for the SB:

---

[17] A wide range of strong and weak hands. About four-fifths of the hands are folded if the BB jams.

SUITED

OFFSUIT

	A	K	Q	J	T	9	8	7	6	5	4	3	2
A	LR	LR	LR	LR	LR	LR	LR	J	J	J	J	J	J
K	J	LR	LR	J	LC	LC	LC	LC	J	J	LCF	LCF	LCF
Q	J	J	LR	LR	LR	LR	J	LCF	LCF	LCF	LRF	LRF	LCF
J	J	J	J	LR	LR	J	J	LCF	LCF	LCF	LCF	LCF	LCF
T	J	J	J	J	LR	J	J	J	LCF	LCF	LCF	LF	LF
9	J	LCF	LCF	LCF	J	LR	J	J	J	LCF	LF	LF	LF
8	J	LCF	LCF	LCF	LCF	LCF	LR	J	J	J	LF	LF	LF
7	J	LCF	LF	LF	LF	LCF	LCF	LC	J	J	LCF	F	F
6	J	LCF	LF	LF	LF	LF	LF	LF	LC	J	J	F	F
5	J	LCF	LF	LF	LF	LF	LF	LF	F	J	J	J	F
4	J	LCF	LF	LF	LF	LF	F	F	F	F	J	F	F
3	J	LCF	LF	LF	LF	LF	F	F	F	F	F	J	F
2	J	LCF	LF	LF	LF	LF	F	F	F	F	F	F	J

J	Jam
LR	Limp and raise, call a jam
LRF	Limp and raise, fold to a jam
LC	Limp and call
LCF	Limp and call a small raise, fold to a jam
LF	Limp and fold
F	Fold

The BB's action if the SB limps:

SUITED

	A	K	Q	J	T	9	8	7	6	5	4	3	2
A	R	R	R	J	J	J	J	J	J	J	J	J	J
K	J	R	R	R	R	R	RF	RF	RF	RF	RF	J	J
Q	J	R	R	J	J	K	K	K	K	K	K	K	K
J	J	J	J	R	J	J	K	K	K	K	K	K	K
T	J	R	J	RF	R	J	J	K	K	K	K	K	K
9	J	RF	K	K	K	R	J	J	J	K	K	K	K
8	J	RF	K	K	K	K	J	J	J	J	K	K	K
7	J	RF	K	K	K	K	K	J	J	J	J	K	K
6	J	RF	K	K	K	K	K	K	J	J	J	J	K
5	J	K	K	K	K	K	K	K	K	RF	J	J	J
4	J	K	K	K	K	K	K	K	K	K	RF	J	J
3	J	K	K	K	K	K	K	K	K	K	K	J	J
2	J	K	K	K	K	K	K	K	K	K	K	K	J

OFFSUIT

J	Jam
R	Raise to 3BB, call a re-raise
RF	Raise to 3BB, fold to a re-raise
K	Check

The BB's action if the SB raises to 3BB:

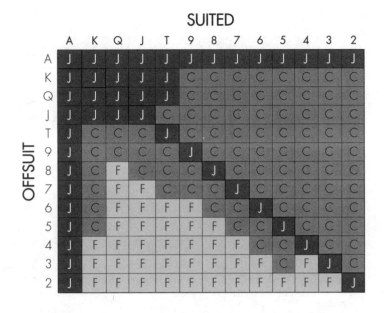

					SUITED								
	A	K	Q	J	T	9	8	7	6	5	4	3	2
A	J	J	J	J	J	J	J	J	J	J	J	J	J
K	J	J	J	J	J	C	C	C	C	C	C	C	C
Q	J	J	J	J	J	C	C	C	C	C	C	C	C
J	J	J	J	J	C	C	C	C	C	C	C	C	C
T	J	C	C	C	J	C	C	C	C	C	C	C	C
9	J	C	C	C	C	J	C	C	C	C	C	C	C
8	J	C	F	C	C	C	J	C	C	C	C	C	C
7	J	C	F	F	C	C	C	J	C	C	C	C	C
6	J	C	F	F	F	F	C	C	J	C	C	C	C
5	J	C	F	F	F	F	F	C	C	J	C	C	C
4	J	F	F	F	F	F	F	F	C	C	J	C	C
3	J	F	F	F	F	F	F	F	F	C	F	J	C
2	J	F	F	F	F	F	F	F	F	F	F	F	J

OFFSUIT (vertical label on left)

J	Jam
C	Call
F	Fold

And finally the BB's action if the SB jams:

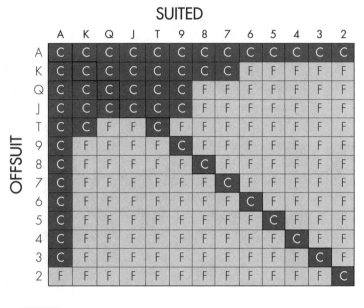

SUITED

	A	K	Q	J	T	9	8	7	6	5	4	3	2
A	C	C	C	C	C	C	C	C	C	C	C	C	C
K	C	C	C	C	C	C	C	C	F	F	F	F	F
Q	C	C	C	C	C	C	F	F	F	F	F	F	F
J	C	C	C	C	C	C	F	F	F	F	F	F	F
T	C	C	F	F	C	F	F	F	F	F	F	F	F
9	C	F	F	F	F	C	F	F	F	F	F	F	F
8	C	F	F	F	F	F	C	F	F	F	F	F	F
7	C	F	F	F	F	F	F	C	F	F	F	F	F
6	C	F	F	F	F	F	F	F	C	F	F	F	F
5	C	F	F	F	F	F	F	F	F	C	F	F	F
4	C	F	F	F	F	F	F	F	F	F	C	F	F
3	C	F	F	F	F	F	F	F	F	F	F	C	F
2	F	F	F	F	F	F	F	F	F	F	F	F	C

OFFSUIT

C Call
F Fold

There are some interesting things to notice about this equilibrium solution.

• The SB never makes the smaller raise to 3BB as the majority action for any hand.

• The SB tries for a limp-reraise with his strongest hands. A limp-reraise is almost never a bluff (like Q3s and Q4s).

• The SB opens with a jam with medium-good hands (low pocket pairs, most aces, and suited connectors).

• If the SB limps, the BB makes a small raise with his best hands and jams with medium-good hands and suited connectors. Even though the smaller raise is almost always a stronger hand than a jam, the smaller raise is frequently called due to pot odds. There's no hand that will call a jam, but fold to the smaller raise.

Although there's no hand that makes a 3BB raise by the SB as the most probable action, a few hands do make that raise a small percentage of the time. So the BB has to be prepared to handle a 3BB raise. It's the BB's response structure that discourages the smaller raise. If the BB doesn't employ an optimal counter-strategy, the SB can make more money by making the smaller raise with more hands. This is often the case in SNGs with sub-optimal players, such as many of the lower-level online SNGs.

Even with all these extra options, the EV of the SB only improves by 0.07BB compared to being restricted to jam-or-fold only. This is ignoring post-flop play and the value of position, and 15BB is probably pushing the limits of what is valuable when solving pre-flop equilibria.

Do smaller raises and limps show enough profit against sub-optimal opponents to make it worthwhile to deviate from jam-or-fold? Let's assume we're in the SB up against the following sub-optimal opponent whom we might find in a low-level SNG. The smaller stack has a CSI of 7. We make the following assumptions about his behavior, derived from studying hand histories of many opponents.

If we limp, he'll raise 30% of the time. A standard raise will pot commit us, so for simplicity we assume he'll push all hands that he intends to raise. In reality, he may mini-raise occasionally and we have the option to flat call. This makes limping with weak hands slightly more profitable than our model predicts, but the difference is small.

• If we raise to 2BB, he'll fold 32%, call 46%, and reraise 22%.

• If we raise to 2.5BB, he'll fold 35%, call 33%, and reraise 32%.

• If we raise to 3BB, he'll fold 38%, call 19%, and reraise 43%.

• If we jam, he'll fold 68% and call 32%.

Assuming this is how he plays, and remember, this is based on our review of actual low-level play, the following is the best strategy to use against him:

SUITED

	A	K	Q	J	T	9	8	7	6	5	4	3	2
A	3	3	3	3	3	3	3	3	3	3	3	3	3
K	3	3	3	3	3	3	3	3	3	2.5	J	J	2F
Q	3	3	3	3	3	2.5	2.5	2.5	2.5	2F	2F	2F	2F
J	3	3	3	3	2.5	2.5	J	J	2F	2F	2F	2F	2F
T	3	3	2.5	2.5	3	J	J	J	J	LF	LF	LF	LF
9	3	3	2.5	2F	J	3	J	J	J	J	LF	2F	2F
8	3	3	2F	2F	LF	J	3	J	J	J	J	2F	2F
7	3	2F	2F	LF	LF	LF	J	3	J	J	J	2F	2F
6	3	2F	2F	LF	LF	LF	2F	J	3	J	J	J	2F
5	3	2F	2F	LF	LF	LF	2F	2F	J	J	J	J	2F
4	3	2F	2F	LF	LF	LF	LF	2F	2F	2F	J	J	2F
3	3	2F	2F	LF	LF	LF	LF	2F	2F	2F	2F	J	2F
2	3	2F	2F	LF	LF	LF	LF	2F	2F	2F	2F	2F	J

OFFSUIT

J	Jam
3	Raise to 3BB and call a re-raise
2.5	Raise to 2.5BB and call a re-raise
2F	Raise to 2BB and fold to a re-raise
LF	Limp and fold to a re-raise

Note that this strategy is highly exploitable by counter-aggression. Our raise size is highly correlated to hand strength (except for jamming). We always fold to a raise whenever we limp or make a mini-raise. An observant opponent will pick up on this.

Also, if our opponent is more aggressive than we predict,

even if he doesn't know we're always weak with small raises and limps, this strategy will end up a loser. However, if he does play exactly as we model, then this strategy has an EV of 0.14BB higher than restricting to jam-or-fold. Therefore, it appears that limping or making small raises isn't worthwhile against an opponent who plays optimally, but can be profitable against a sub-optimal (passive) one.

HEADS-UP WITH DEEPER STACKS

• Aggression is still king. Good cards are hard to come by and most likely neither player has anything. Convincing the other player to fold when no one has a good hand is the easiest road to victory.

• Domination is not that big of a threat. If you have an ace, there's an 88% chance that your opponent doesn't have one. Even if he's taking aggressive action, there's no reason to think he has an ace; it could easily be two big cards or a pair. Pair versus pair isn't all that common either. If you have deuces, there's less than a 6% chance that your opponent has a bigger pair. With pocket sixes, that chance drops to less than 4%.

• Hitting the flop is tough to do. Any pair—even bottom pair—is pretty good and you should think twice before folding it. Middle pair is roughly equivalent to top pair 8-handed and flopping top pair is a monster. Ace-high can also be a winner more times than you might think.

We'll present a couple of different strategies to use against different types of opponents, but beware that heads-up play is all about plays and counter plays—always evolving. Your opponent may switch styles in the match in an effort to throw you off or to try to take advantage of any perceived weaknesses. We'll present a default strategy, as well as more extreme strategies, against two frequently encountered opponent styles.

Our default strategy is fairly balanced. It disguises hand values well and is very useful against a good opponent who'll try to change his strategy to exploit you. It's also a useful starting point if you're unsure how your opponent will play heads-up.

Default Strategy on the Button: Pre-Flop

• Pre-flop raises should usually be 2 to 2.5BB, perhaps 3BB against a very loose player.

• *Top 50% of hands*: Usually raise, but just call sometimes. "Usually" in these heads-up contexts means about 60%-80% of the time. The more straightforward and unobservant your opponent is, the less you need to mix up your play. An exception should be made for very strong hands (QQ+ and AK). With these monsters, usually just call, but occasionally raise.

• If you raise and are re-raised, you need to weigh three factors:

1. pot odds;
2. his aggressiveness (and his view of your aggressiveness);
3. stack depth—play tighter with deeper stacks.

Depending on how these factors stack up, you should probably call with only the top 10%-20% of hands, unless you're being offered better than 2-to-1. With very deep stacks, aces with medium kickers should probably be folded. Whether to put in a third raise (3-bet) with your very strong hands is a judgment call. You could just call for deception, or raise it up if you think your opponent can't let go of a hand.

• *50- to 90th-percentile hands*: Usually call, raise sometimes. If your opponent raises your limp, most of these hands will be folded unless the raise is fairly small. If your hand is suited and you're getting better than 2-to-1, call most of the time.

• *Bottom 10% of hands*: Usually fold, unless your opponent doesn't seem to raise often when you limp. If he's passive, call and try to see a flop. Even 72o is a 60% favorite against a random hand when a 2 flops and a 66% favorite when a 7 flops. Your opponent may also hit the flop, so you may need to let the hand go if he indicates post-flop strength.

Default Strategy for the Big Blind: Pre-Flop

• Pre-flop raises should be slightly more than pot-sized. You're out of position and it's best to end the hand quickly. The value of position heads-up can't be over-emphasized. With your better hands, but out of position, you must play aggressively pre-flop.

• If he just limps, raise almost all the time with the top 30% of hands.

• If he raises to 3BB, call or re-raise with the top 30%, plus suited connectors down to 54s, plus 1-, 2-, and 3-gap suited connectors, with both cards 5 or higher.

• If he raises to 2.5BB, call or re-raise with the top 60%.

• If he raises to 2BB, call or re-raise with the top 80%.

• No matter his raise size, usually re-raise with your best hands (the top 10%-20% hands, depending on his aggressiveness). Against a conservative player, narrow your re-raising range. Against an aggressive raiser, widen your range, but be prepared to call an all-in when you re-raise a hyper-aggressive player.

• If he doesn't seem to be raising frequently from the button, increase your minimum calling standards considerably.

Default Strategy Post-Flop

• My (Tysen) general strategy is to bet frequently on the flop, but I'll often check my best and worst hands. If my opponent bets when I check and I have a very bad hand, I'll frequently fold, but I'll occasionally call or check-raise. If I check a good hand, I'm more likely to check-raise merely good hands (like middle-pair high-kicker) and check-call great hands (like top pair or better).

• Lee often prefers a more aggressive approach and frequently leads at all flops, whether he's hit or missed. If his opponent folds regularly, Lee will keep pounding away. By betting many flops, he wins a lot of pots that he doesn't deserve. This strategy also enables him to win a huge pot when he leads with a monster and his opponent decides to make a stand and play back at him.

• In heads-up play, any pair, even bottom pair, is at least a medium hand. Depending on the pre-flop action, middle pair with a high kicker could be strong enough to be a good hand, and check. Top pair or better is always a great hand. If there's no raise pre-flop, I'll bet about 50% of the time out of position and about 70% of the time on the button if he checks to me. Slow-play frequently to balance out checking your poor hands; heads-up, there's less need to protect your hand from draws. You only have one opponent and often he won't have the draw that's showing on the board.

• Bet frequently with most draws and overcards. If no one raises pre-flop, king-high could easily be the best hand on the flop. I almost always bet all flush draws and most straight draws, even if they're only gutshots. However, just a gutshot with no overcards, such as 64 on a 7-8-K flop, is weak enough to check/fold without a fight.

• On the turn and river, play intelligently and always take into account what has happened on previous streets. It's vitally important that you don't fold too frequently, especially if your opponent is heads-up savvy. Folding too often is probably the biggest mistake you can make in heads-up play, and many players bluff a lot to take advantage of this. Don't fold any pair unless your opponent is showing real strength.

Playing Against a Tight-passive Player

These players frequently have little heads-up experience and may often wonder why they always seem to lose when they get heads-up. If stacks are over CSI 8 and your opponent frequently folds his button, that may be a good indication that he's this kind of player. Folding too frequently heads-up is a mistake; this kind of player often folds too much as stacks get smaller as well, which is an even bigger mistake.

• Raise more frequently from the button, but with a smaller raise size (usually less than 2.5BB).

• Raise *less* frequently from the BB when he limps. He's folding his worst hands, not limping with them, so he's more likely to call after he limps, possibly with a stronger holding. This may be especially true if he views you as a "maniac" and he thinks this might be a good opportunity to trap you with a strong hand.

• Call less frequently when he raises; he's more likely to have a much stronger hand. However, if he shows strength and you've got a very strong hand yourself, don't slow-play; make a larger than normal raise.

• On the flop, frequently try to take down the pot if he's not showing strength, but if he calls on the flop, rarely fire a second barrel on the turn with nothing.

• Whenever he makes a bet or raise, prepare to be shown a good hand.

Playing Against a Loose-aggressive Player

The loose-aggressive style is very effective heads-up and our default strategy is obviously geared that way. Sometimes you'll find yourself against a player who's even more extreme, raising on the button 80% of the time or more. These players are often very aggressive post-flop. Lee's heads-up style fits this mold.

• Always be careful when a very aggressive player *isn't* aggressive on a hand. Players such as Lee and other fast players are also aggressive with their monsters, since their aggressive nature gets them paid off more. But many aggressive players like to get "tricky" and slow-play their monsters. Keep an eye out for what kinds of hands they show down when they haven't been aggressive.

• Trapping and slow-playing are much more effective against these players. Limp/call with a few more strong aces and pairs pre-flop, check/call on the flop, and either check/call or check-raise on the turn. If you check the turn and he checks back, bet the river most of the time, even if you're on a draw that missed. His check on the turn usually indicates weakness or a mediocre hand at best and he's trying to play a small pot. Don't accommodate him.

• Be prepared to see some medium-weak hands to the river. If he raises pre-flop, loosen your calling standards to at least the top 50% of hands. Check/call with some medium hands, such as a low pair post-flop if he's showing strength.

• Be much more aggressive with your medium-strong hands, both pre- and post-flop. Pre-flop, raise with your top 50% hands more often and your bottom 50% less often. If he raises on the button, re-raise with your top 30% and make sure to re-raise more than a pot-sized amount. An aggressive opponent may put you all-in after your re-raise and you'll have to use your judgment based on the pot odds and your assumption of his range.

For example, a very aggressive player raises to 2BB on the button, you make it 7BB, and he pushes to 30BB. Your pot odds are 1.6-to-1. If you assume an aggressive player could do this with the top 8% of his hands, you can actually call him with a fairly large range yourself. Our table on page 136 shows that with 1.6-to-1 pot odds, you can call a top 8% hand with 66+, ATs+, AQo+, and KQs.

9

DETAILED ANALYSIS OF A PROFESSIONAL SNG

The Full Tilt Monte Carlo Invitational

The Full Tilt Monte Carlo Invitational was a rare type of tournament—it was televised live with all the hole cards shown every hand. Viewers were able to see every hand played, rather than just the highlights seen on most poker shows. Most shows eliminate the hands where someone raises and everyone else folds, but those are the bread-and-butter hands of a real tournament. By looking closely at these "boring" hands, you can learn a lot about proper SNG strategy.

The format was similar to an online "turbo" SNG with seven elite players from Team Full Tilt: Phil Ivey, John Juanda, David "Devilfish" Ulliot, Chris Ferguson, Gus Hansen, Phil Hellmuth, and Mike Matusow. The entire tournament had to be completed in four hours, so the blinds went up very quickly. We'll walk you through every hand, starting from the point where there were only four players left[18].

---

[18] We've also reconciled the chip counts. In a few cases, the live chip counts reported on the televised tournament did not agree with the action in future hands. We have accurately tracked the action from hand to hand and believe that our chip counts are more accurate than the live updates.

The prize pool was an impressive *one million dollars* and paid the top three spots:

1ˢᵗ Place	$600,000
2ⁿᵈ Place	$280,000
3ʳᵈ Place	$120,000

This prize structure is a bit more top-heavy than a SNG that pays 50/30/20, so the average bubble factors are smaller at the start. Remember, the more top-heavy the prize structure, the lower the bubble factors.

Players Left	Monte Carlo Bubble Factors	"Standard" SNG Bubble Factors
4	1.53	1.88
3	1.33	1.33
2	1.00	1.00

We pick up the action right after Gus Hansen is eliminated in fifth place. All four of the remaining players are close in chips. David Ulliot has been playing very aggressively and has just lost the chip lead that he has had most of the night. John Juanda and Phil Ivey have both been very tight so far and haven't raised many hands. Commentator Howard Lederer says that he thinks Chris Ferguson has studied the mathematics of short-stacked situations more than the other players and may have an advantage. Ivey, on the other hand, according to Lederer, may be a little out of his element, being much more used to deep-stack play. Howard calls it a "leveling of the playing field," since he considers Ivey to be the best player in the world. Note that no player has a CSI of 10 or greater and when we pick up the action, it's costing 36,000 a round.

Hand 1   Blinds: 8,000/16,000 Ante: 3,000

Player	Chips	CSI	Position	Cards	Pre-flop Action
Ivey	181,000	5.7	Cut-off	Q♠ T♣	Fold
Ferguson	228,000	7.1	Button	3♠ 2♠	Fold
Juanda	296,000	9.3	SB	J♦ 8♣	Fold
Ulliot	295,000	9.2	BB	A♠ 3♣	-

An uneventful hand as everyone folds to Ulliot in the BB. Ivey has a borderline profitable opportunity to push and pick up the blinds. If everyone were playing optimally, Ivey should push his top 27% of hands in this spot and he'd be called by the other players 8%, 10%, and 11%, respectively. QTo is right on the border, but it's likely his opponents will play tighter than the equilibrium solution, since Ivey hasn't been overly aggressive. If we assumed that his opponents were to call only 7%, 8%, and 9%, then not pushing the QTo is a loss of about $6,000 in prize EV... but Devilfish may not play this tightly. Ivey knows that Ulliot has been the most aggressive player at the table, has a reputation of defending his big blind, and is the co-chip leader. He prudently decides to pass.

If Ivey *were* to push, Ulliot shouldn't call with A3o. Ulliot has pot odds of 1.32-to-1 and a bubble factor of 1.18, giving tournament odds of 1.12-to-1. A3o is weaker than the hands included on the charts on pages 136-139, but we can use the chart on page 140. With tournament odds of 1.12-to-1, we can call about 50% as often as he pushes. Since A3o is about the 25th percentile, Ivey would need to be pushing 50% of his hands to make the call profitable.

Hand 2   Blinds: 8,000/16,000 Ante: 3,000

Player	Chips	CSI	Position	Cards	Pre-flop Action
Ferguson	225,000	7.0	Cut-off	7♠ 5♣	Fold
Juanda	285,000	8.9	Button	K♠ 8♦	Fold
Ulliot	312,000	9.8	SB	Q♦ 2♣	Fold
Ivey	178,000	5.6	BB	A♦ Q♣	-

Another hand is folded out. We agree with Juanda's decision not to try and steal the blinds. A button raise may be seen as "suspicious" and Juanda has to worry about Ulliot coming over the top of any raise he makes. In addition, K8o is difficult to play after the flop if either blind calls.

Ulliot misses a profitable opportunity to push from the SB, put pressure on Ivey, and have a positive expectation of collecting some more chips. Ulliot is chip leader again and Ivey is not so short-stacked that he'd be willing to call with weak hands. The equilibrium result in this situation is for Ulliot to push 94% and for Ivey to call 30%. If Ulliot thinks Ivey will call less often than this, he should be pushing any two cards. There's no reason to think Ivey would call more often than 30% and will probably call significantly less often if he doesn't suspect that Ulliot would push any two (which he obviously isn't). Ulliot's failure to push costs him $1,500 EV if Ivey calls 30% of the time and it costs him almost $12,000 if Ivey only calls a seemingly more reasonable 15%. Of course, with Ivey's actual hand, pushing would have been detrimental, but you can't use actual results to determine whether a decision is correct.

Hand 3   Blinds: 8,000/16,000 Ante: 3,000

Player	Chips	CSI	Position	Cards	Pre-flop Action
Juanda	282,000	8.8	Cut-off	J♦ 5♣	Raise to 45,000
Ulliot	301,000	9.4	Button	6♣ 2♠	Fold
Ivey	195,000	6.1	SB	8♥ 3♦	Fold
Ferguson	222,000	6.9	BB	A♥ 6♦	Fold

Juanda makes an uncharacteristic raise and takes down the blinds. Juanda has been tight so far, not raising many pots, and his UTG raise gets respect from everyone. Ferguson gives him credit for a hand and folds his A6o. Juanda makes this raise since he knows that neither blind is going to call him unless they have a hand that's strong enough to go all-in. He can put their entire stack at risk, while only committing a small fraction of his own. Note that if he intends to fold to a re-raise, making this raise with a 72o is just as good as with J5o. His intention is to use his tight reputation to take down the blinds without a contest.

Hand 4   Blinds: 8,000/16,000 Ante: 3,000

Player	Chips	CSI	Position	Cards	Pre-flop Action	
Ulliot	298,000	9.3	Cut-off	Q♣ 9♠	Raise to 40,000	Fold
Ivey	184,000	5.8	Button	J♥ 3♥	Fold	
Ferguson	203,000	6.3	SB	5♥ 2♠	Fold	
Juanda	315,000	9.8	BB	K♣ Q♦	All-in	

Ulliot resumes his aggressive behavior and raises to 40,000. This is a fairly small raise of only 2.5BB and with the ante, it gives the blinds good odds (about 2-to-1) to call. Juanda comes over the top, since he knows that Ulliot is raising aggressively. Since this is a clash of the two big stacks, Ulliot's bubble factor is fairly high (1.73) and Juanda knows that he won't be able to call very often. This is a less extreme version of what we see in satellite problems where a raise that's less than all-in can be tricky.

Hand 5   Blinds: 8,000/16,000 Ante: 3,000

Player	Chips	CSI	Position	Cards	Pre-flop Action
Ivey	181,000	5.7	Cut-off	J♥ 7♦	Fold
Ferguson	192,000	6.0	Button	9♦ 2♣	Fold
Juanda	368,000	11.5	SB	T♥ 8♠	Raise to 48,000
Ulliot	259,000	8.1	BB	5♥ 4♥	Call

Another clash between the big stacks. Ivey and Ferguson have easy folds. Juanda has a playable hand blind-vs.-blind, and both calling and raising seem fine. Because Ulliot will frequently raise if Juanda just calls, Juanda decides to make the more aggressive play of raising. He hopes to win the pot right there, but if he's called, he's got a playable hand, although out of position. Obviously, Juanda would fold if Ulliot re-raises in this spot.

Ulliot also has a standard call, since he's in position with a playable hand that's easy to evaluate on the flop.

The flop is 3♠4♠5♠ and the pot size is 108,000.

Juanda makes a continuation bet of 60,000 and Ulliot goes all-in with his top two pair. Juanda folds, despite having two over cards and a flush draw. Juanda is getting 1.81-to-1 odds and his bubble factor is 1.37, giving him 1.32-to-1 tournament odds. He needs to win about 43% of the time to make the call.

Juanda would be a 51% favorite if Ulliot had a hand like A♦5♥, but if Ulliot has a higher spade or a made hand, Juanda would be in serious trouble. Folding seems right.

Hand 6   Blinds: 8,000/16,000 Ante: 3,000

Player	Chips	CSI	Position	Cards	Pre-flop Action
Ferguson	189,000	5.9	Cut-off	A♠ Q♦	All-in
Juanda	267,000	8.3	Button	Q♥ 4♣	Fold
Ulliot	366,000	11.4	SB	A♦ 8♣	Fold
Ivey	178,000	5.6	BB	Q♣ 2♣	Fold

Ferguson correctly pushes with a strong hand, but gets no action. Note that unlike some beginners, Ferguson didn't try to make a smaller raise with a big hand. He makes the same all-in raise as he would with a weaker hand. When he pushes, the stronger hands help protect the weaker ones and can result in a huge payday if he gets a caller.

Ulliot with his A8o is getting 1.25-to-1 pot odds and has a bubble factor of 1.21 and tournament odds of 1.03. Ulliot would need to think that Ferguson is pushing more than 35% or 40% of the time to make the call correct, so folding is reasonable. No one else is even close to considering a call.

Hand 7   Blinds: 8,000/16,000 Ante: 3,000

Player	Chips	CSI	Position	Cards	Pre-flop Action
Juanda	264,000	8.3	Cut-off	8♦ 5♣	Fold
Ulliot	355,000	11.1	Button	5♠ 2♥	Fold
Ivey	159,000	5.0	SB	Q♣ 3♠	All-in
Ferguson	222,000	6.9	BB	6♥ 2♣	Fold

Here we see Ivey making a good steal from the SB. Perhaps Lederer underestimated Ivey's short-stack play? The equilibrium play is for Ivey to raise 67% and Ferguson to call 35%. Q3o is actually slightly negative EV if Ferguson is calling this often, but once again, most players (even pros) don't call as often as the equilibrium solution recommends. It's usually right to call less often than the equilibrium solution until you've determined that your opponent is an aggressive stealer. This is because most people aren't stealing as often as equilibrium, meaning you need a stronger hand to call when they do steal.

It's a common theme throughout this book: *Most players push less often and call less often than the equilibrium play.* Their calling frequency is probably correct given that, on average, they're up against stronger than equilibrium raising hands . As a result, the correct exploitive play is to *push more often and call less often than the equilibrium play.*

Hand 8   Blinds: 8,000/16,000 Ante: 3,000

Player	Chips	CSI	Position	Cards	Pre-flop Action	
Ulliot	352,000	11.0	Cut-off	A♥ 4♦	Raise to 42,000	Fold
Ivey	184,000	5.8	Button	J♦ 8♣	Fold	
Ferguson	203,000	6.3	SB	A♣ 4♣	Fold	
Juanda	261,000	8.2	BB	A♠ 5♣	All-in	

This is a very interesting hand—three of the players have aces. Ulliot raises as he should, but again it should be a bigger raise so that Juanda doesn't have proper odds to see the flop. Lederer comments that he's surprised Ferguson didn't move all in on this hand. If Ferguson assumes that Ulliot would make his initial raise with a top 30% hand and call a re-raise with a top 10% hand, then pushing the A4s is marginally profitable.

Pushing becomes more attractive if he thinks Ulliot is making his initial raise more frequently. We think this is likely true, making it a mistake, albeit a small one, for Ferguson to fold.

Juanda decides that his A5o is good enough to get Ulliot to back down, just like in Hand 4. Ulliot is getting 1.48-to-1 pot odds and has a bubble factor of 1.40 and tournament odds of 1.05. Ulliot cannot make the call.

Hand 9   Blinds: 12,000/24,000 Ante: 3,000

Player	Chips	CSI	Position	Cards	Pre-flop Action
Ivey	181,000	3.8	Cut-off	K♣ 8♥	All-in
Ferguson	192,000	4.0	Button	A♣ 5♠	Fold
Juanda	320,000	6.7	SB	J♥ 7♣	Fold
Ulliot	307,000	6.4	BB	J♠ 6♦	Fold

The blinds go up on this hand, putting everyone in the Move-in stage and costing 48,000 an orbit. Ivey and Ferguson are getting desperate; Juanda and Ulliot are only slightly uncomfortable. Ivey, finding himself with a CSI of 3.8, pushes with K8o and everyone folds. The equilibrium play is for Ivey to push with 29% and for the others to call him 9%, 13%, and 15% of the time, respectively. K8o is not a top 29% hand and is slightly negative EV if everyone calls by equilibrium, but becomes profitable if your opponents play tighter.

A5o isn't a top 9% hand and Ferguson's fold is correct. He can't be tempted to call here, getting 1.27-to-1 pot odds, a bubble factor of 1.32, and tournament odds of 0.96. As you can see, *it's very hard to properly call on the bubble,* which is why you can often make successful steals. Being first in has great fold equity.

Hand 10   Blinds: 12,000/24,000 Ante: 3,000

Player	Chips	CSI	Position	Cards	Pre-flop Action
Ferguson	189,000	3.9	Cut-off	T♦ 6♣	Fold
Juanda	305,000	6.4	Button	Q♣ J♦	All-in
Ulliot	280,000	5.8	SB	5♦ 2♦	Fold
Ivey	226,000	4.7	BB	6♦ 2♣	Fold

A very straightforward hand. QJo is strong enough to steal from the button and no one else has much of anything.

Hand 11   Blinds: 12,000/24,000 Ante: 3,000

Player	Chips	CSI	Position	Cards	Pre-flop Action
Juanda	350,000	7.3	Cut-off	9♣ 5♣	Fold
Ulliot	265,000	5.5	Button	K♠ 4♠	Fold
Ivey	199,000	4.1	SB	7♥ 6♠	Fold
Ferguson	186,000	3.9	BB	A♣ 8♣	-

At the end of this hand, Ferguson flashes his A8s, disappointed that he didn't get any action. Should someone have pushed?

In Juanda's position as chip leader, the equilibrium play is for him to push 52% and for the others to call him 6%, 12%, and 17%. Not pushing with 95s is a $1,500 mistake if they call this frequently and a $7,800 mistake if they only call 4%, 8%, and 12%.

In Ulliot's position, the equilibrium play is for him to push 56% and for the others to call him 15% and 22%. Not pushing with K4s is a $3,700 mistake if they call this frequently and an $8,500 mistake if they only call 12% and 18%.

In Ivey's position, the equilibrium play is for him to push 79% and for Ferguson to call him 36%. Not pushing with 76o is a $3,900 mistake if he calls this frequently and a $9,900 mistake if he only calls 30%.

Ferguson should call any all-in, unless he thinks that Juanda is tight enough to only be pushing 34% or better here.

Hand 12   Blinds: 12,000/24,000 Ante: 3,000

Player	Chips	CSI	Position	Cards	Pre-flop Action
Ulliot	262,000	5.5	Cut-off	Q♦ 3♦	Fold
Ivey	184,000	3.8	Button	K♠ 3♥	All-in
Ferguson	207,000	4.3	SB	5♦ 4♥	Fold
Juanda	347,000	7.2	BB	T♣ 8♠	Fold

Ulliot has a borderline decision and either pushing or folding is reasonable. If his opponents call at the equilibrium frequencies of 9%, 9%, and 10%, then folding is right, but if they're slightly tighter (say 8%, 8%, and 9%), then pushing shows a small profit. We have no problem with the fold.

Ivey has the same situation, but elects to push. K3o is a $4,200 loss if the blinds call at their equilibrium frequencies (13% and 22%), but shows a $2,700 profit if they're tighter (11% and 17%).

Hand 13   Blinds: 12,000/24,000 Ante: 3,000

Player	Chips	CSI	Position	Cards	Pre-flop Action
Ivey	229,000	4.8	Cut-off	7♥ 5♠	Fold
Ferguson	192,000	4.0	Button	K♠ Q♠	All-in
Juanda	320,000	6.7	SB	J♦ 7♠	Fold
Ulliot	259,000	5.4	BB	K♦ T♣	Fold

Ferguson has an easy all-in on the button and Ulliot takes a long time to consider his call. His pot odds are 1.44-to-1 and his bubble factor is 1.30, giving tournament odds of 1.10-to-1. Ulliot should call if he thinks Ferguson will push 39% or more from the button.

We've run this hand by a number of experts and they all think it's close—some leaning toward a fold, others a call. One reason you might call here is to discourage future steals and, at this point in the tournament, it seems that players are stealing more frequently. The more often you fold your blind, the more it conveys to your opponents that you're tight, so they steal from you more often. By calling with marginal hands (against good opponents), you can discourage others from attempting to steal your blinds. Don't try this against poor opponents; they won't change their behavior based on what you do and they don't steal often in any case. Of course, if Ulliot were to call and lose, he'd have only 67,000 and have other things to worry about.

Ulliot might be considering his table image when he folds. Earlier in the tournament, Ulliot amassed a chip lead and was making some loose calls. The other players would certainly remember his loose blind defense and, therefore, not steal from him with weaker hands. Based on this history, Ulliot may suspect that Ferguson has a hand toward the upper end of his raising range, making a fold correct.

Hand 14   Blinds: 12,000/24,000 Ante: 3,000

Player	Chips	CSI	Position	Cards	Pre-flop Action
Ferguson	237,000	4.9	Cut-off	Q♥ 6♠	Fold
Juanda	305,000	6.4	Button	9♥ 9♦	All-in
Ulliot	232,000	4.8	SB	K♣ 8♥	Fold
Ivey	226,000	4.7	BB	3♦ 2♠	Fold

Another straightforward hand—no one gives Juanda any action.

Hand 15   Blinds: 12,000/24,000 Ante: 3,000

Player	Chips	CSI	Position	Cards	Pre-flop Action
Juanda	350,000	7.3	Cut-off	K♥ 9♥	Fold
Ulliot	217,000	4.5	Button	J♣ J♠	All-in
Ivey	199,000	4.1	SB	Q♣ 8♣	Fold
Ferguson	234,000	4.9	BB	7♦ 3♠	Fold

Lederer comments that he's surprised Juanda doesn't push here with K9s. We are as well. This is a prime opportunity for the big stack to utilize the fear of the bubble. The equilibrium solution is for Juanda to push 56% and for the others to call him 9%, 13%, and 12%. K9s is a top 12% hand and folding it is a $5,500 mistake if they call this frequently, and a $8,500 mistake if they are slightly tighter (7%, 10%, 10%). Of course, it's easy for us to play armchair quarterback—we didn't have our ass in the chair. It's unclear from the broadcast if Ulliot looked at his hand before Juanda took action. Perhaps Juanda was able to pick up a read on him.

Obviously, Juanda is very lucky that he didn't push his K9s, as Ulliot flashes his jacks after they go uncalled.

Hand 16   Blinds: 12,000/24,000 Ante: 3,000

Player	Chips	CSI	Position	Cards	Pre-flop Action
Ulliot	262,000	5.5	Cut-off	8♣ 5♦	Fold
Ivey	184,000	3.8	Button	J♦ 8♠	All-in
Ferguson	207,000	4.3	SB	T♥ 5♠	Fold
Juanda	347,000	7.2	BB	9♠ 2♦	Fold

Ivey continues his aggressive play, hoping that his opponents remain tight. The stacks are identical to Hand 12 and the equilibrium push is still 36% with equilibrium calls of 13% and 22% by the blinds. J8o is a tiny bit stronger than K3o, so pushing is even more correct on this hand, so long as his opponents don't start calling more often because of these frequent steals.

Hand 17   Blinds: 12,000/24,000 Ante: 3,000

Player	Chips	CSI	Position	Cards	Pre-flop Action
Ivey	229,000	4.8	Cut-off	7♦ ??	Fold
Ferguson	192,000	4.0	Button	A♥ 2♣	All-in
Juanda	320,000	6.7	SB	9♦ 8♦	Fold
Ulliot	259,000	5.4	BB	K♣ 9♥	Fold

The computer isn't able to read one of Ivey's cards for the live display, but he folds some hand with a seven in it. Any ace is always a raising hand from the button, so Ferguson has an easy decision to push all-in. Both Juanda and Ulliot give him respect and fold; short-handed with short stacks isn't the time to worry about domination. Any ace is a strong hand; if you have an ace on the button, there's a 77% chance that neither of your opponents will have an ace. Even A2o is rated at the 31st percentile overall for raising.

Juanda is getting pot odds of 1.34-to-1 and has a bubble factor of 1.24 and tournament odds of 1.08-to-1. So with 98s, he needs to believe that Ferguson is pushing at least 86% of the time in order to make the call. Folding is clearly right.

Ulliot is getting pot odds of 1.44-to-1 and has a bubble factor of 1.30 and tournament odds of 1.10-to-1. So with K9o, he needs to believe that Ferguson is pushing at least 47% of the time in order to make the call. That's probably slightly aggressive for Ferguson, so folding seems right, but calling wouldn't be horrible. To an observer who can't see the cards, it looks like the table is getting more aggressive with steals, so perhaps it's time to start calling more frequently.

Hand 18   Blinds: 12,000/24,000 Ante: 3,000

Player	Chips	CSI	Position	Cards	Pre-flop Action
Ferguson	237,000	4.9	Cut-off	7♦ 3♠	Fold
Juanda	305,000	6.4	Button	J♥ 2♣	Fold
Ulliot	232,000	4.8	SB	T♠ 8♣	Raise to 75,000
Ivey	226,000	4.7	BB	K♣ 9♦	Fold

As chip leader, should Juanda have pushed from the button? The equilibrium play here is for Juanda to push 59% and for the blinds to call him 13% and 17%. J2o is not a top 60% hand, but pushing is still profitable if the opponents call less frequently, such as 9% and 12%. Juanda decides not to push this possibility and shows that he's not being a bully. This may help him preserve his fold equity in future hands. Since the players now appear to be stepping up the pace and playing more aggressively, folding in accordance with the equilibrium strategy seems sound.

Ulliot has an easy push from the SB, but instead raises to 75,000. This is a costly mistake as it gives Ivey the option to see a flop and Ulliot will be out of position. The SB is the prime stealing position, because even if Ivey knew that Ulliot was pushing any two cards, he couldn't call more than 37% of the time. The equilibrium solution is to push 80% and to call 27%.

All of the commentators are very surprised at Ivey's fold of K9o. As is, Ivey is getting 1.76-to-1 pot odds and his bubble factor is 1.47, giving tournament odds of 1.19. Note that if

Ulliot had pushed, Ivey's tournament odds would have been reduced to 0.88. Even against an all-in raise, Ivey can call if Ulliot is pushing at least 67% of the time. Ivey is likely choosing between folding and pushing all-in. Based on his fold, Ivey doesn't believe that Ulliot is pushing at least 67% here (and definitely not the 80% equilibrium play). Perhaps he puts Ulliot on a top 50% hand in this spot, which would require at least KTo to call. But if Ulliot is aware that Ivey will fold K9o, he should push everything.

Does the smaller bet suggest more strength than a push? Perhaps Ulliot is counting on that psychological aspect when he makes the small raise.

In a bubble situation, whoever puts in the last raise has an advantage. Amazingly, Ivey does have some fold equity here. If Ivey wants to push pre-flop instead of calling in position, Ulliot would be forced to fold his T8o. Ulliot is getting 2.09-to-1 pot odds and his bubble factor is 1.42, giving tournament odds of 1.48-to-1. With T8o, Ulliot isn't strong enough to call unless Ivey pushes at least 60%.

When bubble factors are high, it's tremendously powerful to be the first one to go all-in. Ulliot would have been better served by preserving this advantage and pushing from the beginning. As it works out, though, Ulliot wins the hand anyway.

Hand 19		Blinds: 12,000/24,000 Ante: 3,000			
Player	Chips	CSI	Position	Cards	Pre-flop Action
Juanda	302,000	6.3	Cut-off	J♦ T♦	All-in
Ulliot	265,000	5.5	Button	8♣ 4♥	Fold
Ivey	199,000	4.1	SB	Q♦ 4♦	Fold
Ferguson	234,000	4.9	BB	3♣ 3♠	Fold

Juanda correctly pushes with JTs and no one calls him. Ferguson is the only one who may be tempted to call, but the bubble factor causes him to fold. In a winner-take-all tournament with a bubble factor of 1, Chris would be more likely to call with the threes. In this situation, he's getting 1.23-to-1 pot odds and has a bubble factor of 1.57, giving tournament odds of 0.78-to-1. Notice from the chart on page 139 that pocket threes need 0.9-to-1 tournament odds in order to call someone who is pushing any two cards. That means Ferguson can't call under any circumstance, even if he thinks Juanda is a maniac. Pocket fours would be enough to call against someone pushing any two, sixes can call someone pushing 50%, and eights are needed to call someone pushing 30%.

Hand 20   Blinds: 20,000/40,000

Player	Chips	CSI	Position	Cards	Pre-flop Action
Ulliot	260,000	4.3	Cut-off	?? ??	Fold
Ivey	180,000	3.0	Button	A♣ 7♥	All-in
Ferguson	210,000	3.5	SB	A♠ 2♦	All-in
Juanda	350,000	5.8	BB	7♠ 5♠	Fold

The blinds go up again, this time to 20,000 and 40,000 with no ante, or 60,000 per round. It doesn't take any time at all for the action to pick up. After Ulliot folds his unknown cards, Ivey has an easy push with A7o and Ferguson calls him with A2o. Ferguson's pot odds are 1.50-to-1; he has a bubble factor of 1.31, giving tournament odds of 1.15-to-1. The call is correct if he thinks Ivey is pushing at least 46%. It's not a clear call, but with these stack sizes, it seems reasonable that Ivey is pushing that often, so the call is reasonable.

The board comes out 3♣9♠7♣5♣K♥ and Ferguson is reduced to 30,000, while Ivey becomes the chip leader. With blinds this high, fortunes change quickly.

Hand 21   Blinds: 20,000/40,000

Player	Chips	CSI	Position	Cards	Pre-flop Action
Ivey	400,000	6.7	Cut-off	A♥ Q♣	All-in
Ferguson	30,000	0.5	Button	9♠ 4♦	Fold
Juanda	310,000	5.2	SB	T♥ 8♥	Fold
Ulliot	260,000	4.3	BB	8♦ 2♣	Fold

Although the action on this hand is boring and predictable when you see the cards, it's actually very interesting to analyze what could have happened. Lederer comments that he feels Ivey as the new chip leader has the power to push any two cards, because he knows that there's very little chance that either of the big stacks will call him. This is the money bubble and with Ferguson so short-stacked, it doesn't make sense for Juanda or Ulliot to get involved unless they have a very good hand. At this point their bubble factors are the highest they've been all tournament:

		Opponent			
		Ferguson	Ulliot	Juanda	Ivey
Player	Ferguson		1.05	1.08	1.11
	Ulliot	1.04		1.93	2.07
	Juanda	1.00	1.41		2.09
	Ivey	1.00	1.24	1.37	

An interesting situation develops if Ivey decides he can push a wide range. Ferguson is getting almost 3-to-1 on his money and can call a wide range as well. If Ferguson folds, both Juanda and Ulliot have to fold all but their best hands (8% for Juanda and 15% for Ulliot, even if Ivey pushes 100%; if they think Ivey is pushing less than 100%, then obviously they should call less often). With Ferguson folding, they cannot unnecessarily risk losing against Ivey and taking fourth place. What's not intuitive about this situation is that *if Ferguson calls, the blinds should be more likely to call than if Ferguson folds*. This is because Ferguson will frequently be in the hand with a weak holding, since he's getting such great pot odds. For example, if Ulliot calls after Ferguson, then one of four situations can occur:

1. Ulliot could win the pot, knock out Ferguson, and more than double up.
2. Ferguson could win the small main pot, but Ulliot could win the big side pot against Ivey.
3. Ivey could knock both players out and Ulliot would earn third-place money, since he started with more chips than Ferguson.
4. Ferguson could win and Ivey wins the side pot, knocking out Ulliot.

The only disastrous situation is #4 and that only happens in the specific situation where Ferguson has the best hand, Ivey has the next best, and Ulliot has the worst.

Calculating the equilibrium solution to this problem isn't trivial, since there's a strong chance of overcalls. Since the larger stacks may come in more frequently than first thought, the equilibrium solution doesn't have Ivey pushing any two cards here; surprisingly, it turns out that somewhere around 50% is optimal. We expect Ivey to push more often than this, perhaps up to 100%, simply because the more frequent overcall situation is not obvious. Ivey (correctly) doesn't expect to be called by anyone with less than a premium hand except Ferguson.

Reality differs strongly from the equilibrium solution, because the blinds are likely to be far tighter than the equilibrium.

Following the equilibrium strategy, if Ivey is pushing 50%, Ferguson should call about 75% of the time, since he's getting good odds. Juanda should call 4% if Ferguson folds and 9% if Ferguson calls. Ulliot should call 7% if Ferguson folds and 14% if Ferguson calls.

While Ferguson follows the equilibrium solution by folding his 94o, it's surprising he folds so quickly. He was getting almost 3-to-1 on his call, and most likely the blinds will not overcall as often as the equilibrium solution suggests. Plus, Ivey is very likely pushing closer to 100%. With Ferguson having to take the big blind two hands later, he needs to be very weak, as he was, to fold after Ivey's push. He now must move in on the next hand, or he'll be all-in on the big blind.

Hand 22   Blinds: 20,000/40,000

Player	Chips	CSI	Position	Cards	Pre-flop Action
Ferguson	30,000	0.5	Cut-off	K♥ Q♦	All-in
Juanda	290,000	4.8	Button	5♣ 5♥	All-in
Ulliot	220,000	3.7	SB	6♠ 4♣	Fold
Ivey	460,000	7.7	BB	T♠ 4♥	Fold

Ferguson picks up a great hand; he moves in and Juanda decides to push all-in after him. Juanda could have risked fewer chips by simply calling, since by pushing he's jeopardizing himself if Ivey picks up a good hand. But by just calling, he risks having Ivey trying to raise him out of the pot. Pushing all-in gives Juanda the best chance to isolate Ferguson heads-up. We agree with Juanda's decision to move in and isolate Ferguson, because small pocket pairs play best heads-up. The chance of either Ulliot or Ivey waking up with a higher pair is less than 9% and the chance of Ivey, the only player who can bust Juanda, having a higher pair is only about 4.5%. Moving in seems clearly correct. Would folding be better? No. Here's why.

Assuming Ferguson is going in more than half the time (Ferguson's minimum hand strength has little impact on everyone else's decisions) and Juanda is forced to choose between pushing and folding, the equilibrium solution has Juanda pushing about 23%. This assumes that he'll be called by the blinds 9% and 10% of the time, respectively. Pocket fives are borderline in this situation. Although pocket fives are normally considered a top 12% hand, they're weaker in this situation, because low pocket pairs don't do as well in multi-way pots. However, since both blinds are likely to be calling less frequently than predicted by the equilibrium model, pushing the fives is better than folding.

Assuming the others follow the equilibrium model, Ferguson can play with about 77% of his hands, including almost any two suited cards. He's happy to see KQo and when Juanda pushes, he's only a slight underdog to almost quadruple up. Unfortunately for Chris, the board comes 8♠J♥3♣9♠J♦ and he's eliminated.

Hand 23   Blinds: 30,000/60,000

Player	Chips	CSI	Position	Cards	Pre-flop Action
Ulliot	200,000	2.2	Button	?? ??	Fold
Ivey	420,000	4.7	SB	J♦ 7♠	Fold
Juanda	380,000	4.2	BB	7♦ 6♥	-

The game is now three-handed and the blinds go up again, costing 90,000 every 3 hands. Ulliot's hand isn't recorded, but the equilibrium is for him to push 36% here. This is expecting Ivey to call 19%, Juanda to call 60%, and Juanda to overcall 13%. Again, the equilibrium solution is probably looser than reality, encouraging more pushing. In addition, this is a situation where ICM doesn't do a great job of modeling Ulliot's situation—Ulliot will have to be BB next hand, so his equity after folding is worse than it appears. This should also encourage more pushing than predicted.

Once Ulliot folds, Ivey makes the mistake of folding J7o. Juanda won't call often, because Ulliot is short-stacked. The equilibrium solution is for Ivey to push 85% and Juanda to call 30%. Not pushing J7o is a $4,200 mistake if Juanda calls 30%, a $14,200 mistake if Juanda tightens up to 20%, and a $20,600 mistake if Juanda will only call 15% (probably the most likely scenario).

Hand 24   Blinds: 30,000/60,000

Player	Chips	CSI	Position	Cards	Pre-flop Action
Ivey	390,000	4.3	Button	T♦ 8♦	Fold
Juanda	410,000	4.6	SB	A♠ 2♣	All-in
Ulliot	200,000	2.2	BB	K♦ 9♦	Call

Ivey misses another opportunity to push. Everyone's CSI is so low that whoever picks up the blinds increases his stack by more than 20%. The equilibrium solution is for Ivey to push 42% and for the blinds to call 11% and 52%. Ivey's not pushing T8s here is a $2,700 mistake, if they call this frequently, but a $12,000 mistake if they're only calling 8% and 35%.

Once Ivey folds, Juanda has an easy push. Ulliot is getting pot odds of 1.86-to-1 and has a bubble factor of 1.25, giving tournament odds of 1.48-to-1.

Ulliot actually calls the raise without looking at his cards. Since he knew he'd be doing that, it would have been more effective to announce this intention *before* Juanda made his raise (after Ivey folds), in order to convince Juanda that he didn't have any fold equity. From Juanda's point of view, the more likely Ulliot is to call, the *less often* he should push. So it's in Ulliot's best interest to tell Juanda he's going to call without looking. He should do everything he can to convince Juanda that he's really committed to calling blind.

However, after Juanda goes through with the raise, calling in the dark is an error. If Ulliot is expecting Juanda to raise with any two cards here, Ulliot can only call 80% of the time, meaning it's correct to fold sometimes. Plus, if he thinks Juanda is more selective, Ulliot should fold more often. Calling in the dark costs a bit more than $3,000 in equity, compared with looking at his cards and making an informed decision.

If Ulliot *had* looked at his cards, the chart on page 139 shows that K9s should call so long as the SB is pushing at least 20%. In this situation, Juanda will raise much more frequently, so the call is automatic.

The board comes 6♦Q♥2♥4♠7♠ and Ulliot is eliminated.

Hand 25   Blinds: 30,000/60,000

Player	Chips	CSI	Position	Cards	Pre-flop Action
Juanda	610,000	6.8	SB	6♣ 5♠	Fold
Ivey	390,000	4.3	BB	Q♣ J♣	-

Once we're down to heads-up, the only thing that matters in terms of the equilibrium solution is the CSI of the shorter stack. As a refresher, the following page shows the equilibrium play tables from Chapter 8.

EQUILIBRIUM RAISING STRATEGY (ALL-IN OR FOLD)
SUITED

OFFSUIT

	A	K	Q	J	T	9	8	7	6	5	4	3	2
A	8	8	8	8	8	8	8	8	8	8	8	8	8
K	8	8	8	8	8	8	8	8	8	8	8	8	8
Q	8	8	8	8	8	8	8	8	8	8	8	8	8
J	8	8	8	8	8	8	8	8	8	8	8	7	5
T	8	8	8	8	8	8	8	8	8	7	7	5	4
9	8	8	8	8	8	8	8	8	8	8	3	3	2
8	8	8	8	8	8	8	8	8	8	8	5	1	1
7	8	8	6	5	6	7	8	8	8	8	8	1	1
6	8	8	6	4	3	3	4	7	8	8	8	1	1
5	8	8	5	4	2	2	2	1	1	8	8	8	1
4	8	8	5	3	2	1	1	1	1	1	8	6	1
3	8	8	5	3	2	1	1	1	1	1	1	8	1
2	8	7	4	3	2	1	1	1	1	1	<1	<1	8

EQUILIBRIUM CALLING STRATEGY (ALL-IN OR FOLD)
SUITED

OFFSUIT

	A	K	Q	J	T	9	8	7	6	5	4	3	2
A	8	8	8	8	8	8	8	8	8	8	8	8	8
K	8	8	8	8	8	8	8	8	8	8	8	7	7
Q	8	8	8	8	8	8	8	7	6	5	5	5	4
J	8	8	8	8	8	8	7	5	4	4	4	3	3
T	8	8	8	7	8	7	6	4	4	3	3	3	3
9	8	8	7	6	5	8	5	4	3	3	2	2	2
8	8	8	6	5	4	4	8	4	3	3	2	2	2
7	8	8	5	4	3	3	3	8	3	3	2	2	2
6	8	7	4	3	3	2	2	2	8	3	2	2	2
5	8	6	4	3	2	2	2	2	2	8	3	2	2
4	8	6	4	3	2	2	2	2	2	2	8	2	2
3	8	5	3	2	2	2	1	2	2	2	2	8	2
2	8	5	3	2	2	2	1	1	1	1	1	1	8

The bubble factors are always 1.0, and with CSIs this low, straying too far from the equilibrium solution can be costly. Remember the cardinal rule of short-stack heads-up play:

Pushing too often is always better than not pushing enough.

We start our heads-up session with Ivey as the short stack with a CSI of 4.3; Juanda, with a CSI of 6.8, has 65o. The equilibrium table above doesn't recommend pushing with 65o with a CSI above 1, but in Juanda's situation, the decision is much closer than the table indicates. Why? Because it's profitable to push if Ivey calls less than 50% of the time, which seems quite plausible. If Ivey only calls 30% in this situation, pushing is worth an amazing $11,000 gain in prize EV. It's important to always keep in mind that actual game conditions can, and usually do, differ significantly from the equilibrium solutions and appropriate adjustments are required. In this hand, Ivey actually has a hand, QJs, with which he'd likely call.

Hand 26   Blinds: 30,000/60,000

Player	Chips	CSI	Position	Cards	Pre-flop Action
Ivey	420,000	4.7	SB	5♥ 4♣	Fold
Juanda	580,000	6.4	BB	Q♠ 9♠	-

This next hand is very similar to the last hand, but with a worse starting hand. This time pushing is profitable if the BB calls less than 45%. If Juanda calls a push only 30% of the time, then pushing is worth $9,400.

Hand 27   Blinds: 30,000/60,000

Player	Chips	CSI	Position	Cards	Pre-flop Action
Juanda	610,000	6.8	SB	Q♣ 6♣	All-in
Ivey	390,000	4.3	BB	K♥ K♠	Call

This time Juanda finds a hand worth pushing (Q6s should push even with a CSI of 8), but runs into pocket kings! This hand illustrates the fact that making the correct decision doesn't assure you of being a favorite. The board comes J♠5♣6♥5♦9♣ and Ivey takes over a 3.5-to-1 chip lead.

Hand 28   Blinds: 50,000/100,000

Player	Chips	CSI	Position	Cards	Pre-flop Action
Ivey	780,000	5.2	SB	5♣ 3♣	Fold
Juanda	220,000	1.5	BB	3♥ 2♦	-

The blinds go up again and Juanda has just over 2BB. After Ivey folds, showing his 53s, Juanda shows his 32o and says he would have been in trouble, because he would have called. Folding the 53s was actually a small mistake, if Juanda will call with any two cards. Assuming Juanda calls all the time, pushing is worth $1,500 more than folding.

Juanda is correct to call with the 32o. That's right! In this situation it's optimal for him to call with the worst possible hand in heads-up play. In order to make folding correct, he has to think that Ivey is so tight as to only raise 17%. It's correct to call 100% of the time in the BB, if the short stack has 2.5BB or less.

Hand 29   Blinds: 50,000/100,000

Player	Chips	CSI	Position	Cards	Pre-flop Action
Juanda	270,000	1.8	SB	T♣ 4♠	All-in
Ivey	730,000	4.9	BB	A♦ 8♠	Call

Here's the final hand of the Monte Carlo Invitational. T4s is an easy push with a CSI of less than 2, and Ivey obviously calls with an ace. The flop and turn are 2♥4♣3♥Q♣, but Ivey spikes the 5♣ on the river to make a straight and win the tournament. If Juanda had won this hand, it would have been very close to dead-even and a literal coin flip at that point, since the blinds are so high that most hands should be played all in.

Monte Carlo Invitational: Summary

I hope you've learned a lot from this analysis. Not to belittle the skills of the players involved, but the play here is very similar to what you will encounter in many SNGs online. With the blinds so high, there are usually no fancy plays or finesse; it's just, "Do I push this hand or not?" The skill factor comes into play by estimating others' playing styles and pushing accordingly.

We've learned that even professionals tend to be tighter than equilibrium when it comes to all-in moves, both in pushing and calling. Being tighter in your calling strategy is certainly justified if you think your opponents aren't pushing as frequently as equilibrium. But the only reason for not pushing at least as much as equilibrium is if you think your opponents are calling more frequently than equilibrium—generally not the case.

Part Three
Other Topics

10

ADJUSTMENTS TO RECENT CHANGES IN NO-LIMIT HOLD 'EM TOURNAMENTS

Over the past couple of years, live tournament play has dramatically changed. Led by a strong contingent of young, aggressive, fearless players (the Scandinavians being the prime example), it's become much more difficult to steal all-important blinds and antes during the middle and latter parts of tournaments. Raises from the "steal positions"—the cutoff, button, and small blinds—are being countered with re-raises. In fact, "re-stealing," which characterizes many of these plays, has become so common that adjustments must be made to remain a winning player. Regrettably, these changes entail a higher degree of risk, but winning tournaments has never been the métier of the faint-hearted. Here are some modifications that can help you stay ahead of the curve.

Steal from Under-the-Gun (UTG)

UTG has become the new steal position. Early-position raises are about the only ones that still command respect. When you need to pick up blinds and antes, raising from up front has a good chance. Once antes have commenced, in addition to normal raising hands, I (Lee) often make a standard

3-times-the-blind raise UTG with a variety of hands, such as any pair, suited connectors including 1-gappers, and suited aces. An UTG raise is unlikely to elicit a re-raise, unless an opponent is holding a big pair or perhaps AK. Hands as strong as ATs, AJo, small to medium pairs, and even AQo are often folded when faced with an UTG raise, making your steal frequently successful. When you do get re-raised, you can usually be confident that you're up against a big hand and fold, but the vast majority of the time, you'll be stacking blinds and antes. Second- and third-position raises aren't as intimidating as UTG raises, but are still often effective.

Be Prepared to Sometimes Re-re-steal

As discussed, re-stealing has become common in tournament play. To prevent aggressive players from continually re-raising you and taking the pot away, you'll have to play back at them with a re-raise of your own. Although this is a high-risk undertaking, you must be prepared to sometimes move in on an aggressive re-stealer pre-flop. Each time you fold when re-raised, you reinforce this aggressive undesirable behavior by your opponents. You must take risks to discourage this move. This means coming back over the top, often with less than a premium hand and frequently for all your chips. If you raise from around back near the button, get re-raised, then go all-in, if he's not already pot-committed, he'll need an extremely powerful hand to call. Most players will need a top 3% hand (JJ-AA or AK) to make this call. I know some tight players who'll even lay down AK and JJ in a spot like this, especially if calling the all-in and losing means elimination.

As I've said, this is a high-risk play. Kenna James tried it twice on me in the 2006 Aussie Millions. Knowing that I'm a situational player capable of re-stealing, he re-re-raised all-in on two occasions after he'd raised from the button and I'd re-raised from the big blind. He had A9o and AQo, respectively.

Both times he ran into pocket kings and lost the race, costing him over 1,000,000 in chips. In Kenna's defense, I didn't *have to* have pocket kings on both occasions to re-raise. I'd have done so with substantially weaker holdings to stop him from stealing. In these instances, Kenna was unlucky. Even given the exact hands, he was almost even money to eliminate me in one of the two hands.

If you don't come back over the top of re-stealers once in a while, they'll cramp your style. Often, it becomes a battle of guts and will power, like a game of chicken. The player who blinks first not only loses the instant pot, but also loses ground in the psychological battle for dominance. This is why the line between maniacal play and great play is sometimes blurred.

The UTG Limp/Re-raise

Players often limp UTG with pocket aces or kings, hoping that after several others follow suit and limp, an aggressive player will take a shot at stealing the pot with a raise. Then the UTG limper springs the trap and re-raises, often by moving all in. Clever players, always looking for an edge, noticed this tendency and started making this limp/re-raise with other hands, such as AK, or speculative hands, such as suited connectors and small-to-medium pairs.

Limp re-raising with AK: Limp/re-raising with AK when UTG or second to act can be a good way to pick up needed chips at an aggressive table, and a method for not only establishing fear equity, but also providing a basis for limping in early position with speculative hands later on without getting raised. After limping up front with AK, getting called by several limpers followed by a raise by an aggressive player, you now move in, representing aces or kings. Faced with this sequence, most players will fold most hands, unless, of course, they have one of the two hands that you're representing. If you do get called by a hand such as JJ or QQ, you'll be a 13/10 underdog, but will be able to see all 5 cards and, if you win, you'll double up. The combination of the big fold equity of the UTG limp/ re-raise, combined with the chance of winning at showdown if called, makes this a positive EV play and a risk worth taking, especially when you have less than average chips and are looking for ways to get chips before you become short-stacked.

If no one raises pre-flop, you'll need to proceed cautiously, but you've got a very well-disguised hand if you hit the flop big. I used this move in a recent tournament in Australia. I limped UTG with A♥K♠ and attracted 4 limpers, including both blinds, but no raisers. The flop came T♦J♣Q♠ and I wound up tripling up when one player pushed with top 2-pair (QJ) and a second player also pushed with K♥9♥, giving him the second nut straight. The UTG limp with AK well and truly trapped the two other players who thought their hands were good. The player with the second nut straight was especially shocked when the cards were shown, when the only hand that could beat him was AK in an unraised pot!

Limp/re-raising with speculative hands: Here's a way to take this ploy one step farther. Consider limp/re-raising with speculative hands, such as suited connectors or small-medium pairs. Limp in UTG and try to see a cheap flop, but if there are multiple limpers followed by a raise from an aggressive player, consider sometimes moving in, especially at times where you're starved for chips.

Say you limp UTG with my favorite hand, 76s. Your intention is to see a cheap flop and, hopefully, win a big pot. You're not desperate, but you're below average in chips and are searching for ways to add to your stack. You're willing to gamble if you flop a big draw, especially if you have fold equity. Three other players limp behind you; then the button, with a stack nearly twice as big as yours, raises. A button raise in a spot such as this, especially one made by an aggressive foe, is often done with a range of hands. If you now move in, representing that you've slow-played aces or kings, the button raiser will be hard-pressed to call.

Ask yourself what hands you'd feel comfortable calling with in his spot? Tens? Jacks? Ace-king? Actually, the button raiser is likely to lay down almost every hand except pocket aces or kings; pocket queens and ace-king might be calling hands for some players, as well. All other hands are likely to be mucked. The range of hands that warrant a call for most players, then, is the top 3% or less, so your gambit will succeed the vast majority of the time, giving you the needed chips to again be a force in the event.

Even if the button decides to gamble with a hand such as AK, your 76s is only a 7/5 underdog—you can still get lucky and double up. The combination of extremely high fold equity and the lesser, but still consequential, chance of doubling up when called makes this a profitable play.

Due to the frequency of being re-raised by UTG limpers, players are now getting gun shy about raising UTG limpers. This provides an opportunity to limp upfront with a number of speculative hands and usually not get raised unless someone has a monster. As you can see, the UTG position now provides great flexibility for either steal/raising, limp/re-raising, or speculative limping, all stemming from the notion that UTG involvement commands more respect than any other position. This phenomenon is less applicable online than in live play, but still applies during the latter stages of tournaments, when better players remain.

Know your table, though—if a number of aggressive players are at your table, especially if they're in late position, don't be surprised if someone raises your UTG limp after multiple limpers. If this is a frequent occurrence, consider pushing a speculative hand, as described above. Always consider table composition as well as stack sizes when determining how much fold equity you have.

Limping with Big Hands When Short-Stacked

Say you've been inactive for a few rounds, your below-average stack has now been further reduced to a CSI of 4-6, and you pick up aces in the hi-jack (2 off the button). Although we generally don't advocate slow-playing big pairs, this is a time when limping may be the best play.

Limping with big pairs from mid-position on is uncommon and unexpected. Usually, a limp from these positions connotes a speculative hand, such as connectors or small-medium pairs. Aggressive players will often raise you, trying to take the pot away, right then or after the flop. Resist the temptation to re-raise. Calling and checking the flop (if you're out of position), or making a weak-looking half pot bet if you're in position and it's checked to you, are generally the best courses of action. What you're looking for in this situation is a way to lure your opponent into making a bet that he thinks you can't call. Aggressive opponents with good chips often attempt to bully short-stacked players by putting them all-in, in the belief that, facing elimination, they won't call. Let them hang themselves! Although you may occasionally take a bad beat, you'll usually double up and be back in the game.

Notice that we started this subsection by stipulating that limping with big pairs is a provocative course of action when you've been *inactive* for a couple of orbits or more. If you've raised a couple of recent times and won unchallenged, a better action path with aces or kings is to make your standard raise. Since this is the third time you've raised, someone may have had enough and play back at you. If so, just call and try to trap them and double up. Changing up your play based on the situation and your history will best accomplish your goal of accumulating chips.

Check/Raise Semi-Bluff on the Turn

This is sophisticated advanced play that's highly effective against the right opponent. Your target should be a solid player who's capable of laying down a hand if he thinks he's beat. Say you have A♥5♥ in the big blind and call a raise from a solid player in the cutoff. The flop comes: K♥8♥2♣. You check and he bets around two-thirds the pot. A lot of aggressive players like to raise it up in this spot. They figure they have 12 outs (9 hearts and 3 aces), are only a 45%/55% underdog, and given their fold equity, have positive EV by raising. While there's some merit to this line of thinking, a solid player with top pair and a strong kicker is likely to strongly suspect that the check/raise represents a draw and may decide to call and move in if a non-heart hits on the turn.

A more deceptive play is to check/call the flop. If you hit the flush on the turn, lead right out, betting 50% -60% of the pot. Since many players who turn the nuts will go for a check/raise, your lead is deceptive and your opponent may think you're bluffing and call. If you miss on the turn, check, but when the solid player bets, raise! Your solid opponent now has a problem. In his eyes, the check/call on the flop, followed by a check/raise on the turn when a *non-heart* comes, belies the fact that you're on a flush draw and substantially increases the likelihood that he's up against a strong made hand, such as a set or 2-pair. Solid players often muck top pair in this situation.

Picking Off Continuation Bets

Ever since Dan Harrington wrote his excellent series of books *Harrington on Hold 'em*, the use of the continuation bet or C-bet has become rampant in poker tournaments. The vast majority of players who raise pre-flop now continue by betting around half the pot if they're first to act post-flop or if it's checked to them, whether or not they hit the flop. In fact, in situations such as a pre-flop raise being called by the big blind,

Chen and Ankenman state in *The Mathematics of Poker* that the pre-flop raiser, if checked to, should bet 100% of the time.

Knowing that the C-bettor misses the flop the majority of the time, there's often an opportunity to check/raise the post-flop C-bet. We especially like this more when we've flopped second pair and neither an ace nor a king has flopped, or when we have a pocket pair that's higher than the lowest two cards that flop.

For example, let's say you've called a mid-position raiser from the big blind holding pocket 7s and the flop comes J-5-2 rainbow. This is an ideal time to check/raise. If your opponent has two overcards to the flop, he'll usually muck. If he has a real hand, such as AJ or an overpair, he'll most likely re-raise and you can throw your hand away with impunity, knowing that you're probably beaten.

In our view, this line of play is often preferable to check/calling the flop and checking the turn, unless you have the balls to check/raise the turn after calling the flop—another strong play.

Sizing Bets to Put Your Opponents Stack at Risk

An advanced play that all top players use is selecting bet sizes that, if called, put their opponent's entire stack at risk. This is done by selecting an amount to bet or raise that would commit 40% or more of an opponent's stack. Many players, especially the better ones, will realize that calling here will commit them to the pot, so they'll think long and hard before calling.

In the 2007 Aussie Millions, 19-year-old Jimmy Fricke used this technique on multiple occasions against Gus Hansen. Seated on Hansen's left and having him well-covered in chips for most of the final table, the hyper-aggressive Fricke continually re-raised Gus, selecting amounts that, if called, would pot-commit Gus. Time after time, Gus backed down, not having a strong enough hand to comfortably play for all his chips.

Here's an example. Blinds and antes are 10,000/20,000 /2,000.

You have 1.8 million and your opponent with 600,000 chips makes it 60,000 to go from the cutoff. You're on the button with KQo. Your opponent may well be stealing, but may also have a number of legitimate late-position raising hands with which he's unwilling to commit his entire stack—hands such as A2s-ATs, 22-88, A8o-AJo, etc. A normal re-raise by you would be to raise to 150,000-180,000, but even the top range will only force your foe to commit 30% of his chips. He can call reasonably comfortably, see the flop, and get away from his hand post-flop if he misses, with the lion's share of his stack still intact.

But what happens if you raise to 250,000 instead? If he calls now, he'll have put more than 40% of his stack at risk. If he calls this bet, there will be about 550,000 in the pot and he'll have only 350,000 left. Getting better than 2.5-to-1 pot odds on the rest of his money if he calls makes it correct to play virtually any two cards, *if he calls.* Of course, he can fold to your re-raise and still have 90% of his original 600K left. Your raise has put him to a move-in or fold decision. If he wants to play, his choice boils down to whether to push pre-flop or on the flop, but either way, he knows all the chips are going in.

Under these circumstances, what range is he willing to commit with? Most players will muck all but their top hands: TT+, AK, AQs. This is a far tighter range than they might have considered had you chosen to raise 25%-30% of their stack. The considered size of your 250,000 bet effectively threatens their entire stack at a time when each rung higher up the payment ladder they climb means big dollars. Using bet sizing to create tougher decisions for your opponents, especially at the final table, is a very useful pro move.

11

TOURNAMENT LUCK

Unquestionably, you've got to be lucky to win tournaments. That's a fact. To be sure, you've got to play well, but you've also got to get your share of the breaks. Luck comes in various guises. For example, if both pocket aces and pocket kings are out in the same hand, it's lucky if you're the one with aces, because four out of five times the kings will be walking, while you'll have doubled up.

Here are some of the key ways that luck plays a role in winning a tournament:

The first bit of luck in a tournament comes right when you sit down—your table draw. If you're lucky, you'll have a table full of unknown Internet players, all of whom have had limited experience in live play. Hopefully, these players will be crawling with tells, like ticks on deer. They'll fumble their chips, telegraph when they're going to raise or fold, and provide you with a host of other readable signals that allow you to dominate the table and build a big stack. That's lucky.

Conversely, you might get a draw that includes Phil Ivey, John Juanda, Michael Mizrachi, Alan Cunningham, and several young Scandinavian guns. Suddenly, instead of licking your chops in anticipation of building a formidable stack, your thoughts become focused on mere survival. Bad luck!

To win, you can't usually afford to get unlucky by getting your money in with the best hand, then losing. For example, early in the main event of the 2006 WSOP, Eric Seidel got all his money in pre-flop with aces against queens. When all the cards were dealt, he was out. He got unlucky.

Later in the same event, 2005 WSOP Champion and friend Joe Hachem was all in pre-flop with AA versus AQs and JJ. Joe was 71% to triple up. When a jack came out, Joe was out, finishing 273rd. Had he won that hand, he'd have been in great position to challenge for a place at the final table.

Barry Greenstein also exited, though a huge favorite when the money went in. None of these players got lucky. Indeed, they all got unlucky.

Another hidden luck factor comes in the form of "cooler hands." A cooler hand is a poker hand where both players have very strong hands, but obviously, one is better than the other. The money is all going in when both hands are too strong to fold. If you've got the better of the two hands, that's luck, because if you had the other hand, you'd be walking instead of stacking chips.

At the final table of the 2006 WSOP Main Event, Jamie Gold had pocket queens twice against an opponent with pocket jacks. His queens held up both times. That was lucky.

When Jason Gray and I got heads-up in the $120,000 winner-take-all Speed Poker event at the 2005 Aussie Millions, Jason was dealt pocket queens and I had kings. All the money was in by the turn and my kings prevailed. If the hands were reversed, there's no way I could have gotten away from queens heads-up with no overcards on the board and he'd have won the tournament. Luck! If you flop a set and someone flops a higher set, you're likely to go broke. That's a cooler. Bad luck!

In addition to the kinds of hidden luck factors we've discussed, over and above not getting unlucky, you'll usually have to get outright lucky at least once in a tournament (and usually more often) when you're the underdog and contesting a huge pot. Here you'll usually be a 2-to-1 or 3-to-1 underdog (e.g., AQ vs. KK, or AQ vs AK) and suck out. Very lucky, but usually a necessity on the slippery slope to tournament victory.

The biggest draw-out I ever made was when we were down to 3-handed at a NLHE tournament at the 2004 St. Martin Open. I moved in with 98o and was quickly called by TT. The flop was something like 772, then a 6 hit on the turn, giving me four outs (the fives) on the river; a ten was of no use, because my straight would be beaten by my opponent's full house. "Five of spades!" I yelled. Wrong—but the five of clubs was close enough. On the flop I was a 50-to-1 underdog. Extremely lucky! I went on to win this event.

Luck has a way of evening out. At the final table of a NLHE event at the Aviation Club in Paris in 2006, I was third in chips when we were down to five players. I'd moved in uncontested pre-flop on three consecutive hands, then picked up two red aces on the button. It was checked around to me and I raised to 4 times the big blind. The second-chip leader in the big blind had had enough of my raising and called. The flop was K♠3♦2♦.

My opponent quickly moved in! I called instantly and he showed me Q♥J♣—a total bluff. A third ace was *not* what I wanted to see on the turn (but it came), followed by a fatal ten on the river. This was almost the mirror image of the St. Martin miracle. Most unlucky!

You'll need to win some races. Besides getting lucky as a 2-to-1 or greater underdog at least once, you'll usually have to win a few close encounters—pair versus two overcards and vice versa. Here, you'll generally be up to a 13/10 favorite or underdog, but not more. You'll usually have to win several of these, both as a favorite and as an underdog. Johnny Chan won 12 such close encounters on his way to winning the World Championship.

In the 2006 WSOP Main Event, Alan Cunningham was

knocked out in fourth place. He had pocket tens and was up against AQo. Although Cunningham was about a 13/10 favorite, he lost this race. Winning it would have given him a very real shot at the bracelet and almost an extra $9 million. Bad luck!

There's no question that luck plays a significant role on who gets there on any given occasion. Of course, overall, the luck factor balances out and the better players get their share of the pie. But short term, it can be very humbling. As Phil Ivey succinctly put it when he was knocked out of the $100,000-buy-in high-stakes Speed Poker event at the 2006 Aussie Millions on the second hand when he called an all-in by Tony G. and lost as a 2-to-1 favorite: "I'm glad I didn't come all this way only for this!"

12

PLAYING AGAINST BETTER PLAYERS

You're cruising along nicely in a major tournament. Approaching the bubble, your chip position is in the top 10% of all remaining players. Your table is playing tightly and you're steadily adding to your stack with selected steals, both pre- and post-flop. Other players seem afraid of you and generally stay out of your way. Life is good!

Then it happens. Nightmare! You've been moved. The non-descript conservative players you were dominating have been replaced by some steely-eyed pros. Alan Cunningham, with a mountain of chips, is seated on your immediate right and on your left you stare down at murderer's row: Chris Ferguson, Mark Vos, Patrik Antonius, and Joe Hachem. Unreal! What bad luck. Your brimming confidence now dwindles with each ratcheting up of your testicles, as they slowly ascend upward into your body, as fear sets in. Damn! What to do?

Kill Phil-Style

In *Kill Phil*, Blair Rodman and I present a push-or-fold strategy based on hand selection at various CSI levels that definitely levels the playing field when confronting players with superior talent. Much of the advantage enjoyed by great play-ers stems from post-flop play. Their ability to read opponents and make highly accurate judgment calls is legendary. They're able to sense subtle nuances of weakness and capitalize on it by strategically betting, raising, or re-raising to take pots away from nervous less experienced opponents.

T op players also excel at deep-stack play and regularly claim orphaned pots while extracting maximum value from their big well-disguised hands. Their chips are their primary weapons. Because of this, they absolutely despise confrontations that put their stack at risk, unless they're holding the nuts or close to it. For this reason, the all-in raise or re-raise are potent weapons against them. Fold equity is always on the side of the all-in bet-tor and there are precious few hands a top pro will call with, if all or most of his chips are at stake.

Following the guidelines discussed in detail in *Kill Phil*, especially in the "Kill Phil Expert" section, goes a long way toward neutralizing a pro's edge.

Countering Aggression with Aggression

In the modern tournament game, top players, practically universally, play a lot of pots, especially when they'll have posi-tion post-flop. By playing many hands in position, they can pick up a great number of pots on the flop or turn when an op-ponent shows weakness. They know their opponent will miss the flop two-thirds of the time if they don't have a pocket pair, and even though their foes may have the courage to bet the flop, they'll usually chicken out on the turn, either by checking or making a weak bet. Betting or raising in situations such as these is lucrative and routine for better players.

Additionally, because pros are capable of playing any two cards and often do, their opponents can't rule out hands that contain a deuce on a flop of 2-2-9, or 65 on a flop of 2-3-4, even in raised pots. Such holdings are quite possible for these clever players, though unlikely for more conventional foes. Constantly keeping their weaker competitors off balance, they pick up pot after pot, while instilling the opposition with fear and trepidation.

To combat this, aggression is called for early in a hand. Calling, especially when out of position, should generally be avoided. Re-raise or fold is a better approach—not necessarily an all-in re-raise, but a substantial bet that's likely to get most pros to fold marginal hands. It's sometimes worth taking a shot and re-raising with hands as weak as KTo, A8o, A2s, 66, and occasionally even with suited connectors, to try to slow down these aggressive players. If you re-raise them off a few hands, they may become a little gun shy and afford you a modicum of respect.

Look at it from their point of view: There are probably many players at the table they can pick on. If you show you're willing to fight back, they'll search for easier prey. If you don't find ways to periodically come over the top of these savvy pros, they'll just keep mercilessly pounding away.

When you re-raise with hands such as these and get called, you'll need to find the gumption to bet the flop. A bet of around two-thirds of the pot is about right, whether you've hit the flop or not. If called, be prepared to bet the turn as well. Strong players will frequently call your flop bet to see what you'll do on the turn. If you check the turn, they'll take the lead. By betting the turn, you'll usually convince them that you have a strong hand and they'll give it up, unless they've got a big hand.

An even stronger play is a check/raise semi-bluff on the turn. If you've got a second pair or a big draw, check-raising the turn is often a viable option against aggressive foes who are likely to bet the turn trying to take the pot away.

When you re-raise pre-flop with suited connectors or a small-to-medium pair and hit the flop hard (2-pair, set, or big draw), you've got an opportunity to win a lot of chips. Make your standard two-thirds pot bet on the flop, then check the turn. If your opponent bets the turn, put in about a pot-sized raise. If he checks behind you on the turn, you have options on the river. Often an all-in bet is your best option. This may look like a bluff and you may get called. Alternatively, you can make a bet of around 80% of the pot. Paradoxically to many players, however, this bet may actually represent a stronger hand than an all-in bet.

Checking the turn after betting the flop with a big draw with the intention of raising—such as with a pair and a flush or straight draw, both a flush and a straight draw, or a draw with overcards—is also a strong play. If your opponent checks behind you, it gives you a free card to draw to your hand. If he bets, a big raise provides both fold equity and allows you to take control of the hand. An all-in check-raise on the turn, whether you've hit your draw or not, puts your risk-averse opponent to the test. Tournament veterans despise having to guess, especially when an incorrect assessment will severely reduce their armament of chips. By playing top 2-pair or a set the same way as a big draw, you won't provide them with the information they need to differentiate and make accurate decisions. If they're unsure, they'll usually muck.

A third alternative to consider against hyper-aggressive opponents is to check the river with a made hand, hoping to induce a bluff. If your opponent bets, you should just call his river bet, unless you have the nuts. If you raise, you'll probably only get called by hands that beat you, unless the turn and/or river have made your hand a monster. If you check a flush that you made on the river, super-aggressive opponents may try to represent that *they* have the flush and may even move in. Other less aggressive foes may value bet with top pair and a good kicker with the intention of folding if raised. As mentioned though, it's usually a mistake to raise in situations such as this without the nuts, because you may suddenly find yourself on the rail!

At a recent big tournament in Singapore in the first few minutes of play, it was passed around to me in middle position. With blinds of 25/50 and everyone holding around 10,000 chips, I raised to 125 with A♣2♣ and was called by the player on my left and the small and big blinds. The flop was: 9♠3♣2♥.

It was passed around to me and I bet 300; only the player on my left called. The turn: J♣.

Now I bet 900 and was quickly called. The river was the T♣. Bingo! I bet 1,800 and to my surprise my opponent made it 5,000! Holding the immortal nuts, I gave it due deliberation, then moved in, and was insta-called. He showed Q♣9♣.

This is a situation where it would have been far better for my opponent to have just called on the river. Holding only the third nuts just isn't enough to go broke with this early in the tournament, especially against an opponent who could have any two cards.

You may be thinking that the river raise is justifiable based on the fact that I could well be betting a set or an overpair. After all, I raised pre-flop and bet every round, indicating strength long before the river. If I have a set, it might be difficult for me to release it and my opponent may pick up an additional 3,500.

The problem with this line of thought is that I might very well lay down a set in a spot like this. I'd bet all the way indicating strength, yet my opponent now makes a big raise on the river. I must assume that he *expects* me to call. Since my most likely holding is a set or an overpair, his raise on the river indicates he can beat these hands. Even though the possible flush would be by way of the back door (only one club on the flop), his raise represents either a made flush or perhaps a set of either tens or jacks, or a made straight—all hands that would beat me if I flopped a set. An outright bluff on the river is highly unlikely, given this betting sequence and board. Considering all this, and the fact that I'd still have plenty of chips left this early in the tournament, I'd have thought long and hard before calling with a set.

The flip side of this coin is that the river raise pretty much commits my opponent to the pot. With 6,200 already invested, he's committed 62% of his chips in the hand. Should he call my all-in re-raise? Tough spot. Although he's getting almost 5-to-1 odds, I can't be bluffing and certainly wouldn't risk my tournament on a set or straight, and if I have a flush, I'd undoubtedly just call, unless it was the nuts (which it was). What hand could I have that I'd move in with and that he could beat? In a situation such as this, he might have considered saving his last 3,800, especially with blinds of only 25/50 and a CSI of over 50.

By simply calling my river bet, my opponent would have been risking a total of only 30% of his stack in the hand. If he had the winner, he'd have added a healthy 3,000 to his stack. At times such as these, early in a tournament, discretion is often the better part of valor.

Interestingly, a raise on the flop by my opponent (the way I'd have played his hand) wins the pot right there.

Keep Fold Equity on Your Side

An important corollary of aggressive play is to keep fold equity on your side of the equation. Putting a superior opponent to a difficult decision, especially if his tournament life is on the line, is an effective tactic. Great players hate guessing. In fact, a key part of their repertoire is putting *you* to a guess for all or most of your chips. By moving in first, you not only take this important weapon away from the pros, but you also turn the tables on them by putting them under great pressure where a mistake in judgment may be fatal. Unless they're really sure they have the best hand, they'll almost invariably fold. They know that they'll be able to outplay their weaker opponents on subsequent hands and pick up a lot of easy pots, so they're loath to risk such easy pickings on just one hand against an opponent who has represented extreme strength. When in doubt, push.

As discussed previously, do this with both your big hands and your bluffs. Fold equity is an amazingly effective ally. An excellent example of this principle occurred at the 2006 Aussie Millions. Jerry Fitt, an amateur player who has had some success at tournament poker due to his aggressive style, was involved in a pot with Phil Ivey who had a big stack in excess of 350,000. Fitt also had a good-sized stack of around 200,000. With 6,000 in blinds and antes (1,200/2,400/300). Fitt made it 12,000 to go from late position, holding KK. Ivey, seated on Fitt's left, called with 77. The pot size was now 30,000.

The flop: 5-4-3 rainbow.

Fitt now bet 20,000, two-thirds of the pot. At this point he'd committed around 15% of his chips to the hand. Ivey made it 70,000, a 50,000 raise. Fitt went into the tank. If he called this raise, he'd have 40% of his chips in the pot. Knowing Ivey, Fitt must have also been convinced that the rest of Ivey's chips were highly likely to go in on the turn. Fitt decided that if he called the 50,000 raise, he'd be pot-committed and compelled to call Ivey's probable all-in bet on the turn. Having worked this out, he decided to move in himself, and to do so on the flop. He announced, "All in!" for his last 122,000.

Now it was Ivey's turn to sweat. The pot contained 291,600 and it cost Ivey 122,000 to call. Unless Fitt was bluffing, Ivey likely had only six outs—two 7s and four 6s—making Ivey more than a 3-to-1 underdog. With the pot offering Ivey only 2.4-to-1, Fitt had given Ivey the wrong price to call. Of course, from Ivey's perspective, he couldn't be certain that Fitt had an overpair. He could have a hand such as A6, 66, or being the aggressive sort that he is, even AK. Also perhaps going into Ivey's decision mix was the fact that losing this hand, although damaging, would not be fatal.

Ivey did wind up calling and lost the hand. This was a very close decision for Phil and he could just as easily have folded. From his reaction after the hand, he probably thought folding would have been the better choice.

Have the Courage of Your Convictions

When playing against aggressive great players, a sound tactic is making plays likely to be misinterpreted. When you make such a play, however, you must steel yourself to the chip onslaught you may have to endure that results directly from such deception.

Here are two actual examples, both involving my favorite player to analyze—Phil Ivey.

Example 1: At the final table of a WPT event several years ago, Peter Giordano, an aggressive amateur, was seated on Ivey's left. As usual, Ivey had a mountain of chips and had Giordano well-covered. In the subject hand, Ivey raised from late position with Q6 offsuit. Giordano, holding AQ, decided to set a trap for Phil and just called. The other players all folded. The flop was perfect for Giordano: A-6-2.

Ivey bet the flop and Giordano now sprung the trap, putting in a big raise. Ivey thought for a while, then moved in! Now, with his tournament life and tons of money on the line, it was Giordano's turn to cogitate. The more he thought, the more visibly agitated he became. He seemed tortured with indecision. Did Ivey flop 2-pair or a set? Possibly. Would he move in with less? Ultimately, Giordano talked himself out of calling and mucked the winning hand.

Let's now have a look at this hand from Ivey's perspective. He raised pre-flop from late position with garbage. As the table captain, this is a routine steal. Giordano just calls, representing a mediocre hand. The flop helps Ivey, giving him middle pair with a decent (queen) kicker. Ivey bets and gets raised. What hand does he put the aggressive Giordano on, given this sequence? He probably quickly eliminates a big ace, because he thinks Giordano would re-raise pre-flop with an ace and a big kicker. Pocket sixes or pocket deuces are possible, but with such a strong hand, it's likely that Giordano would have been reluctant to make a big raise on the flop. Why take Ivey off the lead when he's likely to also bet the turn? Ivey probably reasoned, based on the betting, that Giordano held an ace with a mediocre kicker—a hand he might call with pre-flop and raise with post-flop. Ivey undoubtedly believed that he could blow Giordano off such a marginal holding. The hands that probably concerned him were A6 or A2, hands with which Giordano would likely have called pre-flop and raised post-flop.

AQ probably never entered Ivey's mind as a possibility. Ivey's play of the hand makes perfect sense given the misinformation he'd been fed. Giordano set the perfect trap, then let his wily quarry escape the noose. Once you decide on a decision path, it's essential to see through the flurry of chips that's likely to come your way. No-limit hold 'em is not for the faint-hearted!

Example 2: Aussie Millions 2006. With around 10% of the field left, Phil Ivey gets involved in a hand with the 2005 Aussie Millions winner, New Zealander Jamil Dia. Phil has never played with Jamil before. Both have big stacks, but Jamil has Phil covered by a significant margin when this hand comes down. With blinds and antes of 1,200/2,400/300, Ivey raises to 8,000 from the small blind with Q♠7♥ (sound familiar?). Dia, in the big blind with A♥K♣, decides to trap and calls.

The flop is J♦2♦2♥.

Ivey bets 15,000 into a pot of about 23,000. Dia thinks and calls. It's quite possible that this flop missed Ivey. Dia with position and two overcards thinks he may have the best hand, has position, and makes a reasonable call.

The turn: A♦!

Ivey has absolutely nothing, but Dia hasn't shown any strength. Ivey bets 40,000 into the 53,000 pot. Surprisingly, Dia, after pondering a bit, just calls. Perhaps the three diamonds on the board have frozen him. After his call, there's 133,000 in the pot. Ivey only has an additional 98,000. If Ivey has a diamond (which we know he doesn't), Jamil will put Phil to a tough decision if he moves in on the turn. If Ivey already has the flush, trip deuces (or better), Dia is likely to double him

up by calling his all-in river bet anyway, but if Ivey is still drawing, he'd be getting the wrong price to continue after the turn.
An ace (or king) is the card Jamil's hoping for. I'd have taken
full advantage of it and pushed on the turn. If Ivey has a flush
or makes a flush on the river, so be it.

Dia's call brings the river card: K♦!

Ivey, after a long dwell-up, announces, "All in!"

Now it's Jamil's turn to think … and think … and think …
He's got top 2-pair, but any diamond beats him, let alone trip
deuces or a full house. Given the betting sequence, pocket aces
or kings may have seemed more likely to Jamil than a diamond.
With the ace, king, and jack of diamonds all on the board,
the only starting hands that fit the betting are pocket queens
with the queen of diamonds, pocket aces, kings, or deuces, or
perhaps a hand such as A2, K2, or J2. At long last, time is
called and Jamil is given one additional minute to act. With ten
seconds left, the floorman starts the countdown. Jamil's hand
is dead if he reaches zero. Jamil seems racked with indecision.
Ultimately, the fact that he'll still have chips left (and the fact
that Jamil hates to lay down a hand once he's involved in a pot)
may have tipped the scales. With the count at two, Jamil announces, "I call."

Ivey takes a cheap shot and says, "Kings full," then immediately smiles and reassuringly puts his hand on Jamil's arm as
he mucks. Jamil, after recovering from heart failure and visibly
shaken by Ivey's comment, rakes the pot, eliminating Ivey.

This last hand took an incredible 14 minutes to play. In the
end, Jamil set a trap and stuck with his plan, despite a fright-
ening board and intense pressure from perhaps the best in the
game.

No one can accuse him of not having courage.

In summary, here are the ways to help neutralize the advantage that the better players enjoy:

• Avoid calling raises pre-flop, especially out of position.
Either re-raise (perhaps all-in) or fold.

• Keep fold equity on your side. Move in on the flop or turn with strong hands that may be outdrawn or vulnerable to scare cards and an all-in bet by your opponent.

• When in doubt, call an all-in. If you're not sure what to do after your superior opponent has moved in and put you to a decision for all your chips, suck it up and call. This takes great courage and sometimes you'll be walking, but more often than not, you'll double up. Generally speaking, an unknown player should be less concerned about an all-in river bet by an aggressive pro than he should be by a bet of half to two-thirds of the pot that's begging to be called. The all-in is more often a bluff, while the lesser bet often accompanies the nuts.

Playing Against "Hyper-LAGs"

A new and expanding group of tournament players out there has taken tournament poker to a new level—the loose hyper-aggressive player, or hyper-LAG, for short. This new breed plays an extraordinary number of hands, is super-aggressive and fearless, and won't back down very often when challenged. The hallmarks of this style are fear, intimidation, and a barrage of chips. Folding, though on occasion they do so, isn't a prominent part of their game. Theirs is pressure poker—an onslaught from start to finish. They're dangerous and unpredictable and, since they're involved in so many pots, impossible to avoid. This group differs from the small-ball pros, who are often averse to playing big pots without the nuts or close to it. The hyper-LAG integrates both small-ball and long-ball poker, putting maximum pressure on his opposition.

In the 2007 Aussie Millions, I encountered two of these loose canons—the Finn Patrik Antonius, and the 19-year-old American online phenom Jimmy Fricke.

Patrik is an awesome player who combines a loose hyper-aggressive style with great reads and deception. I played with him for more than 10 hours and he literally played around

75% of his hands! He'd almost invariably open-raise when first in and would frequently call a raise when he had position on the raiser, with the intention of outplaying him as the hand evolved. He relied heavily on having position, as do all good players, but hyper-LAGs like Patrik have honed this powerful weapon to precision, using it to make bets that consistently put their opponents' stacks at risk. When out of position, he'd become a bit more cautious, especially when re-raised.

Since he can have any two cards, it's difficult to put him on a hand. Like Ivey, who also plays a variation of this style, Patrik has integrated both small ball and long ball into his game, with devastating effectiveness. Regardless of his hand value, he's perfectly capable of shoving it all-in if he thinks you can't call.

An excellent example of this type of play occurred on the bubble at the Millions. With 81 players remaining and 80 getting paid a minimum of $15,000 each, Patrik raised *every hand* for two orbits, picking up 10,000 chips per hand. I was the only player with a stack big enough to hurt him, although he had me well-covered. Patrik undoubtedly has a good understanding of bubble factors and was acting accordingly. When he button-raised to 13,000 for the 16th straight time with blinds and antes of 2,000/4,000/500, I re-raised from the big blind to 41,000 off a stack of 235,000, holding ATo. My bubble factor was 1.42, meaning I needed to be about a 3-to-2 favorite to play for all my chips. As you read a few pages earlier on page 241, this is the recommended play against an aggressive blind stealer who's likely to pass with marginal hands. Against the hyper-LAG, however, you've got to be prepared for him to come back over the top with a wide range of hands. If he doesn't, he may be perceived as being vulnerable to a re-raise, an impression that might tarnish his reign of fear. Patrik studied a while, asked how many chips I had, then moved in.

Now I was faced with a dilemma. If I folded, I'd still have above average chips; if I played, I'd probably be either a 60/40 favorite (if Patrik had a hand such as KQo or K7s). There was also a chance that I'd be either a 3-to-1 favorite or a 3-to-1 dog, if Patrik had an ace. Weighing it all up, I opted to fold, even though probabilities favored my having best hand and thinking that I was, on average, a 3-to-2 favorite. We'd been playing for 14 hours and, despite my conditioning, I could feel it. Knowing that the day would end when the bubble burst (which it did soon thereafter) and still having a respectable stack, I decided there'd be better opportunities.

Defending Against the Hyper-LAG

Defense 1—The Check-call: Although I think re-raising most aggressive players who raise from late position is often the best play, it may not be optimal against the hyper-LAG. In retrospect, I think I made a sub-optimal play against Patrik Antonius by re-raising with that ATo. A better play would have been to have smooth-called, then checked the flop regardless of what came, or to just have moved in pre-flop. I should have realized that Patrik was likely to move in at the first sign of resistance. For the hyper-LAG, backing down would set an unwanted precedent. To continue to suppress the table, he needed to preserve his fear equity. If he backed down at the first sign of resistance, his fear equity would undoubtedly suffer.

He also knew that there were precious few hands with which I'd be willing to risk my tournament life, since I'd still have above-average chips if I folded. He may have figured that I'd probably have to have AJs+, AQ+, or TT+ to call. Pocket 8s or 9s would be a tough decision. AT, the hand I had, was borderline, given the circumstances. Against a hyper-LAG, if you re-raise you've got to be prepared to call an all-in bet, because this is a play they're prepared to make, both with a legitimate hand or on air.

I want to emphasize that this is different from playing against most pros, who'll usually fold marginal holdings when re-raised. *Fold equity* and *fear equity* play such a large part in a hyper-LAG's game that they'll often take big risks in order to squelch resistance. Putting opponents to a decision for all their chips plays a big role in the way they maintain dominance. Like the alpha-male in a society of gorillas, pugnacious upstarts can't be tolerated and must be chip-bludgeoned back into line, so there was little merit in re-raising with the AT, unless I was willing to go all the way with the hand pre-flop. Had I moved in, I'd have kept fold equity on my side and put Patrik to a guess for a significant portion of his stack. His calling range in this instance would probably be something such as 99+, AQ+, AJs+. In other words, I'd pick up the pot more than 90% of the time.

Why would smooth-calling and checking the flop have been better than a standard re-raise? Loose hyper-aggressive players rarely put on the brakes and can throw off a lot of chips before realizing that, on this occasion, their bullying isn't getting the job done.

If I flopped an ace or a ten with zero overcards or one, check-calling all the way would probably have won a lot of chips. He'd certainly bet the flop, would likely fire a second barrel on the turn, and might fire a third (perhaps even moving in) on the river, if he thought I couldn't call. I've fired three barrels on numerous occasions, getting a foe to lay down the best hand on the river. Of course, I could still get busted. On a board of A7259 at showdown, he might turn over 75, 97, AJ, 22, etc., but the vast majority of the time my hand figures to be good.

Alternatively, if I missed the flop, a check/all-in bluff is another reasonable line of play. That formidable ally, fold equity, would have been on my side, and by moving in first, his decision would have been reduced to call or fold. Considering the power of his chips, he'd need a strong hand to call, had I selected this approach.

Wouldn't this all-in check-raise bluff be risky? Absolutely! To defend against the hyper-LAG, you must be willing to go broke. Period.

Defense 2—Bullying the Bully: Another way to defend against hyper-LAGs is to give them a dose of their own medicine. This is a variation of the fighting-aggression-with-aggression theme discussed previously, but hyper-LAGs call for hyper-aggressive counter-punching.

At the start of Day 3 of the Aussie Millions, I was seated two to the left of 19-year-old online hyper-LAG Jimmy Fricke. I'd heard reports about plays he'd made against Eric Seidel the preceding day, 3-betting him pre-flop, getting him to lay down, then showing Q5s.

Jimmy was chip leader at our table with more than 550,000. I started with 192,000. It didn't take long for Fricke to start the domination dance. Very soon after play began, he started asserting himself, open-raising frequently. About the third time he did so, I picked up AK and moved in. Jimmy said, "That's not cool, Lee," and folded.

A few hands later, UTG, here he comes again, opening with a raise. I put in a big re-raise with AQs and the player on the button thought for about five minutes before mucking AKo! Instantly, Fricke announced, "All-in!" and just as quickly, I called. Jimmy's face now paled and he didn't want to show his hand, waiting for me to show mine. "I called," I said and waited. Very reluctantly, he showed pocket 5s. Though still a marginal favorite, he looked shaken that I was able to make this call. I won the race and now had a stack that could threaten him. Unfortunately, I was unable to see whether these dynamics would affect his play as I was moved to another table. But I can tell you this: Having an unafraid foe seated two to your left is not what a hyper-LAG wants to see. Jimmy continued to dominate, playing very aggressively, but with well-thought-out bet sizing, and wound up winning $1,000,000 by finishing second. Impressive! And it's two more years before he's even old enough to play in a U.S. casino.

Defense 3—Trapping a Hyper-LAG: Hyper-LAGs can be trapped. If you're lucky enough to flop a set or 2-pair (using both cards in your hand), you can win a big pot from a hyper-LAG. Check-raising the turn is usually the best approach, although calling the turn and leading out on the river is another reasonable alternative. Often the hyper-LAG has accumulated enough chips to withstand such chip-bleeding encounters. Big hands don't come down too often and the hyper-LAG is usually replete with chips from all the pots he's stolen. Marginal or weak hands are far more frequent than monsters.

13

TELLS AND READS

In tournament poker, how important is the ability to read hands and pick up tells?

First, it's important to realize that, although they both require keen focus and observation, these are different skills. Hand reading is the ability to assess the strength or weakness of opponents' hands based on their betting patterns and the composition of the board. Tell reading is the ability to detect physical or verbal cues that correlate with the quality of opponents' hands. Both are valuable skills in no-limit hold 'em tournaments.

Daniel Negreanu is a superb hand reader. Not only is he very observant, he's got the gift of gab and is superb at eliciting information from players unwary enough to get caught in his interactive web. He's enjoyable to play with—light, likable, joking, complimentary … fun. But while he's creating a party atmosphere, he's soaking up information. He'll show hands hoping that his opponents will reciprocate. Often, he'll tell them what he thinks they have (he's correct with uncanny accuracy) and it's difficult for many players to resist either confirming or, more rarely, disproving his predictions by exposing their hole cards when the hand's over. Before long, Daniel's got an accurate read on what a player's checks, bets, raises, re-raises, and check-raises mean and he uses this formidable knowledge to make extraordinarily accurate decisions.

Picking up tells is different. "Old timers," such as Doyle Brunson and T.J. Cloutier, excel at this art. As discussed by Blair and me in *Kill Phil*, reading tells pivots around the ability to detect micro-expressions—small, inadvertent, physical changes that give away the strength of an opponent's hand.

With more and more players moving from the Internet to live tournaments, tells are becoming more prevalent. Let's look at some of the more common tells in today's game.

CHIP TELLS

Fumbling Chips

One of the most common but often overlooked tells, especially for players who are relatively inexperienced in handling chips, is fumbling chips when bluffing. Because they're more nervous than usual, it may be more difficult for them to make their bets in a smooth flowing motion, and a chip or two may fall off from either their bets or their stacks. I'm more likely to call a big bet from a player who has fumbled his chips and appears to be a bit nervous than from one who has smoothly executed. This tell is especially reliable if, by being observant in hands where I'm uninvolved, I notice a correlation between fumbling and weakness and/or non-fumbling and strength.

Bluffers, especially those inexperienced with live bluffs, are fighting a battle to conquer their inherent nervousness by attempting to control physical movements, and betting is the most frequent activity where the effect of this battle to compel apparent physical calmness is manifested. Although the bettor is trying his damndest to look cool and controlled, his underlying discomfort is often revealed in his chip handling.

Be aware, however, that on occasion, players holding an

absolute monster will shake uncontrollably. While bluffers may try to freeze their actions, these hyper-excited players are, obviously, far less concerned about disastrous consequences. An uncharacteristic visible shaking is unlikely to be associated with a bluff. Here, you're more likely to be shown the World's Fair!

Tidying Up

A corollary to fumbling is tidying up, or fixing a muffed bet. When chips fall off a pile that's been bet, bluffers will very frequently hurriedly attempt to put things back in order by tidying up. This trait, combined with the fumbled chips, is highly indicative of weakness. Bluffers, rather like criminals, often want the scene of the crime to have the appearance of normalcy, so they fix their piles of chips. For me, the combination of fumbling plus cleaning up is enough presumptive evidence of a bluff to usually make the call.

Conversely, if the scattered chips are left unattended, I'm a bit less suspicious of a bluff.

Interestingly, fumbling and tidying are difficult to execute with intention as a reverse tell. A reverse tell is when a player intentionally behaves according to a known tell, but instead of having the hand that a mannerism might indicate, he has the opposite (see "Reverse Tells" later in this chapter). Reverse tells must appear natural to be effective. This is easier said than done. Bad actors give away even more information than players with tells. In the case of the fumble/tidy-up combo, it's particularly difficult to convincingly execute as a ruse.

The Force of The Bet

Look for patterns in the way opponents put their chips in the pot. One thing to notice is the force with which they set their chips down. Mike Caro has written a lot about "strong is weak and weak is strong" and forcefully executed bets often are associated with weakness. Conversely, softly placed seemingly non-threatening bets often mean a strong hand. This is not as reliable as other tells; sometimes a player with a strong hand can't wait to get his chips in the middle. This isn't done as an intentional reverse tell, but rather out of the ignorance of what his body language reveals.

Splashing, Scattering, or Spinning

Another weak/strong tell is splashing or scattering chips into the pot, often a sign of weakness (strong means weak). A variant of this is spinning, where a player delivers chips into the pot with spin of his fingers, as opposed to straight in. This also correlates with weakness.

Bet Placement

It's important to notice where in relation to the betting line chips are placed. Bets that are made barely into the field of play are generally stronger than bets made farther in, yet another variant on the strong-is-weak theme. Generally speaking, the more threatening the bet appears, the less substance in the player's holding.

Loading Up

A common chip tell in inexperienced players is to get a bet or a raise ready before it's their turn to act. Referred to as "loading up," this tell is particularly useful in no-limit hold 'em. If I can see that a player is preparing to bet, I can modify my actions accordingly. If I'm thinking about stealing, I might fold instead, as it's likely that I'm about to be called or raised. On the other hand, if I've got a monster, I can smooth call, knowing that there's a good chance I'll be raised.

A word of caution. This is one of the most common and easily performed reverse tells, so if I see a wily experienced veteran loading up, it's probably designed to keep me from betting. Because the seasoned player realizes that I'll interpret this action as strength, he may use it as a ploy to play a pot cheaply. Beware!

Glancing Down at Chips

Another very common tell is when players check their hole cards, then immediately glance down at their chips. This usually means that they like their hand and are preparing to bet. This tell can be utilized in much the same way as loading up.

Speed of Bet

By bet speed, we mean the elapsed time between the time a player looks at his hand or sees board cards and his bet. By closely observing opponents, you'll get a good idea as to what's the usual interval between his assimilation of information and his bets. Some players, such as Chris "Jesus" Ferguson, seem to wait a standardized interval before calling, raising, or folding, while others routinely act quite quickly. When normally thoughtful players suddenly move in very quickly, it's often suspicious; red flags indicating bluff are waving.

Conversely, if a player normally bets quickly, then suddenly ponders for a uncharacteristically long time, look out!

ALL-IN TELLS

All-in tells are unique to big-bet poker. Although some of these are also applicable to limit poker, these are particularly applicable to no-limit.

Moving Chips

When a player goes all-in, he can do so in a number of ways. One way is to say, "All-in" or "I'm all-in." Another is to push all his chips into the pot. Some players always announce; some always push. But a number of players sometimes move their chips, while at other times announcing. Why? Generally speaking, with these players, announcing is associated with a stronger hand than pushing. The pushing is often done to convey non-existent strength. Like a frill lizard puffing up to appear maximally threatening to a dangerous foe, pushing a large stack of chips into the pot may be meant to scare off an opponent. Lean toward calling.

At the Aussie Millions a couple of years back, Billy "the Croc" Argyros, an Australian pro, and Tony Bloom, an excellent British player, had advanced deep into the heads-up tournament and locked horns in a match-up. Billy had moved in pre-flop over a raise by Bloom. Bloom had him well-covered, but if he called and lost, Billy would take the lead. Bloom, holding A9, thought for a long time. On several occasions, it appeared as though he was ready to lay it down. Then he asked Billy for a count. Billy pushed his chips to the center and started counting. When Billy moved his chips, Bloom's body language changed. Perking up, he quickly called. In discussing this hand, Billy and I both agreed that it was the movement of his chips to the middle that convinced the canny observant Englishman to call.

Voice Changes (All-in and Betting Tells)

This tell applies both to announced bets and all-ins. Change in voice is perhaps the most significant class of tells, because it arguably affects the greatest number of players and is often made in key situations. There are a myriad number of such voice tells. Here are some of the most common:

Strength of voice: Bets and all-ins announced forcefully may indicate weakness.

Direction: An all-in announced to the dealer may represent a stronger hand than an all-in directed at the opponent. A forcefully announced all-in directed squarely at an opponent and accompanied by a glare from an inexperienced player is a trio of tells that will often convince me to call. These are some of the subtle signs that support some of the amazing calls a pro may make on television. They're not operating in a vacuum, but at times it may appear as though they're clairvoyant.

Clearing throat or breaking voice: Players who are nervous sometimes can't quite get words out clearly, even only two important words, such as "All-in." A cracking voice or an attempt to clear their throat may indicate a bluff. If in doubt, call.

Stating an amount: A number of verbal tells revolve around stating an amount of a bet or an all-in. A player can silently push his chips into the pot or he can announce the amount. An announcement of an all-in for "two hundred seventy-five thousand dollars" may be made to discourage a call, whereas a quiet declaration "I'm all-in," or "I'm all in for two seventy-five" may be designed to encourage a call.

Announcing the amount in thousands is more suspect than just announcing the number of thousands. For example "three hundred fifty-thousand" more likely correlates with weakness than "three fifty."

Adding dollars to the declaration is further cause for suspicion. "Three hundred and fifty-thousand *dollars*" is not only a mouthful, it also smacks of "please don't call this."

Promising to show: Say an opponent has moved in on you and you're contemplating whether or not to call. Suddenly, he says, "If you fold, I'll show you." What does this mean? Coming from an unknown player, it often connotes weakness, once again by conveying strength. From a pro, of course, it can mean anything and is best ignored.

Calling for the clock when a player is deliberating: Decisions involving all or most of your chips frequently take time. Sometimes an opponent may call "time" on a pondering player. In such a case, the player faced with a decision has one minute to act or his hand will be declared dead. Common sense would mandate giving a player all the time in the world if you're holding the nuts or close to it. So what does it usually mean when the player who's moved in calls for the clock?

Paradoxically (as is the case with many tells), calling for the clock is commonly used to elicit a call. The player appears to be anxious and you're supposed to pick up on this and call. Tread carefully in such instances.

Threats or berating: On numerous occasions players may make a variety of threatening or berating comments when an opponent is considering making a big call. Comments such as, "Throw your hand away," or "You know you're going to fold; why hold up the game?" or "You don't have a clue how to play," and the like are, as a rule, meant to goad you into calling.

Acting like a jerk: More and more in televised tournaments players are acting like jerks. In search of a moment of TV stardom and in part perhaps seduced by the antics and success of the poker bad boys, such as Hellmuth, Matusow, or Tony G, they act like utter jerks while an opponent is deliberating. Look out, though! Usually they're wanting a call.

Talking to opponents: More often than not, an inexperienced player who talks during a hand is nervous and gives out considerable information to the sharks. Our considered opinion is that the vast majority of players would be best served by keeping their traps tightly shut. You need to be extremely competent to be able to talk and not give up more than you receive. True, guys such as Negreanu, Lindgren, Goehring, and Gouga (Tony G) can do it and it mainly works in their favor, but those who are truly successful at this art can probably be counted on one hand. For the rest, talking is a significant negative.

It's amazing, though, when a talking maestro works his magic. One of my favorites was a hand played by Alan Goehring against Ted Forrest in season one of the WPT in the $25,000-buy-in championship event at Bellagio. Forrest had bet top pair and Goehring had moved in on a bald-ass bluff. Forrest took his time and was thinking the hand through. He gave Goehring a long stare-down, searching for clues. Suddenly, Goehring broke the tension. "You look like you could use some help," he quipped.

Without taking his eyes off Goehring, Forrest responded, "Yes, I sure could."

As naturally as if he were talking with his mother and with a genuine smile, Goehring replied, "I'd like to help you, Ted, but I'm involved in a hand right now."

Forrest nodded and, after another pause, folded.

Goehring's performance was masterful. He seemed totally comfortable, delivering that line with consummate ease. It seemed to be all that Ted needed to push him toward folding.

Goehring may have practiced this line prior to the tournament. To me, it seemed too facile to be spontaneous. But Goehring is very good at talking, so it's possible it was off the cuff. In any event, it was impressive. A reverse tell par excellence!

PHYSICAL TELLS

When faced with a big decision, I have a blank mind. Frankly, I don't know what I'm going to do. I replay the hand and correlate what I know about my opponent's betting pattern and tendencies with what I've observed in the hand. Then I study him. A stare-down like this may take several minutes. What am I looking for? Physical signs that might tip me off to the strength of his hand. As with each of the previous categories, this discussion alone could fill a book.

Comfort Level

First off, I check his apparent comfort level. Does he appear to be tense or relaxed? If I'm not sure, I may try to get him to move or talk. One effective way to do this is to ask, "How much is it?" This query, used by many pros, rarely bears any relationship to the amount bet. Rather, it's designed to force him to move and, hopefully, talk. A pro's not looking for content at times like this; he's looking for affect. Specifically, he's attempting to estimate comfort level.

Tension is difficult for most non-professional poker actors to convincingly pull off. If there are signs of tension, they're probably real. Reading tension is not only reliable, it's near the top of my hierarchy of tells. Tension can be manifested in a multitude of ways—eyes, voice, chip handling, twitching and ticks around the mouth, posture, and so on. We'll cover a few of these below. Reading tension is a learned art and develops with experience at live tournaments.

Posture Tells

Alterations in body posture can be revealing. A player who leans slightly forward after seeing the flop, for example, is often showing real interest.

Arms folded across the chest is a classic defensive posture. In psychotherapy, patients entering an area of discussion where they feel vulnerable often take this posture. Poker players are no exception and this pose may be a harbinger of vulnerability.

Interestingly, in the hand discussed previously between Goehring and Forrest, Goehring had his arms crossed over his chest. Vulnerable? You can bet on it.

Twitching

It's true. Some players actually start to inadvertently twitch when they're nervous. Sometimes, it's a muscle that contracts uncontrollably, or an eye that starts blinking frenetically, or a slight twitch in the corner of the mouth.

If this is atypical, it's a sign of tension and you'll often be well-served by calling, if you're undecided. Be mindful, however, that some players have an abnormality, such as a twitch, tick, or a tremor, that they have all the time. It doesn't take much observation to notice this, though, so you shouldn't be deceived if they twitch when all-in.

Smiling

As discussed in *Kill Phil* and elsewhere, a genuine smile generally means a strong hand, while a forced smile often indicates weakness. A real smile is difficult to fake. A fake smile appears forced and unnatural, more like a grimace than a smile, and not involving the corners of the eyes. Genuine smiles, with a bit of practice, are readily recognizable.

Eye Tells

There are a number of common eye tells. As previously discussed, glancing down at chips often signals a hand worth betting (strength). Here are a few others:

Staring at the flop: Often, when less experienced players stare at the flop, they've missed it. When a player hits the flop, his natural tendency is to look away or toward his chips. If I'm up against only one opponent and he's taking a long hard stare at the flop before either checking or betting, I may be inclined to test him with a bet or a raise, respectively. For this reason, I watch my opponents looking at the flop before I do so myself. I've picked up some valuable clues as to the value of their hands using this simple procedure.

Staring at you: As a rule, a player who stares at me after making a large or all-in bet is, more often than not, weak rather than strong. On several occasions, this tell has tipped me toward calling rather than folding a close decision.

Be aware, though, that some players, especially ones wearing dark sunglasses, stare at their opponents all the time. As with most tells, it's the variance from usual behavior that's key. This is where focus and the power of observation pay dividends, allowing you to detect differences that make a difference.

Blink frequency: A common law-enforcement technique is to observe blink frequency in people being interrogated. Frequent blinking is often associated with lying. In poker, "lying" equates to bluffing. Careful observation of opponents when you're not in the hand will give you a baseline reading. It's especially useful to compare blink frequency (or lack thereof) with hands shown down. If you can match blink frequencies with hand values at showdown, you've got a potent weapon. It's not difficult to understand why it's an advantage for most players to wear sunglasses. Not having to worry about their eyes is big.

REVERSE TELLS

In *Kill Phil*, Blair and I covered ways to use intentional tells to your advantage. Basically, any of the tells mentioned in the above discussion can be used to induce an action opposite to what the tell would normally indicate. Reverse tells are best utilized against players who are most likely to understand the meaning of the mannerism. Against someone struggling to determine whether his hole cards match the flop, sending false signals is a useless endeavor. Save such subtleties for the pros.

And speaking of subtlety, don't lay it on too thick. While an expert might view a hint of indecision as weakness, he'll see right through you, as though he's Superman with x-ray vision, if your act seems unnatural.

Moves to Induce a Call or Fold

Any reverse tell, if convincingly pulled off, can induce an opponent to make a mistake. Here are a few subtle ones that are easy to pull off and are likely to produce the desired action.

The freeze play: While we advise all but the most skillful players to refrain from talking when involved in a hand, if you happen to have had a few words with an opponent and he makes a comment that indicates he's strongly considering calling, freezing up and refusing any further interaction may induce a call. Your adversary may well interpret this sudden change in demeanor as a sign of weakness, as if you're dreading being called.

Freezing up can also be accomplished without conversation. An action as minor as gum chewing or sucking on a mint can provide the needed catalyst. Abruptly stop chewing or sucking when you're loaded and your opponent searchingly says something such as, "I can beat a pair." An observant foe will notice this sudden freeze and is likely to call.

Another variant of the freeze play uses chips. Many players incessantly shuffle a stack of chips in rhythmic fashion. Perhaps this is done to diffuse tension or just out of boredom. If you've moved in and are convinced that you have the best hand, you can use chip shuffling to create a freeze play. When it seems as though your rival is about to make a decision, suddenly stop shuffling your chips and freeze. This artful bit of behavior modification may be enough to elicit a call.

The water ploy: While an unexpected act of tension can lead to a desired call, conversely, a relaxed action can often push a competitor toward folding.

Perhaps the easiest and one of the most convincing relaxed actions is reaching for a bottle or glass of water and drinking. We first saw this used successfully by Kirill Gerasimov, a Russian pro, during the first season of the WPT. When heads-up with Alan Goehring, a player we greatly respect, Kirill made big all-in bluffs on several occasions. While Goehring was sizing him up, he'd casually reach over for water. The relaxed nature of this move conveyed that he was comfortable about being called, when in truth, he was terrified. Kirill timed this move perfectly to Goehring's decision point and in each instance, Alan folded, allowing Kirill to accumulate a lot of chips with the worst hand. I've never seen anyone as thirsty as Kirill appeared to be during that heads-up battle!

Paradoxical intention: Tony Gouga (Tony G) is one of the pro players highly skillful at using talk as a weapon. Although he's become known for his attacking antics and acerbic tongue, he can also cajole an unsuspecting foe into a trap. At critical times, I've seen him make truthful comments that seem so out of character that they seem totally unbelievable. This is especially true when relatively inexperienced players are involved.

At a recent major event in Singapore, Tony got heads-up with an aggressive local player who had little live-tournament experience. Chips went back and forth for a while. There was about a $200,000 difference between first and second.

A hand came up where the local player raised on the button and Tony, as he often did, called to see a flop, confident that he could outplay his less seasoned opponent. The flop was T-T-A. Tony checked; his opponent made a pot-sized bet and Tony called. The turn was an insignificant rag. Tony checked again, but after his opponent again made a pot-sized bet, Tony put in a huge raise—not all-in, but enough for his opponent to realize that a call would put all of his chips at risk, as Tony's next bet would surely be all-in.

The Singaporean went into the tank. To me, it looked as though he was trying to find a way to call. Tony, who'd been quiet up to now, suddenly piped up. "You have an ace?" No response. Tony continued, "It's all right. You can tell me. You've got an ace, right?" Another pause. "Look, if you've got an ace, you're a winner. Just move in. It's as simple as that." After another pregnant pause, the Singaporean showed an ace and mucked. Tony turned over 86, a total bluff!

This move seemed to totally deflate his opponent, who seemed psychologically devastated, and it wasn't long before Tony had all the chips—a good example of the use of paradoxical intention.

The weak steal ploy: This reverse tell was successfully used by Ben Roberts, a savvy British pro, to trap me in a hand at the VC Cup in London a few years ago. In a 6-handed format, I was seated on Ben's left. A hand came up where Ben was on the button and I was the small blind. After the first player folded and while the next two players were squeezing their cards, Ben held his cards slightly off the table, as though ready to discard them. This is commonly a tell indicating a weak hand that a player has lost interest in and is ready to discard at the first opportunity. But when the first three players all folded, Ben suddenly regained interest in the pot and raised.

With no one else yet in, it looked like a steal. I had a couple of face cards and decided to play. I hit top pair on the flop and bet out; Ben called. The turn was a blank and I bet again. Now Ben raised. I called this bet and his well-calculated smallish value bet on the river. Ben showed me AA. What had appeared to be a pre-flop steal as an afterthought when the first three players folded actually turned out to be a trap, well-baited with a clever reverse tell.

The list of tells and reverse tells goes on *ad nauseam*. We hope this brief analysis provides you with sufficient tools and ideas to craft your own repertoire of reverse tells and inducements to pull out of your bag of tricks when situations warrant.

14

TOURNAMENT PREPARATION

HELPFUL HINTS FOR PEAK TOURNAMENT PERFORMANCE

Tournaments are grueling and 13-hour-plus days are common. There are a number of critical decision points that you'll undoubtedly be faced with during this protracted, high-stress, taxing saga. Small nuances in body language, facial expressions, or chip handling can be the difference between winning and losing. Obviously, intense focus is essential and this requires mental clarity. Products are currently available that, in my view, will help keep you optimally perceptive, focused, and free from fatigue, even though you may have traveled halfway around the world.

Overcoming Jet Lag

I'm 64 years old now and frequently travel through 10-12 time zones. Day is night and night is day, wreaking havoc with my circadian rhythms and resulting in jet lag—a dull headache, inability to sleep at night, sudden intense mid-afternoon sleepiness, hunger at odd times, etc. I'm sure all poker players who travel great distances to play a tournament know the drill. Anyone who tells you that they play as well after traveling a long way is either out of touch with reality or lying. Just look at the record of top American players who travel to Europe or Australia to play tournaments—definitely sub-par showings.

Your body adjusts slowly to abrupt time changes. The recovery time is about one day per hour of time change, so if you're traveling from Las Vegas to Paris to play a WPT event, a nine-hour time change, ideally you'd arrive nine days prior to the tournament. Unfortunately, most players can't afford the luxury of such an early arrival. Most pros are scrambling from tournament to tournament and can only manage to arrive a day or two early, if that. Internet qualifiers may have to beg for sufficient time off work to be able to play the main event. Requesting an additional nine days off is a non-starter. Given the fact that most often there won't be sufficient time to adjust, what can you do? Here are a few things that I've found helpful.

Melatonin: Sleeping well in your new time zone is pivotal to overcoming the effects of jet lag. Melatonin, a naturally occurring substance produced by the pineal gland, controls circadian rhythm. Taken at bedtime, it will help most people sleep, although there's substantial individual variance in the quantity needed to re-regulate your body cycles. After a long trip I stay awake until at least 9 p.m., then I take a three-mg sustained-release melatonin tablet and sleep until about 6 a.m. The next night I shift to a one-mg tablet, which I take each night thereafter until I've fully adjusted.

Exercise: Although initially you may not feel like doing it, light exercise upon arrival at your destination is helpful in minimizing the effects of jet lag. Exercise increases the circulation of oxygenated blood throughout the body, including the brain. Increased oxygen supply to the brain aids in improving mental functioning, adaptation, and focus. Outdoor activities, such as swimming, jogging, or walking, are excellent.

My travel routine combines an aerobic exercise shortly after arrival with stretching exercises, such as yoga, followed by shower, massage (preferably shiatsu or acupressure), a light dinner, an hour of high-tech meditation (see below), melatonin, and bed. In terms of adjustment capacity, a couple of days using these tools is probably equivalent to five days without them.

High-tech meditation: Brain-wave synchronization in the form of brain entrainment is a great adjunct for acclimatizing to time change, as well as reducing stress and improving focus. In *Kill Phil* we discussed this technology and provided source details. Since then, I've discovered a source that I consider to have an even better product. This technology, known as "holosync," synchronizes the two hemispheres of your brain into deep meditation patterns that would ordinarily literally take years to master. Developed by Bill Harris of Centerpointe, CDs containing this technology are readily available. For a free sample, contact www.centerpointe.com[19].

Awareness and Focus: I regularly exercise, but religiously do so the day of tournaments. This increases the oxygen supply to the brain and improves mental clarity and focus. If you don't like to exercise, try sex! Vigorous sex produces similar results.

I meditate using brain entrainment CDs for at least one hour prior to playing. My routine before playing also includes time in the gym, combined with either walking or swimming. I eat very modestly and avoid coffee, sugar, and starchy foods, such as potatoes, pasta, and rice, while playing. Heavy meals divert blood flow to the stomach to aid the digestive organs. When playing, I want maximal cerebral blood flow. Eating

---

[19] None of the authors are affiliated with, nor receive remuneration of any kind for, recommended products.

lightly, combined with some specific supplements, helps accomplish this.

Diet and Supplements for Cognitive Enhancement

All serious poker players are looking for an edge. Optimizing mental capacity is an edge within the control of each of us, providing we have sufficient knowledge and determination. Like the engine of a fine car, our brains can be "tuned" by providing proper nutrients and oxygenation. Exercise can provide oxygenation and diet and supplements can supply the required nutrients. Also, eliminating counterproductive behavior that diminishes cognition, such as alcohol, sleeping pills (other than melatonin), and recreational drugs, is essential for optimal performance. Like any other athlete, a top poker player must be prepared for peak functioning over an extended period of time in a high-stress environment. Regrettably, I've seen some extremely talented young players blow major tournament opportunities due to partying during an event, late nights, and alcohol abuse.

Improving your diet is a great way to lay the groundwork for peak performance. In my book *Prostate Cancer Prevention and Cure,* there are more than 100 pages on nutrition, which provide detailed diet and supplement information that's not only "prostate friendly," but is also likely to help reduce the incidence of heart disease, other cancers, and Alzheimer's disease. Here are some simple guidelines for dietary changes that may improve mental function:

Eat less meat and more fish and vegetables: Omega-3-rich foods, such as oily fish, are rich in brain nutrients. Sardines, mackerel, anchovies, herring, wild salmon, and cod are all loaded with beneficial omega-3 fatty acids. DHA and EPA, the two main omega-3 fatty acids, are found in these fish. Being low down on the food chain, they contain relatively little heavy metal (mercury, cadmium, etc.) contamination and are ideal "brain foods." Farmed salmon has significantly less omega-3 fatty acids than wild salmon, due to dietary differences between wild fish and those raised in captivity.

In the April 2007 issue of the *Journal of Neuroscience,* a study was reported on mice that had been genetically modified to accumulate proteins associated with memory loss. Mice fed a "typical American diet," high in omega-6 fatty acids and low in omega-3 fatty acids, had a significantly higher build-up of these memory-impairing proteins than mice whose diet was supplemented with the omega-3 fatty acid DHA.

DHA and EPA enhance the membranes of brain cells, helping repair brain cells and increasing cognitive abilities to reason and calculate.

Omega-3s also have cardiovascular benefits and studies show a reduction in atherosclerosis and heart disease from regular consumption. They also appear to lower the levels of "bad cholesterol" (VLDL cholesterol) and triglycerides.

If you dislike fish, DHA and EPA are available in supplement form (see Appendix for reliable sources). Walnuts are also a good source of omega-3s, but must be eaten while fresh.

Vegetables and fruits, such as pomegranates and blueberries, provide antioxidants that help keep brain cells healthy. The combination of regular ingestion of fish, vegetables, and selected fruits is optimal for brain function.

I take all these supplements, a number of which can be obtained in a single capsule (see Appendix). I'm convinced that they help keep me mentally sharp and capable of dealing with the difficult decisions presented by tournament poker.

Zen and Poker

Zen adepts achieve a state of "mu" or no-mind. This is a constant state of presence or a capacity free from the distraction of extraneous thoughts. The clear centered focus of Zen masters is like a blank screen upon which the things/events that comprise the movie of life play out. In this undistracted detached way, they are capable of fully attending to each passing moment.

This state of total awareness without discursive thoughts is remarkably useful at the poker table. It facilitates the ability to observe small nuances in other players, while exuding a quiet inscrutable confidence than unnerves foes.

Long-time players such as Doyle Brunson and T.J. Cloutier talk about having a "feel" for the game. They "intuitively" know when someone has a big hand or when they're bluffing. They counsel players to stick with their first impression and not to second-guess themselves.

It seems to me that "feel" and "intuition" are misnomers for what they are actually observing. Rather, they've developed the ability to read micro-expressions—minuscule fleeting changes in the demeanor of their opponents. These can be extremely brief, often lasting only fractions of a second.

Paul Ekman of San Francisco is the pioneer of work on micro-expressions. He has found that individuals have different innate aptitudes for reading them. He's also found that a person's ability to read these subtle changes can be improved with practice.

It's my contention that poker players can improve their ability to read other players either by quieting the mind through meditation, learning how to better read micro-expressions, or both. Ekman has some CDs available that can aid in learning how to recognize micro-expressions (see Appendix).

When a top player on the World Poker Tour circuit was asked by a friend why he didn't bet a particular hand that seemed to the probable winner, then correctly folded as the hidden cameras revealed, he confided that he had observed a slight shift in the way his opponent was sitting when the final card hit the board. "This subtle change in posture seemed to indicate strength," he said, "so I decided to check. My suspicions were confirmed by his bet, so I threw my hand away."

These types of observation are well beyond the ability of most players. But imagine how much the ability to read micro-expressions can be enhanced if all extraneous thoughts are removed, as is the case with Zen adepts. Simply put, an uncluttered mind is far more capable of astute observation than one cluttered with thoughts. This is probably why the advice of some experts to go with your first impression is sage. In that fraction of a second before thoughts flood in, you may have had the benefit of clear Zen-like insight, but it's so fleeting that its hard to feel confident about the observation. Imagine, though, the power if the state became constant and perpetual. This is the power that Zen, or other meditation techniques that instill an on-going state of no-thought, can bring to the poker table.

iPod or Not?

If you aren't inclined to devote time to learning how to meditate, even with the aid of brain-entrainment technology, is there anything else you can do to relieve tension and increase awareness during tournaments?

Many players use an iPod while playing. Although they often claim that they listen to music to overcome boredom, we believe there may be more to it than that. Music tends to block out distracting thoughts, at least partially, resulting in a degree of freedom from thought. Constant thinking is actually quite fatiguing, so any respite provided by music may help conserve mental energy during those exhausting 15-hour marathon days that frequently occur during tournaments.

Some players have found that they're more observant when listening to music and are better able to pick up tells. This also makes good sense to us. Discursive thinking is distracting. If you've got constant chatter clacking around your head, how can you effectively focus both on this self-talk and also pick up the subtle signals that opponents may be inadvertently sending? Well, you can't. So anything that produces a degree of freedom from unwanted thought, or a "fasting of the mind," is useful both in improving your powers of observation and in increasing your stamina. Staying focused for long periods of time is one of the key ingredients to winning tournaments. By helping to clear the mind of thoughts, music can play a role in this mental housekeeping process.

There are a couple of disadvantages to being hooked up with an iPod. One problem is that you may miss revealing conversation at the table. Nuances, such as changes in a player's voice when announcing a bet or raise, may be masked or go unheard. Sometimes this can lead to a critical mistake, such as acting out of turn when another player has announced "raise," but you didn't see that he still had cards and didn't hear the announcement. Playing music softly enough to hear most table conversation may help compensate, but it's hard to imagine that an occasional important clue won't be overlooked.

Music, in itself, can also become a distraction. If it's got words, your focus can be diverted from the game to the lyrics. Replacing discursive thinking with a repetitive lyric that reverberates in your cerebrum may be a distinction without a difference. All you may be doing is replacing one distraction for another. For this reason, non-verbal music played at low volume may be an improvement for some—reducing thoughts without creating new ones.

Many of the top players don't use an iPod at the table. They just don't want to miss anything. You won't see one on the likes of Brunson, Reese, Cloutier, Ferguson, Greenstein, or Ulliot, just to name a few. Erick Lindgren goes one step further. He leans over and tries to see what type of music his opponents are listening to in an attempt to pick up clues as to their present state of mind. When I'm at the table, I try to ask a player with an iPod some questions. If they pull the earphones out and say, "What was that?" I know that they won't be fully able to pick up on auditory information.

iPod use is common among online players who may be playing live for only the first or second time and have become accustomed to listening to music while playing. There are some very good players who do tune in, such as Phil Hellmuth and Marcel Luske. They don't miss much at the table, so they may have the music turned down very low. I've observed that Marcel often has only one earpiece in when he's involved in a hand.

A useful alternative to listening to music at the table is the brain-synchronizing technology. This can be downloaded to your iPod and used as either a substitute for music or as a rejuvenating respite when your attention span starts to fade a bit. Listening to these CDs during breaks can also be quite useful in reducing stress and tension. I suggest experimenting with this at home and in smaller tournaments so that you can work out how to personally optimize the use of this product. Some may use it as an effective replacement for music, while others may find it helpful on a more periodic fatigue-relieving basis.

I don't use an iPod at the table, as my base state is now one of internal silence. But if I had constant mental chatter, as many players do, I'd definitely use these CDs, either prior to or during a tournament. I think you'll be amazed at how much more you can observe when you minimize unwanted thinking.

Part Four

Online Short-Handed No-Limit Hold 'Em Cash Games

15

ONLINE SHORT-HANDED NO-LIMIT HOLD 'EM CASH GAMES

INTRODUCTION

As discussed in the previous sections, tournaments differ from cash games because chips change value. This has a real rational effect on optimal play, because small stacks will limp along meekly trying to "fold into the money." The big stacks will get more aggressive, bullying the small stacks, occasionally playing chicken, but mostly avoiding each other. Equilibrium tournament strategy involves stack and chip management as much as it involves pure poker skills.

In addition to the rational game-theory effects, tournaments also have psychological effects. Darwinian selection culls the ranks so that the tightest and most paranoid players remain as the bubble approaches. Players will be tight, tired, and edgy after playing for several hours or even several days. They know that one mistake can wipe out all their success. And they can't just reach into their pockets for another buy-in. For these reasons tournament players may be extra tight.

In sum, tournament play often involves tight opponents with shorts stacks where it pays to be extra aggressive. In contrast, cash play usually involves deep stacks with more resilient opponents. Cash play doesn't follow a tournament clock, so it requires more patience. Players need to pick their spots. Good players are still aggressive, but they must use position and be able to get away from a hand cheaply, while searching for ways to trap their opponents for their whole stacks.

Mark Vos plays these deep-stack games regularly and is a consistent big winner. He specializes in 6-max online cash games, where the action moves a little faster than full ring games. As we just said, cash games require patience in addition to skill. Multi-tabling 6-max games compensate for the patience factor (which Mark admits isn't his strongest asset) and lets him leverage his talent. Hopefully, there will be something in this chapter for beginning players, experienced online players, and those who've played only live poker for most of their lives. Now let's hear from Mark.

Format

The format for this chapter is to break down the different parts of the short-handed cash game—pre-flop, flop, turn, and river—into separate sections. In each section I go through the basic things you should focus on and then, by way of example, elaborate on these concepts and clarify their purpose and application.

I also include a brief discussion of online poker-specific tools, such as Poker Tracker, multi-tabling, and bankroll management.

For most of this chapter, the assumption that all players have approximately 100BB is used.

In almost every poker book, the style of play recommended is "tight-aggressive." A player of this type online is referred to as a TAG. As the name suggests, it means playing few hands, but entering a pot aggressively. This allows you to control the action and play the pot on your own terms.

Although it's true that most winning players are TAGs,

at the top of the pinnacle, the truly great online players are LAGs, or loose aggressives. Another style that works well against loose, weak, and passive players is an *ultra*-tight but aggressive style. Players using this style are often referred to as "nits," a semi-derogatory term.

The common denominator of all these styles is aggression, the offshoot of which is control, the ability to manipulate the action in your favor.

PRE-FLOP

When you look at your cards pre-flop and are required to act by folding, calling, or raising, you need to figure out what your intentions are for the hand. If you're unsure of your action plan, you should avoid getting involved in the hand. Confusion and indecision lead to mistakes on which your opponents will capitalize and this will cost you a lot of money.

The situations you'll be faced with are:
- pots where no one has entered before you;
- pots where there's been a raise before you;
- pots with limpers in front of you;
- pots with multiple raises before the action gets to you;
- pots where you raise and get re-raised.

Pots Where You're the First to Enter

First and foremost, this is a situation where you should *fold or raise,* almost exclusively. Occasionally, due to extreme circumstances (a complete maniac at the table, or for deception), you can limp in, but this should be the exception and never the norm.

When I enter a pot, I almost always open with a pot-sized raise of about 3.5 times the amount of the big blind (BB). This size of raise isn't etched in stone, but I think that pre-flop raises should be standardized so as not to give away information. As a general rule, the amount you decide on should be between 3 and 4BB in a 6-handed format. This is similar to Lee's preferred tournament raising structure of 2-2.5BB from up front at a full table, 3 times the BB from mid-position, and 4 times the BB from the cutoff and button. Smaller than that and you don't create sufficient pressure, bigger than that and you can easily find yourself overcommitting too frequently.

On the rare occasion that I do mix up the size of my opening raise, it's usually because of the presence of a short stack. For example, a raise to 3.5BB with a 15BB stack in the blinds is probably too large, as the BB will be in a push-or-fold situation most of the time.

KEY POINT: If you're first to enter, almost always enter with a standardized raise of about 3-4 the big blind.

The hands you should be opening with depend on your position and the specific table dynamics. If you're getting re-raised a lot, you need to tighten up your opening requirements, but if you're running over the game and your opponents fear you, you can open up your range of raising hands. When I'm under the gun (UTG) or UTG+1, 2 off the button in a 6-max game, my range is quite small. I usually open with ATs, KQs, AJo+, or 77+, but also fairly regularly throw in a raise with suited connectors or smaller pairs. The frequency of my early-position raises with speculative hands, such as tiny pairs and suited connectors, depends on the texture and flow of the game and my table image. It's important to stay far away from hands that are easily dominated and are hard to play out of position, such as A7o or KTo. This costs many players a great deal of money.

> **KEY POINT:** When you're out of position, avoid playing hands that are easily dominated.

When in the cut-off or on the button, you can be fairly liberal with your raises. I raise with hands that have any sort of strength. In the cut-off, I'll raise with hands such as JTo+, any pair, any suited ace, or any suited connector down to 54s; on the button, I loosen up slightly more, playing hands such as 1-gap suited connectors and marginal hands such as Q9o. The reason for my wide ranges here is that I almost certainly play the pot in position if called and I have a good chance of just picking up the blinds.

When it's folded to me in the SB, even though I'm faced with only one opponent, I think it's a good time to err on the side of caution and play tight. The reason for this is twofold: First off, the big blind knows it's just heads-up and will significantly open his hand range for calling or raising; and secondly, I'll have to play the hand out of position. It's usually correct to throw away most marginal hands here, unless you're against a particularly weak opponent.

Review—When You're First To Enter

You are: UTG+1 holding A9o. What should you do?

• Fold all of the time in early position. It's not worth getting involved, as hands that call will usually dominate you.

You are: In the cut-off with 98s.

• Raise most of the time; this hand plays well post-flop; you can win a big pot and it helps vary your play, making you more unpredictable. Unpredictable players are considered dangerous and, as Lee is fond of saying, fear equity is an asset in poker.

You are: On the button with K7s, T8s, or QTo.
• Raise with these hands nearly every time; use your position to keep pressure on the blinds.

You are: In the SB with A2o, 96o.
• Throw these hands away; it's not worth getting involved out of position unless your opponent is especially weak. I'd play all suited aces, but fold weak non-suited aces.

Facing a Raise

When someone raises in front of you, the range of hands you can play decreases substantially. To gauge how liberal your hand range can be, you need to be aware of the players' level of aggression and their skill post-flop. If I decide to re-raise in position, I usually raise the amount of the pot or just under. When I re-raise out of position, I raise the size of the pot or slightly more. This is to try to make it harder for a player who holds position over me to remain in the pot.

In Position

Against a player who's unable to release hands post-flop, it's in your interest to see a number of flops, so calling behind with hands such as suited connectors or small pairs is a profitable play. I only re-raise this type of player if I'm confident I have the best hand and am raising for value or protection. If the player is tight aggressive and skilled post-flop, speculative holdings lose a lot of value, because the skilled players seldom pay you off by losing their entire stack. However, against this type of player, I occasionally make re-raises with suited connectors, as I'm unlikely to be called pre-flop and, even if I am, I have a playable post-flop hand. I will, of course, also re-raise this type of player with a hand I'm confident is ahead.

Out of the SB

Facing a raise in the SB, I exercise extreme caution and play a very small number of hands. This is both because I'll have to play the hand in the worst position post-flop and I don't get to close out the action pre-flop, which could allow the big blind to force me off my hand. Faced with an early-position raise, I throw away almost all hands except really big hands, such as AQs+ or 99+. I re-raise here only if I'm confident my hand is substantially ahead, as I'm very likely to be called and be faced with playing a big pot out of position.

When dealing with a late-position raise, I open up my range, but not by much. I still throw away small pairs from 77 on down, while hands such as AT are KJ are definite folds; hands such as AJs+, AQo+, or 88+ should be played. However, it can be profitable to occasionally throw in a re-steal by re-raising a late-position raiser with a marginal hand that plays easily post-flop and can win a big pot, such as suited connectors or small pairs. It's preferable to re-steal with this type of hand than with one that may be dominated. I'm constantly looking for plays that will allow me to win big pots.

In the BB

In the big blind you can open your hand range substantially when compared with the small blind, both because it's slightly less to call and you close out the action. As a result, you won't get re-raised off your hand. Against an early-position raiser, it's almost always correct to defend with any pair and, against anyone but the top opponents, with suited connectors. Against an early-position raiser, the intention is to try and flop a big hand and win a big pot. Against late-position raisers, I'd defend with more hands that are likely to be ahead. Hands such as KQo now become playable. When playing late-position raisers, you're often up against a marginal hand and the implied odds with speculative holdings often aren't there, because your opponents usually won't have a good enough hand to commit a large portion of their stack when you hit the flop big, such as flopping a set. It's actually better to defend with 22 versus an UTG raise than it is against a button raise!

KEY POINT: With speculative hands, it's better to defend from the big blind against an early-position raiser than a late-position raiser.

In both the big blind and small blind, there are often opportunities for the squeeze play. I wouldn't try this too often, but if you have a tight image and there's a middle-position raise and a caller or two, you might want to throw in a sizable raise to try and steal the pot. You'll pick up the pot quite often with this move and, even if you get called, you could either take a stab at a post-flop bluff (the texture of the board and type of opponent will determine how likely this is to succeed) or you may even hit something!

Review

You're in: late position with ATo or KJo facing an early-position raiser. What should you do?

• Fold unless the player is very poor.

You're in: the SB with AJo and facing an early position raise.

• Fold with the same proviso as before.

You're in: the BB with 5♠4♠ facing a raise from UTG.

• Call and try to play a big pot if you flop 2-pair or a big draw.

Limpers in Front of You

This is a very similar situation to being the first to enter a pot. My raising ranges change almost meaninglessly from when I'm first to enter. Be wary of tricky or scared players who are limping, hoping that they'll be raised so they can then re-raise. This issue is especially prevalent when dealing with short stacks. In a situation where you suspect some sort of limp re-raise ploy or when there are multiple limpers, it's OK to limp behind with a mediocre hand, such as connected cards, or suited semi-connectors, to see a flop.

Facing a Raise and Re-Raise or Being Re-Raised

When there's a raise and a re-raise in front of you, it's time to throw away almost every hand, regardless of your position. In situations such as this, the only time you need to make a decision is when you have a hand such as QQ or AK and you're trying to decide if your hand is best. Usually, you're not giving up much by throwing these hands away.

In a standard game, a raise and a re-raise mean that you're faced with a total raise of around 13BB. Assuming the stacks are 100BB, putting in a further raise with these hands means you need to put in about 30BB. If you're then raised again, you're almost always beat and must either fold and lose your large investment or call and most likely lose an even larger pot. Even if you're ahead more than 50% of the time, the fact that you'll probably force all hands worse than yours to fold, while all better hands get you in trouble, means the best play is just to throw them away and see the next hand.

With hands such as AA and KK, which you're obviously going to play, you just have to do what you feel is the best thing to get all your money in, depending on your table image at the time. Folding KK, although occasionally the correct play, isn't something you should look to do in a 100BB-deep game, unless the situation is absolutely once-in-a-blue-moon perfect. The number of times I've regretted not folding it are far outnumbered by the number of times someone has managed to get all their money in with a worse hand.

When you're the opening raiser and you get re-raised, there are a few things you have to consider. First, do you have position; second, does your hand play well in a big pot; and third, is your hand likely to be best? If you can't answer yes to at least two of these questions, you should immediately throw it away.

In general, when you get re-raised and you're out of position, the best play is to fold. It might feel a bit weak, but unless you have a monster, you're faced with incredibly hard post-flop decisions. Against bad players where I think I have a big edge post-flop, I might defend with pairs and some suited connectors, but against good players I'm unlikely to defend unless I'm confident I have the best hand. With position, I play a few more hands and almost certainly defend with pairs and suited connectors. If you're defending with a drawing hand, you really want implied odds of about 10-1. To calculate this, compare the lesser of the two stacks (his and yours) to the size of the bet. If the smaller stack is at least 10 times the amount of the bet, go ahead and call.

When you get re-raised and have a hand you're pretty sure is ahead, you need to decide the best way to extract value. Sometimes raising again, sometimes calling, or at times just pushing all in will be the best play. You need to make this decision based on the feel of the game and your table image. I tend to re-re-raise or move in against players I know are unlikely to release a hand. But against better players, I may just call the re-raise and try to get the rest of my money in on the flop.

Review

With AQo UTG facing a re-raise from the cut-off:

- Fold almost all of the time. The cut-off has to give you

credit for a big hand and you're probably dominated. Even if you happen to be ahead, you're unlikely to win much, since you can't be confident about any pair you hit.

With 88 from the cut off facing a button re-raise:
• Usually fold, unless you think the player is weak and is likely to stack off if you hit your set.

With 22 or 56s in the cut-off confronting a re-raise from the SB:
• Call if you're getting at least 10-1 odds on the amount of the re-raise relative to your opponents stack.

THE FLOP

Assuming you play hands in the style I suggest pre-flop, you should be faced with these situations: Either you're the pre-flop raiser, caller, 3-bettor, or caller of a 3-bet.

Pre-flop Raiser

Whether you're in position or out of position, you'll almost always be allowed to act first, as blind defenders will usually check it to you. The decision you're faced with is, should I continuation bet (cb)?

The key to making the correct decision is to mix up your play. Your aim should be to cb around 60%-90% of the time, depending on how aggressive you choose to play, by betting around two-thirds to three-quarters the pot. You should bet with sets, under-pairs, flush draws, no draws, 2 over-cards, no over-cards, etc., but then at times, you should also check these hands. You really want to have your opponent guessing and not knowing what you're doing, thus causing him to make mistakes. Although you want to vary your play, there are situations where a continuation bet is more profitable than others.

98s on a Q-2-3 flop: This is a spot where you should usually fire. If the flop missed your opponent, you'll usually pick up the pot; if the flop hit your opponent and you get raised, you can throw your hand away. With a hand such as this, I'd bet similar flops around 80% of the time.

QJo on a T-9-2 flop: This is a good flop for you; fire almost every time, but you could check occasionally for deception. I'd bet this flop about 90% of the time.

77 on a 7-3-A board: Many players would check this flop, but as Lee advises for tournaments, I virtually never do. I fire almost every time and very rarely check for deception. Playing this way, my big hands protect my weak hands, as observant opponents are unable to distinguish a betting pattern between the two.

As you can see, the logic behind betting or checking changes, but the objective is to put pressure on the opposition most of the time no matter what you hold!

Pre-flop Caller

On the flop, the betting lead is usually in the hands of your opponent. When faced with a flop bet, you need to make a decision: Should I fold as my hand has no value or should I continue with the hand?

If you decide that you should continue with the hand, you then need to choose between calling and raising. The trick here is, don't raise if a 3-bet forces you to lay down a hand with outs or showdown value. If your hand is total trash and you're putting in a bluff, then it's OK to raise and fold if your opponent plays back at you.

If your hand is super strong and you're happy to go all-in, then it's OK to raise, hoping to be re-raised. But if you have, say, a weak flush draw or top pair with which you're not comfortable committing your stack on the flop, be cautious about raising. If the player re-raises big or all-in and you have to fold, you're giving up a lot of equity. In situations such as this, a call is almost certainly the best play.

Being in position should make a big difference in your decision whether to call or fold. Position allows you to be far more liberal, and calling with gutshot straight draws, especially with over-cards and other marginal hands such as that, is justifiable, because you can often take control of the hand on later streets. When you're out of position, you won't get full value for your hands and will find yourself faced with tougher decisions.

Review

You have: Q♥J♥ on the button on a flop of 9♣8♥2♠ and your opponent bets.

• You can legitimately raise, call, or fold here, depending on how you evaluate your opponent's hand. Be wary about raising though, because if he re-raises, you'll have to throw your hand away.

You have: Q♠J♠ on a K♥2♦7♣ board.

• You should raise or fold. The hand has no showdown value, so either give up or try to steal.

You have: J♠T♠ or 9♣9♦ on a 9♥8♠2♠ flop.

• You should usually raise in spots such as this. You're happy to be 3-bet and are willing to play for all your chips; occasionally you can call to mix up your play.

Preflop 3-Bettor

If you 3-bet pre-flop, you should try and make sure that you've either done so with a hand that you're highly confident is best or a hand that you're sure is not. Marginal hands, such as AJ, play very badly in big pots! Assuming you've followed these rules, it's quite easy playing pots of this nature. Virtually always, come out firing. Usually, there will be around 25-30BBs in the middle and betting 80% of the pot is a good approach. If your opponent decides to raise, you need to consider the board and your hand in order to make the correct decision. It will be around 65BB to call to win a 200BB pot. If you think your hand will win the pot a third of the time, you should make the call; if you have complete air (i.e., a bluff), just throw it away and move on.

Review

You have: 98s, or KK, on a flop of A-K-2 or T-6-2.

• Lead at this board almost every time! Re-evaluate if your opponent raises.

Pre-flop Caller of a 3-Bet

This is a situation I don't like to be in without a hand that's easy to play post-flop. You'll almost certainly be facing a bet, similar to the type described in the previous paragraph. You just need to judge what strength hand he might have based on his previous play and either muck a hand that is likely no good or try and extract full value if you feel confident in your holding.

TURN PLAY

When You're the Aggressor on the Flop

The turn is where you really need to use some hand-reading skills and can't just rely on formulaic moves. The pots are usually much bigger and your decisions are often stack-defining. When you have the betting lead, the questions you need to ask yourself are:

• Am I trying to extract value or protect my hand?
• Am I trying to force a fold with a weak hand?
• Should I be done with the hand?

If you're trying to extract value, you need to gauge the situation and decide how best to do so, whether it's a check-raise, a standard lead, a small bet, or a big bet. This is really opponent-dependent and you need to take into account your history with a particular opponent and his betting and calling frequencies.

If you're trying to induce a fold with a marginal hand and are firing a second barrel on a bluff, the key is to try and exert maximum pressure on your opponent. Bet an amount that makes it look like you're likely to force him to commit his stack on the river or make a bet that looks like its screaming for a call. Again, you need to learn this through trial and error and your own judgment. Against weaker players, the bigger bet may look more threatening, while better players may be more concerned about the smaller bet. Of course, this isn't a hard-and-fast rule. So much depends on your history and what that player thinks he knows about you. At the top level, this dynamic can become a complex mind game.

If you think you can't carry on in the hand, just check-fold. In poker, there's no reward for blind stubbornness.

When You're the Flop Caller

The two most important situations that come up here are when you're facing a bet and when you're checked to or decide to lead out.

When you're facing another bet on the turn, obviously you can now fold, call, or raise. It's much harder to call with a marginal hand on the turn, because the bet is far bigger, the pot is bigger, and the implied odds are diminished. You really want to have a hand that you think is the best or fold. If you decide your hand is likely to be ahead, it's important to find a balance between extracting value and protecting your hand. If there's an obvious flush or straight draw, you should generally make a raise to ensure you don't let yourself go broke to a cheap draw! If, however, you believe that a raise will cause him to fold a weaker hand than yours, but it's likely that he'll either bet or call a bet on the river, calling on the turn is the better option.

If your opponent checks to you on the turn, you have to make the decision whether to bet or check behind. I bet with high frequency in this situation, but I make my decision based on two things:

• the likelihood my opponent will call, fold or check raise;
• the value of a bet, considering the cards I hold.

It's impossible to set rules for what your opponents will do; the best way to be able to judge what their action will be is through observation of their play. I try to watch players and see how easy it is to get them off their hands, how much I need to bet to make them fold or call, how often they like to trap with a check-raise, and so on. In order to gather this information about your opponent, try to focus on big pots they play, even when you aren't involved, to see how they react in different circumstances.

When making the decision whether to bet the turn based on my holding, I generally bet either to gain value from and protect a hand I believe is ahead or to push an opponent off a marginal hand that I can't beat. In situations where I think my hand is best, I bet almost every time—the very rare checks would usually be for deception or to gain value on the river. When I'm fairly sure I don't have the best hand, I'll still bet with regularity, but not with the same frequency as when I think I'm ahead.

The decision whether to bluff comes down to how likely I think my opponent will fold. However, when deciding whether to semi-bluff when I have outs, there's another important factor to consider. The secondary consideration is the likelihood of a check-raise. I really need to be confident that the player won't check-raise me off my draw, because I give up a massive amount of value when this occurs.

Leading out on the turn after calling on the flop is an interesting play. It goes against the flow of most hands and is probably an underused tactic. The positives are that it allows you to take gain some control of the hand and vary your play, while also preventing your opponent from checking behind, but the negatives are you might lose value by making your opponent fold or miss an opportunity to check raise with a big hand. Some players lead the turn after they check-call the flop and hit their draw; others do it with weak hands, such as middle or bottom pair, when worried about an opponent making a bigger bet, if checked to. This tactic, known as a blocking bet, is designed to keep the size of the pot down, while maintaining a modicum of control of the hand.

I think the key to leading on the turn after calling on the flop effectively is to mix it up. If you choose to use it, you should occasionally check-call the flop and lead the turn with top pair big kicker, a set, or a made draw, but also non-connected draws and marginal hands.

Review

You're facing a bet with 5♠5♥ on a T♠9♣5♣2♦ board:

• This is a spot where you must certainly raise both for value and protection. Against 2-pair, an over-pair, a straight draw, or a flush draw, a raise is the best play. On the river, if a draw card hits, he won't pay you off with the pair hands, but if this card completes his draw, you'll likely lose a lot of money!

You're facing a bet with AJ on a A-7-7-J board:

• Here you'd be much better off calling. Hands like Ax will probably fold to a raise, but call a bet on the river. A hand that has you beat will also cost you far more if you raise.

You're checked to with 55 on a 7-7-2-T board:
• Although a lot of lesser experienced players might check this hand, this is definitely a spot where you should bet, unless you suspect your opponent is trapping. You need to protect your hand against overcards.

You're checked to with A♣6♣ on a J♣6♠3♦3♣ board:
• Here you should almost certainly check. There's a decent chance of your hand being either ahead or behind. If you're ahead, your opponent has very few outs. If you're behind however, and your opponent check raises, you might get pushed off a very strong draw.

RIVER PLAY

When making a decision about how to act on the river, you no longer have to concern yourself with protecting your hand, implied odds, speculative hands, etc. Fundamentally, you want to achieve one of three things:
• gain value from a hand that is likely to be ahead;
• force a fold from an opponent who has you beat;
• avoid calling with the worst hand.

Truly great players come to the fore in this final round of betting, because this is the moment when the most information is present. Hand-reading skills are of paramount importance and situations are so varied that standardized rules can no longer really assist with decision-making. However, forming a logical structure for your play is critically important. I've chosen to briefly touch on the three concepts you need to understand, then by using examples, work through some hands.

Gaining Value

When deciding whether to bet or raise for value, the question you have to ask yourself is, "Are there more hands that will call or raise this bet that I beat than beat me? Also, what is the chance I get re-raised and how will I deal with that?" Many players make the mistake of betting or raising on the river, because they think they have the best hand without considering what hands their opponents can call with.

If you believe you have the best hand, but only a few hands can call your bet (even if you have the nuts, as this applies to an opponent with a busted draw of some sort), the only way to get money out of the hand is to check and try and get a bluff, or a very thin-value bet, out of your opponent.

KEY POINT: On the river, don't bet a hand just because you believe it's ahead; you don't need to protect against draws anymore. Bet a hand for value, only if it can be called by weaker hands.

Bluffing

Usually, it's quite difficult to get players to fold their hands on the river, because the pots are fairly large and your opponents often feel committed, since they frequently already have a lot invested. However, along with the increased risks come increased rewards, both instant and in the future. Not only can you pick up a number of large pots without the best hand, but when you do get caught, the likelihood of being paid off in the future, when you actually have a made hand, increases. It's very important to mix up your play and throwing in river bluffs with some regularity is an important part of this.

An example of a randomizing play I like to make occasionally is if I flop a flush draw and there's a straight draw on the board too, I'll raise a river bet if either the flush or the straight draw hits. This puts a lot of pressure on my opponent and he'll have no way of knowing if I missed or made my draw. Also, in cases such as this, your bet should be large, often all-in, whether you're bluffing or have hit your draw. This will provide you with the highest return, as discussed earlier in the tournament section of the book.

Avoiding Calls with the Worst Hand

This is a situation that, more than any other, requires information gathering and processing. You need to know your opponent and how he plays hands. Take into account his level of aggression, the strength of your hand relative to the board, and all the actions that have taken place in the hand up to that point. Use the information to make an informed logical decision about calling, taking into consideration your hand, the pot odds, and your opponent's tendencies.

Review

You've raised with A♠5♠ on the button and been called by the big blind. The flop comes down A♣T♥7♥; the big blind checks, you bet 75% of the pot, and get called. You decide to check behind after the big blind checks the 6♠ that falls on the turn. The river is the A♦ and the board now reads A♣T♥7♥6♠A♦. Your opponent now leads out for 80% of the pot. You know this player is aggressive; do you fold, call, or raise?

• Your hand is strong and is certainly worth at least a call. You know this player could be betting any number of hands, most of which you beat—aces and tens, a busted flush draw or other obscure missed draw, and some pocket pairs. The less likely, but possible, holdings he would bet and that beat you are a full house of some sort, a straight with 98, or a strong ace.

Now you should think about how the hands you could be up against would react to a raise. If, in the less likely event he has a hand that is better than yours, he will certainly at least call and possibly re-raise, which will cost you money. However, if he has one of the hands that you beat, he's far less likely to call your raise. A busted draw will definitely fold and most 2-pair-type hands will release as well. This is almost certainly a situation where you should call your opponent's bet, as the long-term cost of raising will be higher than the rewards.

You have K♣K♥ in the big blind; an aggressive player raises from UTG+1. You re-raise slightly more than the pot and your opponent calls. The flop comes 5♠5♣T♣. You bet 70% of the pot; your opponent calls. The turn is the T♠, now putting 2 spades out as well. You bet 50% of the pot and again your opponent calls. You both now have half your stacks committed. The river is an ugly-looking A♠. Should you bet or check?

• This is definitely a spot to check; if your opponent has you beat he will certainly call any bet, and if he can't beat your kings, it will be very hard for him to call after the ace falls.

You check and your opponent moves all in for his remaining stack, about half the pot. Do you call or fold?

• Now you need to assess all the information you have at your disposal. From the pre-flop action and your opponent's call of your re-raise, it's likely he has a pair, big or small, a big ace, or less frequently, strong suited connectors. After he calls your bet on the flop, his range probably includes pocket pairs, suited connectors with a draw, suited connectors that hit the flop by pairing, or a flush draw. If he had an ace-high flush draw with A♣Q♣ or A♣J♣, he would probably have raised your flop bet, so although possible, it's unlikely this is his holding. When he calls your weak turn bet, you don't really gain any more information; all of the previous holdings are still plausible.

Now you check to him on the river and he goes all-in.

Why would he go all-in? The two most compelling reasons are to win the pot with the second-best hand or to gain value from a strong hand. You played the hand in a way that seems logical for a pair such as JJ, QQ, or KK, so he may believe the ace scared you. He would certainly push a full house, but how likely is he to have it, really? You made a large re-raise pre-flop, which probably would have pushed him off almost all holdings with a ten or a 5. Although unlikely, he could possibly have an ace; however, he would probably check it back with a weak ace, worried you could only call with a better hand. If he had a medium pocket pair and was calling the bets, hoping you had big cards, and you check to him, he might re-evaluate the situation and realize he's behind and most likely up against a bigger pair. In this case, a strong player could easily go all-in trying to scare you off the hand range you appear to hold. If he flopped a flush draw that missed, he would know he had no showdown value and might attempt a steal, trying to represent the ace.

Looking at all the possible holdings and their relative probabilities and knowing he's an aggressive player, a call is certainly the right play, especially considering the pot is laying you 3-to-1 to call.

You have 6♠7♠ on the button and open raise; both the SB and the BB call you. The flop comes A♥8♠9♠ with the 8♠9♠ and your opponents check to you. You bet around 80% of the pot and the SB calls you. The turn comes a 4, your opponent checks, and you check behind. The river comes the Q♠; your opponent bets out 80% of the pot. Do you raise or call?

• You have a very strong hand that beats almost all the holdings your opponents could have, such as a big pair, 2-pair, sets, or a straight. The only hand that you fear is a bigger flush. It's possible that this is occasionally worth only calling, but generally I would raise, as there certainly are a number of hands that would call my raise that I beat in this button-versus-blind confrontation.

You make a triple raise and your opponent immediately pushes all-in for about the size of the pot. Do you call or fold?

• You've played your hand pretty straightforwardly on all streets, bet your straight-flush draw, checked when you missed the turn, and raised when you hit your flush on the river. It looks like extreme strength and your opponent would feel very confident of getting called when he pushes all-in. He almost certainly has a big flush, more likely than not the nut flush. Some crazy or super-tricky players might not have your hand beat in this spot, but in general this is a good spot to lay your hand down, as you're almost certainly beat and the 2-to-1 the pot is laying you is not enough.

OTHER CONSIDERATIONS

Bankroll Management

There are many different schools of thought on this topic. There are also many different definitions of bankrolls. My idea of a bankroll is an unreplenishable pool of money set aside and readily available for playing poker. If this bankroll runs out, your money for poker runs out and you're busted. As a result, a very conservative approach needs to be taken to ensure you never hit a brick wall where you need to either quit poker or go down the ugly path of borrowing money.

As a general rule, I suggest having at least 50 maximum buy-ins. For example, if you're playing $5/$10 no-limit (nl) with a $1,000-maximum buy-in, you need to have $50,000. If you want to move up to $10/$20nl, you should wait until you get to at least $100,000 before making it your regular game. If you drop below 35-40 buy-ins in your regular game, you should consider stepping down and playing lower until you rebuild to a safer level. The higher the limit, the more buy-ins you should have, because the games get more aggressive and the swings are higher. I'd feel more comfortable with a bankroll of $125,000 in a $10/$20nl game, and for a $25/50nl $350,000-$400,000.

While I suggest at least 50 buy-ins, this doesn't mean that if you have enough for 200 buy-ins for your regular game, you're obliged to move up. You should always play where you feel comfortable and never feel compelled to play higher. Although some of the best players in the game moved up the limits aggressively, took risks, and came through to prove themselves, for every success story there are hundreds of failed attempts and collapsed careers. Stay within your comfort zone and you can avoid many of the pitfalls that you'll face in this game.

Multi-Tabling

Playing more than one table at a time is a great way to play more hands and increase your profits. However, as you play more and more tables, the level of attention you can give to each game decreases. Also, it can be harder to play long sessions and it can be a more stressful, or less pleasurable, experience. You won't be able to collect as much information about your opponents or the table dynamics and errors from a rushed decision occasionally creep in.

Your win rate per table is in some way inversely proportional to the number of tables you play. At some point your overall win rate will be maximized. For example, you play a game in which you win $60 per hour on a single table, $50 per hour per table over two tables, or $20 per hour per table over three tables. One table makes you $60 per hour, two make you $100 an hour, and three earn you $60 per hour. The best number of tables to play at one time is clearly two.

KEY POINT: The purpose of multi-tabling is to maximize profitability and comfort, not the number of tables you play.

Online Poker Tools

The key to winning at online poker is the ability to gather, analyze, and process a large amount of information faster and better than your opponents. In all forms of poker, information is power. When playing online poker, especially when multi-tabling, it can be very hard to keep track of all your opponents and how they play.

Poker programs have been created that can be used to gather and process large of amounts of historical information about your opponents. Almost every online pro, and an ever-increasing number of amateur players, use these tools to some degree.

While a number of tools all do similar things, the two that I've found two of them to be the most useful.

Poker Tracker (PT): Poker Tracker is a program that collects hand histories written to your hard drive from when you play on an online poker table, then sorts, categorizes, and displays statistical data on the tendencies that you and your opponents have shown. When you have a large number of hands on your opponents, you'll have meaningful information that will allow you to pinpoint the weaknesses in your opponents' playing styles, as well as their pre-flop and post-flop tendencies. This enables you to structure your game to take advantage of their weaknesses and avoid or counteract their strengths.

Poker Tracker presents the information in hundreds of different ways. Due to this, it can be daunting at first to use the software. Most online poker players who use PT use only a fraction of the information available, but as you get more used to the program, the greater your understanding of the stats will be and the greater success you'll have playing online poker.

PokerAce HUD (Heads Up Display): PokerAce HUD is a program that can be used in tandem with Poker Tracker to overlay important statistics about your opponents over their seat at an online poker table in real time.

You can customize which PT stats you would like to see

displayed. The default stats that give a good basic idea of your opponents playing style are:

• VPIP (Voluntarily Put In Pot): This tells you how often your opponent voluntarily puts money in a pot by either calling or raising pre-flop. You can use this to instantly determine whether your opponent is loose or tight pre-flop.

• PFR (Pre-Flop Raise): This tells you how often your opponent raises pre-flop. You can use this to determine whether your opponent is passive or aggressive pre-flop.

• AF (Aggression Factor): This tells you your opponent's overall aggression factor, including his or her post-flop aggression. Poker Tracker uses a formula to determine this number; under 2.0 is generally considered passive and over 2.0 generally considered aggressive.

• Total Hands: This heading tells you the total hands of your opponent's play you've logged. It is meaningful, because the greater number of hands you've logged, the more value you can place on the information Poker Tracker is giving you. You'll generally want to have a few hundred hands before you put too much importance on the information PT has collated, but even after a few hands the stats have some significance.

Poker Tracker and PokerAce, along with a number of other poker tools, are available for purchase online. They can be easily found with a quick search.

Appendix 1

EQUILIBRIUM SOLUTION FOR MOVING-IN FAR FROM THE MONEY

Pushing With CSI 3

Position	No Antes
Small Blind	22+,A2+,K2+,Q2+,J2+,T6o+,T2s+,96o+,93s+,86o+, 84s+,76o,74s+,64s+,53s+ (73.2%)
Button	22+,A2+,K4o+,K2s+,Q8o+,Q5s+,J9o+,J7s+,T9o,T8s+, 98s,87s (42.7%)
Cut-Off	22+,A2+,K8o+,K3s+,QTo+,Q8s+,JTo,J8s+,T8s+,98s,87s (33.9%)
Hijack	22+,A2+,KTo+,K7s+,QTo+,Q9s+,JTo,J9s+,T8s+,98s (30.0%)
3 off	22+,A3o+,A2s+,KTo+,K9s+,QJo,Q9s+,J9s+,T9s (26.1%)
4 off	22+,A7o+,A5o,A2s+,KJo+,K9s+,QJo,Q9s+,J9s+,T9s (22.5%)
5 off	22+,A8o+,A3s+,KJo+,KTs+,QTs+,JTs,T9s (18.6%)
6 off	33+,A9o+,A5s+,KJo+,KTs+,QTs+,JTs (16.3%)
7 off	33+,A9o+,A7s+,KQo,KTs+,QTs+,JTs (14.8%)

Pushing With CSI 3 (cont'd)

Position	Antes
Small Blind	22+,A2+,K2+,Q2+,J2+,T5o+,T2s+,96o+,92s+,86o+, 84s+,75o+,73s+,65o,63s+,52s+,43s (77.4%)
Button	22+,A2+,K2+,Q8o+,Q2s+,J9o+,J6s+,T9o,T6s+,96s+, 86s+,75s+,65s,54s (48.4%)
Cut-Off	22+,A2+,K7o+,K2s+,Q9o+,Q6s+,JTo,J7s+,T9o,T7s+, 97s+,86s+,76s,65s (39.4%)
Hijack	22+,A2+,K9o+,K5s+,QTo+,Q8s+,JTo,J8s+,T8s+,97s+, 87s,76s (33.0%)
3 off	22+,A2+,KTo+,K8s+,QTo+,Q9s+,J9s+,T8s+,98s,87s (29.1%)
4 off	22+,A4o+,A2s+,KJo+,K9s+,QJo,Q9s+,J9s+,T8s+,98s (24.9%)
5 off	22+,A7o+,A2s+,KJo+,K9s+,Q9s+,J9s+,T9s,98s (21.0%)
6 off	22+,A8o+,A3s+,KJo+,KTs+,QTs+,J9s+,T9s (18.9%)
7 off	33+,A9o+,A7s+,A5s,KQo,KTs+,QTs+,JTs,T9s (15.4%)

Pushing With CSI 4

Position	No Antes
Small Blind	22+,A2+,K2+,Q2+,J5o+,J2s+,T7o+,T2s+,97o+,95s+, 86o+,84s+,76o,74s+,64s+,53s+,43s (68.3%)
Button	22+,A2+,K6o+,K2s+,Q9o+,Q6s+,JToJ7s+,T7s+,97s+, 86s+,76s (39.1%)
Cut-Off	22+,A2+,KTo+,K6s+,QTo+,Q8s+,JToJ8s+,T8s+,98s,87s (31.2%)
Hijack	22+,A4o+,A2s+,KTo+,K9s+,QJo,Q9s+,JToJ9s+,T8s+, 98s (26.7%)
3 off	22+,A7o+,A2s+,KJo+,K9s+,QJo,Q9s+,J9s+,T8s+,98s (22.2%)
4 off	22+,A9o+,A3s+,KJo+,K9s+,Q9s+,J9s+,T9s (18.6%)
5 off	33+,ATo+,A7s+,A5s,KQo,K9s+,Q9s+,J9s+,T9s (15.4%)
6 off	44+,ATo+,A8s+,KQo,K9s+,Q9s+,J9s+,T9s (14.3%)
7 off	44+,AJo+,A9s+,KQo,K9s+,QTs+,JTs,T9s (12.5%)

Position	Antes
Small Blind	22+,A2+,K2+,Q2+,J5o+,J2s+,T6o+,T2s+,96o+,93s+,86o +,84s+,76o,74s+,65o,63s+,53s+,43s (71.9%)
Button	22+,A2+,K5o+,K2s+,Q9o+,Q4s+,J9o+,J7s+,T9o,T7s+, 96s+,86s+,75s+,65s,54s (43.6%)
Cut-Off	22+,A2+,K9o+,K5s+,QTo+,Q8s+,JToJ8s+,T7s+,97s+, 86s+,76s (33.6%)
Hijack	22+,A3o+,A2s+,KTo+,K9s+,QTo+,Q9s+,JToJ8s+,T8s+, 98s,87s (29.1%)
3-off	22+,A7o+,A5o,A2s+,KJo+,K9s+,QJo,Q9s+,JToJ9s+,T8s+, 98s (24.0%)
4 off	22+,A9o+,A2s+,KJo+,K9s+,Q9s+,J9s+,T8s+,98s (19.5%)
5 off	22+,ATo+,A5s+,KJo+,K9s+,Q9s+,J9s+,T9s,98s (17.3%)
6 off	33+,ATo+,A7s+,KQo,K9s+,Q9s+,J9s+,T9s (15.1%)
7 off	55+,ATo+,A9s+,KQo,K9s+,Q9s+,JTs,T9s (13.3%)

Pushing With CSI 5

Position	No Antes
Small Blind	22+,A2+,K2+,Q3o+,Q2s+,J7o+,J2s+,T7o+,T3s+,97o+, 95s+,87o,84s+,76o,74s+,64s+,53s+,43s (64.4%)
Button	22+,A2+,K9o+,K4s+,QTo+,Q8s+,JTo,J7s+,T7s+,97s+, 86s+,76s,65s (34.5%)
Cut-Off	22+,A3o+,A2s+,KTo+,K8s+,QTo+,Q9s+,JTo,J8s+,T8s+, 98s,87s (29.4%)
Hijack	22+,A7o+,A5o,A2s+,KJo+,K9s+,QJo,Q9s+,J9s+,T8s+,98s (23.1%)
3 off	22+,A9o+,A3s+,KJo+,K9s+,QJo,Q9s+,J9s+,T9s,98s (19.8%)
4 off	33+,ATo+,A7s+,A5s,KJo+,K9s+,Q9s+,J9s+,T9s (16.3%)
5 off	44+,ATo+,A8s+,KQo,K9s+,Q9s+,J9s+,T9s (14.3%)
6 off	55+,AJo+,A9s+,KQo,K9s+,QTs+,JTs,T9s (12.1%)
7 off	66+,AJo+,A9s+,KQo,KTs+,QTs+,JTs (11.0%)

Position	Antes
Small Blind	22+,A2+,K2+,Q3o+,Q2s+,J7o+,J2s+,T7o+,T3s+,97o+, 94s+,86o+,84s+,76o,74s+,65o,63s+,53s+,43s (66.8%)
Button	22+,A2+,K8o+,K3s+,QTo+,Q6s+,JTo,J7s+,T9o,T7s+,96s+, 86s+,75s+,65s,54s (38.2%)
Cut-Off	22+,A2+,KTo+,K7s+,QTo+,Q8s+,JTo,J8s+,T8s+,97s+,87s, 76s (31.5%)
Hijack	22+,A7o+,A5o,A2s+,KTo+,K9s+,QJo,Q9s+,JTo,J9s+,T8s+, 98s (24.9%)
3 off	22+,A8o+,A2s+,KJo+,K9s+,QJo,Q9s+,J9s+,T8s+,98s (21.3%)
4 off	33+,ATo+,A7s+,A5s,KJo+,K9s+,Q9s+,J9s+,T9s,98s (16.6%)
5 off	44+,ATo+,A8s+,KQo,K9s+,Q9s+,J9s+,T9s (14.3%)
6 off	55+,AJo+,A9s+,KQo,K9s+,QTs+,JTs,T9s (12.1%)
7 off	55+,AJo+,A9s+,KQo,K9s+,QTs+,JTs (11.8%)

Pushing With CSI 6

Position	No Antes
Small Blind	22+,A2+,K2+,Q6o+,Q2s+,J8o+,J3s+,T7o+,T4s+,97o+, 95s+,87o,85s+,76o,74s+,64s+,53s+,43s (59.9%)
Button	22+,A2+,KTo+,K5s+,QTo+,Q8s+,JTo,J8s+,T7s+,97s+, 86s+,76s (32.7%)
Cut-Off	22+,A4o+,A2s+,KTo+,K9s+,QJo,Q9s+,JTo,J8s+,T8s+,98s (27.0%)
Hijack	22+,A9o+,A2s+,KJo+,K9s+,QJo,Q9s+,J8s+,T8s+,98s (20.7%)
3 off	22+,ATo+,A7s+,A5s,KJo+,K9s+,Q9s+,J9s+,T9s (16.7%)
4 off	33+,AJo+,A8s+,KQo,K9s+,Q9s+,J9s+,T9s (13.9%)
5 off	55+,AJo+,A9s+,KQo,K9s+,QTs+,JTs,T9s (12.1%)
6 off	66+,AJo+,A9s+,KTs+,QTs+,JTs (10.1%)
7 off	77+,AQo+,ATs+,KTs+,QTs+,JTs (8.4%)

Position	Antes
Small Blind	22+,A2+,K2+,Q5o+,Q2s+,J8o+,J2s+,T7o+,T3s+,97o+, 95s+,87o,84s+,76o,74s+,63s+,53s+,43s (62.0%)
Button	22+,A2+,K9o+,K4s+,QTo+,Q7s+,JTo,J7s+,T9o,T7s+, 96s+,86s+,76s,65s (36.0%)
Cut-Off	22+,A4o+,A2s+,KTo+,K8s+,QTo+,Q8s+,JTo,J8s+,T8s+, 97s+,87s (29.1%)
Hijack	22+,A8o+,A2s+,KJo+,K9s+,QJo,Q9s+,J8s+,T8s+,98s (21.6%)
3 off	22+,ATo+,A7s+,A5s,KJo+,K9s+,Q9s+,J9s+,T9s,98s (17.0%)
4 off	44+,ATo+,A8s+,KQo,K9s+,Q9s+,J9s+,T9s (14.3%)
5 off	55+,AJo+,A9s+,KQo,K9s+,QTs+,JTs,T9s (12.1%)
6 off	66+,AJo+,A9s+,KQo,KTs+,QTs+,JTs (11.0%)
7 off	66+,AQo+,ATs+,KTs+,QTs+,JTs (8.9%)

Pushing With CSI 7

Position	No Antes
Small Blind	22+,A2+,K2+,Q8o+,Q2s+,J8o+,J3s+,T8o+,T4s+,97o+, 95s+,87o,85s+,76o,74s+,64s+,53s+ (56.9%)
Button	22+,A2+,KTo+,K6s+,QTo+,Q8s+,JTo,J8s+,T7s+,97s+, 86s+,76s (32.4%)
Cut-Off	22+,A7o+,A5o,A2s+,KJo+,K9s+,QJo,Q9s+,JTo,J8s+,T8s+, 98s (24.3%)
Hijack	22+,ATo+,A4s+,KJo+,K9s+,Q9s+,J9s+,T9s,98s (17.6%)
3 off	33+,ATo+,A8s+,KQo,K9s+,Q9s+,J9s+,T9s (14.8%)
4 off	55+,AJo+,A9s+,KQo,K9s+,QTs+,JTs,T9s (12.1%)
5 off	66+,AJo+,A9s+,KTs+,QTs+,JTs (10.1%)
6 off	88+,AQo+,ATs+,KTs+,QTs+,JTs (8.0%)
7 off	88+,AQo+,ATs+,A5s,A4s,KTs+,QJs (8.0%)

Position	Antes
Small Blind	22+,A2+,K2+,Q8o+,Q2s+,J8o+,J3s+,T8o+,T4s+,97o+, 95s+,87o,84s+,76o,74s+,64s+,53s+,43s (57.5%)
Button	22+,A2+,KTo+,K5s+,QTo+,Q8s+,JTo,J7s+,T9o,T7s+,97s+, 86s+,76s,65s (34.2%)
Cut-Off	22+,A7o+,A5o,A2s+,KTo+,K9s+,QJo,Q9s+,JTo,J8s+,T8s+, 98s,87s (25.5%)
Hijack	22+,A9o+,A3s+,KJo+,K9s+,QJo,Q9s+,J9s+,T8s+,98s (20.1%)
3 off	44+,ATo+,A7s+,KJo+,K9s+,Q9s+,J9s+,T9s (15.5%)
4 off	55+,AJo+,A9s+,KQo,K9s+,QTs+,J9s+,T9s (12.4%)
5 off	66+,AJo+,A9s+,KQo,KTs+,QTs+,JTs (11.0%)
6 off	66+,AQo+,ATs+,KTs+,QTs+,JTs (8.9%)
7 off	88+,AQo+,ATs+,A5s,KTs+,QJs (7.7%)

Pushing With CSI 8

Position	No Antes
Small Blind	22+,A2+,K3o+,K2s+,Q8o+,Q2s+,J8o+,J4s+,T8o+,T6s+, 98o,95s+,87o,85s+,74s+,64s+,53s+ (53.2%)
Button	22+,A2+,KTo+,K7s+,QTo+,Q8s+,JTo,J8s+,T8s+,97s+, 87s,76s (31.5%)
Cut-Off	22+,A8o+,A2s+,KJo+,K9s+,QJo,Q9s+,JTo,J8s+,T8s+,98s (22.5%)
Hijack	33+,ATo+,A7s+,A5s,KJo+,K9s+,Q9s+,J9s+,T9s (16.3%)
3 off	44+,AJo+,A8s+,KQo,K9s+,Q9s+,J9s+,T9s (13.4%)
4 off	66+,AJo+,A9s+,KQo,KTs+,QTs+,JTs (11.0%)
5 off	88+,AQo+,ATs+,A5s,KTs+,QTs+,JTs (8.3%)
6 off	88+,AQo+,ATs+,A5s,A4s,KTs+,QJs (8.0%)
7 off	99+,AQo+,ATs+,A5s,A4s,A3s,KJs+,QJs (7.5%)

Position	Antes
Small Blind	22+,A2+,K3o+,K2s+,Q8o+,Q2s+,J8o+,J4s+,T8o+,T5s+, 98o,95s+,87o,85s+,76o,74s+,64s+,53s+ (54.4%)
Button	22+,A2+,KTo+,K5s+,QTo+,Q8s+,JTo,J8s+,T9o,T7s+, 97s+,86s+,76s (33.6%)
Cut-Off	22+,A8o+,A2s+,KJo+,K9s+,QJo,Q9s+,JTo,J8s+,T8s+,98s, 87s (22.8%)
Hijack	22+,ATo+,A7s+,A5s,KJo+,K9s+,QJo,Q9s+,J9s+,T9s,98s (17.9%)
3 off	44+,AJo+,A8s+,KQo,K9s+,Q9s+,J9s+,T9s (13.4%)
4 off	55+,AJo+,A9s+,KQo,KTs+,QTs+,JTs (11.5%)
5 off	66+,AQo+,ATs+,A5s,KTs+,QTs+,JTs (9.2%)
6 off	88+,AQo+,ATs+,A5s,A4s,KTs+,QJs (8.0%)
7 off	TT+,AQo+,ATs+,A5s,A4s,KJs+,QJs (6.8%)

Appendix 2

EQUILIBRIUM CALLING STRATEGIES FOR FAR FROM THE MONEY

Calling a 3 CSI Push

No Antes			
Pusher's Position	No Blind	Small Blind	Big Blind
Small Blind			22+,A2+,K2+,Q2+, J4o+,J2s+,T6o+,T2s+, 97o+,95s+,87o, 85s+,75s+,65s,54s (66.8%)
Button		22+,A2+,K5o+, K2s+,Q9o+,Q6s+, JToJ8s+,T8s+,98s (38.2%)	22+,A2+,K2+,Q7o+, Q2s+,J8o+,J4s+, T8o+,T6s+,98o,96s+, 85s+,75s+,64s+,54s (53.2%)
Cut-Off	22+,A2+,KTo+, K8s+,QJo,QTs+, JTs (26.4%)	22+,A2+,K9o+, K4s+,QTo+,Q8s+, JToJ9s+,T9s (31.5%)	22+,A2+,K5o+, K2s+,Q8o+,Q3s+, J9o+,J5s+,T9o,T6s+, 96s+,86s+,75s+, 64s+,54s (46.0%)
Hijack	22+,A4o+,A2s+, KTo+,K9s+,QTs+ (23.1%)	22+,A2+,K9o+, K6s+,QTo+,Q9s+, J9s+,T9s,98s (30.0%)	22+,A2+,K6o+, K2s+,Q9o+,Q4s+, J9o+,J7s+,T9o,T7s+, 96s+,86s+,75s+, 65s,54s (42.7%)

Calling a 3 CSI Push (cont'd)

Pusher's Position	No Antes		
	No Blind	Small Blind	Big Blind
3-off	22+,A7o+,A2s+, KJo+,KTs+,QJs (18.9%)	22+,A3o+,A2s+, KTo+,K9s+,QJo, Q9s+,J9s+,T9s (26.1%)	22+,A2+,K9o+, K3s+,Q9o+,Q6s+, J9o+,J7s+,T9o,T7s+, 96s+,86s+,75s+, 65s,54s (39.1%)
4-off	22+,A8o+,A5s+, KQo,KTs+,QJs (16.1%)	22+,A5o+,A2s+, KJo+,K9s+,QTs+,JTs, T9s (21.9%)	22+,A2+,K9o+, K4s+,QTo+,Q6s+, JTo,J7s+,T9o,T7s+, 97s+,86s+,76s,65s (36.0%)
5-off	33+,A9o+,A7s+, KQo,KJs+ (13.6%)	22+,A8o+,A3s+, KJo+,KTs+,QTs+,JTs (18.3%)	22+,A3o+,A2s+, KTo+,K5s+,QTo+, Q8s+,JTo,J8s+,T7s+, 97s+,86s+,76s, 65s (32.1%)
6-off	44+,ATo+,A8s+, KQs (10.7%)	22+,A9o+,A4s+, KQo,KTs+,QTs+,JTs (16.1%)	22+,A5o+,A2s+, KTo+,K6s+,QTo+, Q8s+,JTo,J8s+,T8s+, 97s+,87s,76s (29.1%)
7-off	44+,ATo+,A9s+, KQs (10.4%)	33+,A9o+,A7s+, A5s,KQo,KTs+,QTs+ (14.8%)	22+,A7o+,A2s+, KTo+,K6s+,QJo, Q9s+,J8s+,T8s+, 98s,87s (24.6%)

Calling a 3 CSI Push (cont'd)

Pusher's Position	Antes		
	No Blind	Small Blind	Big Blind
Small Blind			22+,A2+,K2+,Q2+, J4o+,J2s+,T7o+,T3s+, 97o+,95s+,87o, 86s+,76s (64.4%)
Button		22+,A2+,K4o+,K2s+, Q9o+,Q5s+,J9o+, J8s+,T8s+,98s (40.3%)	22+,A2+,K2+,Q8o+, Q3s+,J9o+,J6s+,T9o, T7s+,97s+,86s+,76s (46.6%)
Cut-Off	22+,A2+,K9o+, K6s+,QTo+,Q9s+, JTs (29.1%)	22+,A2+,K7o+,K3s+, QTo+,Q8s+,JTo,J8s+, T9s (33.9%)	22+,A2+,K6o+, K2s+,Q9o+,Q6s+, JTo,J7s+,T8s+,98s, 87s (37.9%)
Hijack	22+,A2+,KTo+, K8s+,QJo,QTs+, JTs (26.4%)	22+,A2+,K9o+,K6s+, QTo+,Q9s+,J9s+,T9s (29.7%)	22+,A2+,K8o+, K4s+,QTo+,Q8s+, JTo,J8s+,T8s+, 98s,87s (33.6%)
3-off	22+,A5o+,A2s+, KTo+,K9s+,QTs+, JTs (22.5%)	22+,A3o+,A2s+, KTo+,K8s+,QJo, Q9s+,JTs,T9s (26.1%)	22+,A2+,K9o+, K5s+,QTo+,Q8s+, JTo,J8s+,T8s+,98s (32.1%)
4-off	22+,A7o+,A3s+, KJo+,KTs+,QTs+ (18.9%)	22+,A5o+,A2s+,K Jo+,K9s+,QTs+,JTs (21.6%)	22+,A3o+,A2s+, KTo+,K7s+,QJo, Q9s+,J9s+,T9s,98s (27.0%)
5-off	33+,A8o+,A5s+, KQo,KJs+ (15.1%)	22+,A8o+,A3s+,K Jo+,KTs+,QTs+,JTs (18.3%)	22+,A7o+,A5o, A2s+,KJo+,K9s+, Q9s+,JTs,T9s (21.3%)
6-off	33+,A9o+,A7s+, KQo,KJs+ (13.6%)	22+,A8o+,A5s+, KQo,KTs+,QTs+ (16.4%)	22+,A8o+,A2s+, KJo+,KTs+,QTs+,JTs (18.6%)
7-off	44+,ATo+,A8s+, KQs (10.7%)	33+,A9o+,A7s+, KQo,KTs+,QJs (14.2%)	22+,A8o+,A4s+, KQo,KTs+,QTs+,JTs (17.0%)

Calling a 4 CSI Push

No Antes			
Pusher's Position	No Blind	Small Blind	Big Blind
Small Blind			22+,A2+,K2+, Q4o+,Q2s+,J7o+, J4s+,T8o+,T6s+,98o, 97s+,87s (54.4%)
Button		22+,A2+,K8o+,K5s+, QTo+,Q9s+,J9s+,T9s (30.9%)	22+,A2+,K6o+, K2s+,Q9o+,Q7s+, JTo,J8s+,T8s+, 98s (37.0%)
Cut-Off	22+,A5o+,A2s+, KJo+,KTs+,QTs+ (21.0%)	22+,A3o+,A2s+, KTo+,K8s+,QJo,QTs+, JTs (25.5%)	22+,A2+,K9o+, K4s+,QTo+,Q8s+, JTo,J9s+,T9s,98s (31.8%)
Hijack	33+,A7o+,A4s+, KQo,KTs+ (16.6%)	22+,A5o+,A2s+, KJo+,KTs+,QTs+,JTs (21.3%)	22+,A2+,KTo+,K7s+, QJo,Q9s+,J9s+, T9s (27.6%)
3-off	33+,A9o+,A7s+, KQo,KJs+ (13.6%)	22+,A8o+,A4s+, KQo,KTs+,QTs+ (16.7%)	22+,A7o+,A5o, A2s+,KTo+,K9s+, QJo,Q9s+,JTs (22.8%)
4-off	44+,ATo+,A8s+, KQ (11.6%)	33+,A9o+,A5s+, KQo,KTs+ (14.5%)	22+,A7o+,A2s+, KJo+,KTs+,QTs+,JTs (19.5%)
5-off	55+,AT+,KQs (9.7%)	44+,ATo+,A8s+, KQo,KJs+ (11.9%)	33+,A9o+,A4s+, KQo,KTs+,QTs+ (15.4%)
6-off	66+,AJo+,ATs+, KQs (8.3%)	55+,ATo+,A9s+,KQs (10.0%)	44+,ATo+,A7s+, A5s,KQo,KTs+,QJs (13.1%)
7-off	77+,AJo+,ATs+ (7.5%)	66+,AJo+,ATs+,KQs (8.3%)	55+,ATo+,A9s+, KQo,KJs+ (11.2%)

Calling a 4 CSI Push (cont'd)

Pusher's Position	Antes		
	No Blind	Small Blind	Big Blind
Small Blind			22+,A2+,K2+, Q4o+,Q2s+,J7o+, J4s+,T8o+,T6s+, 97s+,87s (53.5%)
Button		22+,A2+,K7o+, K4s+,QTo+,Q8s+, JTo,J9s+ (33.0%)	22+,A2+,K7o+, K2s+,Q9o+,Q8s+, JTo,J8s+,T9s (35.1%)
Cut-Off	22+,A4o+,A2s+, KTo+,K9s+,QTs+ (23.1%)	22+,A2+,KTo+, K8s+,QJo,QTs+,JTs (26.4%)	22+,A2+,K9o+, K7s+,QTo+,Q9s+, JTs (28.8%)
Hijack	22+,A7o+,A2s+, KJo+,KTs+,QJs (18.9%)	22+,A5o+,A2s+, KJo+,K9s+,QTs+ (21.3%)	22+,A4o+,A2s+, KTo+,K9s+,QJo, QTs+,JTs (24.3%)
3-off	33+,A8o+,A5s+, KQo,KTs+ (15.4%)	33+,A8o+,A3s+, KJo+,KTs+,QJs (17.2%)	22+,A7o+,A2s+, KJo+,KTs+,QTs+, JTs (19.5%)
4-off	44+,A9o+,A8s+, KQo,KJs+ (12.8%)	33+,A9o+,A7s+, A5s,KQo,KJs+ (13.9%)	33+,A8o+,A4s+, KQo,KTs+,QJs (16.0%)
5-off	55+,ATo+,A9s+, KQs (10.0%)	44+,ATo+,A8s+, KQo, KJs+ (11.9%)	44+,A9o+,A5s+, KQo,KTs+,QJs (14.3%)
6-off	66+,AT+,KQs (9.2%)	55+,ATo+,A9s+, KQs (10.0%)	55+,ATo+,A9s+, KQo,KJs+ (11.2%)
7-off	66+,AJo+,ATs+ (8.0%)	66+,AJo+,ATs+, KQs (8.3%)	66+,AT+,KQs (9.2%)

Calling a 5 CSI Push

No Antes			
Pusher's Position	No Blind	Small Blind	Big Blind
Small Blind			22+,A2+,K2+, Q7o+,Q3s+,J8o+, J7s+,T9o,T8s+,98s (46.6%)
Button		22+,A2+,KTo+,K8s+, QJo,QTs+,JTs (26.4%)	22+,A2+,K9o+, K6s+,QTo+,Q9s+, J9s+,T9s (29.7%)
Cut-Off	33+,A7o+,A4s+, KQo,KTs+,QJs (16.9%)	22+,A5o+,A2s+,KJo+, KTs+,QTs+ (21.0%)	22+,A3o+,A2s+, KTo+,K9s+,QJo, QTs+,JTs (25.2%)
Hijack	44+,A9o+,A7s+, KQo,KJs+ (13.1%)	33+,A8o+,A5s+,KQo, KTs+,QJs (15.7%)	22+,A7o+,A2s+, KJo+,KTs+,QTs+,JTs (19.5%)
3-off	55+,ATo+,A9s+, KQs (10.0%)	44+,A9o+,A7s+,KQo, KJs+ (13.1%)	33+,A8o+,A3s+, KJo+,KTs+,QJs (17.2%)
4-off	66+,AT+,KQs (9.2%)	55+,ATo+,A9s+,KQs (10.0%)	44+,ATo+,A7s+, KQo,KJs+ (12.2%)
5-off	66+,AJo+,ATs+ (8.0%)	66+,AJo+,ATs+,KQs (8.3%)	55+,ATo+,A9s+, KQo,KJs+ (11.2%)
6-off	77+,AQo+,AJs+ (6.3%)	77+,AJo+,ATs+,KQs (7.8%)	66+,AJo+,ATs+,KQs (8.3%)
7-off	88+,AQo+,AJs+ (5.9%)	88+,AQo+,AJs+ (5.9%)	77+,AJo+,ATs+,KQs (7.8%)

Calling a 5 CSI Push (cont'd)

Pusher's Position	Antes		
	No Blind	Small Blind	Big Blind
Small Blind			22+,A2+,K2+, Q7o+,Q3s+,J8o+, J7s+,T9o,T8s+,98s (46.6%)
Button		22+,A2+,K9o+, K8s+,QJo,Q9s+, JTs (27.6%)	22+,A2+,K9o+, K6s+,QTo+,Q9s+, J9s+ (29.4%)
Cut-Off	33+,A7o+,A2s+, KJo+,KTs+,QJs (18.4%)	22+,A5o+,A2s+, KJo+,K9s+,QTs+ (21.3%)	22+,A4o+,A2s+, KTo+,K9s+,QJo, QTs+,JTs (24.3%)
Hijack	44+,A8o+,A7s+, KQo,KJs+ (14.0%)	33+,A8o+,A4s+, KJo+,KTs+,QJs (16.9%)	33+,A8o+,A3s+, KJo+,KTs+,QTs+ (17.5%)
3-off	44+,ATo+,A8s+, KQo,KJs+ (11.9%)	44+,A9o+,A7s+, KQo,KJs+ (13.1%)	33+,A9o+,A7s+, A5s,KQo,KTs+ 14.2%)
4-off	55+,ATo+,A9s+, KQs (10.0%)	55+,ATo+,A9s+,KQs (10.0%)	55+,ATo+,A8s+, KQo,KJs+ (11.5%)
5-off	66+,AJo+,ATs+, KQs (8.3%)	66+,AJo+,ATs+,KQs (8.3%)	66+,AT+,KQs (9.2%)
6-off	77+,AJ+ (7.2%)	77+,AJo+,ATs+ (7.5%)	77+,AJo+,ATs+, KQs (7.8%)
7-off	88+,AQo+,AJs+ (5.9%)	77+,AQo+,AJs+ (6.3%)	77+,AJ+ (7.2%)

Calling a 6 CSI Push

No Antes			
Pusher's Position	No Blind	Small Blind	Big Blind
Small Blind			22+,A2+,K4o+, K2s+,Q8o+, Q6s+,J9o+,J8s+, T8s+ (40.6%)
Button		22+,A5o+,A2s+, KTo+,K9s+,QTs+ (22.2%)	22+,A3o+,A2s+, KTo+,K8s+,QJo, QTs+,JTs (25.5%)
Cut-Off	44+,A8o+, A7s+,KQo,KJs+ (14.0%)	33+,A7o+,A4s+, KJo+,KTs+,QJs (17.8%)	22+,A7o+,A2s+, KJo+,KTs+,QTs+ (19.2%)
Hijack	55+,ATo+,A8s+, KQs (10.3%)	44+,A9o+,A7s+, KQo,KJs+ (13.1%)	33+,A8o+,A4s+, KQo,KTs+,QJs (16.0%)
3-off	66+,AT+,KQs (9.2%)	55+,ATo+,A9s+, KQs (10.0%)	44+,ATo+,A8s+, KQo,KJs+ (11.9%)
4-off	77+,AJo+,ATs+ (7.5%)	66+,AJo+,ATs+, KQs (8.3%)	55+,ATo+,A9s+, KQs (10.0%)
5-off	88+,AQo+,AJs+ (5.9%)	77+,AJo+,ATs+, KQs (7.8%)	66+,AJo+,ATs+, KQs (8.3%)
6-off	88+,AQ+ (5.6%)	88+,AQo+,AJs+ (5.9%)	88+,AQo+,AJs+ (5.9%)
7-off	99+,AQ+ (5.1%)	99+,AQ+ (5.1%)	99+,AQ+ (5.1%)

Calling a 6 CSI Push (cont'd)

Pusher's Position	Antes		
	No Blind	Small Blind	Big Blind
Small Blind			22+,A2+,K4o+, K2s+,Q8o+,Q6s+, J9o+,J8s+,T8s+ (40.6%)
Button		22+,A4o+,A2s+, KTo+,K9s+,QJo, QTs+,JTs (24.3%)	22+,A3o+,A2s+, KTo+,K8s+,QJo, QTs+,JTs (25.5%)
Cut-Off	33+,A8o+,A5s+, KQo,KTs+,QJs (15.7%)	33+,A7o+,A3s+, KJo+,KTs+,QJs (18.1%)	33+,A7o+,A2s+, KJo+,KTs+,QJs (18.4%)
Hijack	44+,A9o+,A8s+, KQo,KJs+ (12.8%)	44+,A9o+,A8s+, KQo,KJs+ (12.8%)	44+,A9o+,A7s+, KQo,KJs+ (13.1%)
3-off	55+,AT+,KQs (9.7%)	55+,ATo+,A9s+, KQs (10.0%)	55+,ATo+,A9s+, KQo,KJs+ (11.2%)
4-off	66+,AJo+,ATs+ (8.0%)	66+,AJo+,ATs+, KQs (8.3%)	66+,AJo+,ATs+, KQs (8.3%)
5-off	77+,AQo+,AJs+ (6.3%)	77+,AJo+,ATs+ (7.5%)	77+,AJo+,ATs+, KQs (7.8%)
6-off	88+,AQ+ (5.6%)	88+,AQo+,AJs+ (5.9%)	88+,AQo+,AJs+ (5.9%)
7-off	99+,AQ+ (5.1%)	99+,AQ+ (5.1%)	88+,AQ+ (5.6%)

Calling a 7 CSI Push

	No Antes		
Pusher's Position	No Blind	Small Blind	Big Blind
Small Blind			22+,A2+,K6o+, K2s+,Q9o+,Q7s+, JTo,J8s+,T9s (36.3%)
Button		33+,A6o+,A2s+, KJo+,KTs+,QJs (19.3%)	22+,A5o+,A2s+, KTo+,K9s+,QTs+ (22.2%)
Cut-Off	44+,A9o+,A8s+, KQo,KJs+ (12.8%)	44+,A9o+,A7s+, KQo,KJs+ (13.1%)	33+,A8o+,A4s+, KJo+,KTs+,QJs (16.9%)
Hijack	55+,ATo+,A9s+, KQs (10.0%)	55+,ATo+,A9s+,KQ (10.9%)	44+,ATo+,A7s+, KQo,KJs+ (12.2%)
3-off	77+,AJo+,ATs+ (7.5%)	66+,AJo+,ATs+,KQs (8.3%)	55+,AT+,KQs (9.7%)
4-off	88+,AQo+,AJs+ (5.9%)	77+,AJo+,ATs+ (7.5%)	77+,AJo+,ATs+, KQs (7.8%)
5-off	88+,AQ+ (5.6%)	88+,AQ+ (5.6%)	88+,AQo+,AJs+ (5.9%)
6-off	99+,AKo,AQs+ (4.2%)	99+,AQ+ (5.1%)	99+,AQ+ (5.1%)
7-off	TT+,AKo,AQs+ (3.8%)	99+,AQ+ (5.1%)	99+,AQ+ (5.1%)

Calling a 7 CSI Push (cont'd)

Pusher's Position	Antes		
	No Blind	Small Blind	Big Blind
Small Blind			22+,A2+,K6o+, K2s+,Q9o+,Q8s+, JTo,J8s+,T9s (36.0%)
Button		33+,A6o+,A2s+, KJo+,K9s+,QTs+ (19.9%)	22+,A5o+,A2s+, KTo+,K9s+,QTs+ (22.2%)
Cut-Off	44+,A9o+,A7s+, KQo,KJs+ (13.1%)	44+,A8o+,A7s+, KQo,KTs+ (14.3%)	33+,A8o+,A5s+, KJo+,KTs+,QJs (16.6%)
Hijack	55+,ATo+,A9s+, KQs (10.0%)	55+,ATo+,A8s+, KQo,KJs+ (11.5%)	44+,ATo+,A8s+, KQo,KJs+ (11.9%)
3-off	66+,AJo+,ATs+, KQs (8.3%)	66+,AJo+,ATs+,KQs (8.3%)	66+,AJo+,ATs+, KQs (8.3%)
4-off	77+,AQo+,AJs+ (6.3%)	77+,AJ+ (7.2%)	77+,AJo+,ATs+, KQs (7.8%)
5-off	88+,AQ+ (5.6%)	88+,AQ+ (5.6%)	88+,AQo+,AJs+ (5.9%)
6-off	99+,AKo,AQs+ (4.2%)	99+,AQ+ (5.1%)	99+,AQ+ (5.1%)
7-off	TT+,AKo,AQs+ (3.8%)	99+,AQ+ (5.1%)	99+,AQ+ (5.1%)

Calling an 8 CSI Push

No Antes			
Pusher's Position	No Blind	Small Blind	Big Blind
Small Blind			22+,A2+,K7o+, K4s+,QTo+,Q8s+, JTo,J9s+ (33.0%)
Button		33+,A7o+,A3s+, KJo+,KTs+,QJs (18.1%)	22+,A6o+,A2s+, KJo+,KTs+,QJs (19.8%)
Cut-Off	55+,ATo+,A8s+, KJs+ (10.6%)	44+,A9o+,A8s+, KQo,KJs+ (12.8%)	44+,A9o+,A7s+, KQo,KTs+ (13.4%)
Hijack	66+,AJo+,ATs+, KQs (8.3%)	66+,AT+,KQs (9.2%)	55+,ATo+,A9s+, KQs (10.0%)
3-off	77+,AQo+,AJs+ (6.3%)	77+,AJo+,ATs+ (7.5%)	77+,AJo+,ATs+,KQs (7.8%)
4-off	88+,AQo+,AJs+ (5.9%)	88+,AQo+,AJs+ (5.9%)	88+,AQo+,AJs+ (5.9%)
5-off	99+,AKo,AQs+ (4.2%)	99+,AQ+ (5.1%)	99+,AQ+ (5.1%)
6-off	TT+,AKo,AQs+ (3.8%)	TT+,AQ+ (4.7%)	99+,AQ+ (5.1%)
7-off	TT+,AK (3.5%)	TT+,AKo,AQs+ (3.8%)	TT+,AKo,AQs+ (3.8%)

Calling an 8 CSI Push (cont'd)

Pusher's Position	Antes		
	No Blind	Small Blind	Big Blind
Small Blind			22+,A2+,K7o+, K4s+,QTo+, Q8s+, JTo,J9s+ (33.0%)
Button		33+,A7o+,A3s+, KJo+,KTs+,QJs (18.1%)	33+,A6o+,A2s+, KJo+,KTs+,QTs+ (19.6%)
Cut-Off	55+,A9o+,A8s+, KQo,KJs+ (12.4%)	44+,A9o+,A8s+, KQo,KJs+ (12.8%)	44+,A9o+,A8s+, KQo,KJs+ (12.8%)
Hijack	66+,AJo+,ATs+, KQs (8.3%)	66+,AT+,KQs (9.2%)	55+,ATo+,A9s+, KQs (10.0%)
3-off	77+,AQo+,AJs+ (6.3%)	77+,AJo+,ATs+ (7.5%)	77+,AJo+,ATs+, KQs (7.8%)
4-off	88+,AQo+,AJs+ (5.9%)	88+,AQo+,AJs+ (5.9%)	88+,AQo+,AJs+ (5.9%)
5-off	99+,AKo,AQs+ (4.2%)	99+,AQ+ (5.1%)	99+,AQ+ (5.1%)
6-off	TT+,AKo,AQs+ (3.8%)	99+,AQ+ (5.1%)	99+,AQ+ (5.1%)
7-off	TT+,AKo,AQs+ (3.8%)	TT+,AKo,AQs+ (3.8%)	TT+,AKo,AQs+ (3.8%)

Appendix 3

ASSUMED RANK ORDER FOR PUSHING HANDS

Percentile	Power Numbers	Hands (in order)
Top 5%	Always push with CSI <8	AA, KK, QQ, JJ, AKs, TT, AKo, 99, AQs, AQo
Top 10%	PN 50+	AJs, KQs, ATs, QJs, KJs, KTs, 88, JTs, QTs, 77, 66, AJo, A9s
Top 15%	PN 32-48	KQo, 55, K9s, T9s, J9s, Q9s, 44, A8s, ATo, 33, A7s
Top 20%	PN 26-31	A5s, KJo, 98s, 22, A6s, A9o, A4s, A3s, T8s, QJo
Top 30%	PN 16-24	A2s, A8o, JTo, A7o, J8s, A5o, KTo, 87s, A6o, A4o, K8s, 97s, QTo, A3o, Q8s
Top 40%	PN 10-15	76s, A2o, T7s, 86s, K7s, K6s, K5s, K9o, J7s, 65s, T9o, K4s, 54s, Q7s, 96s, 85s, T8o, 98o, 64s, K3s, K8o
Top 50%	PN 8-10	75s, Q6s, J6s, 87o, T6s, 74s, 95s, K2s, K7o, Q9o, T5s, K6o, K5o, J9o, Q5s, Q4s, Q3s, J8o
Top 60%	PN 6-8	K4o, Q2s, K3o, Q8o, J7o, J5s, 97o, J4s, T4s, K2o, J3s, 43s, Q7o, Q6o, T7o

Percentile	Power Numbers	Hands (in order)
Top 70%	PN 3-6	Q5o, 84s, J2s, T3s, Q4o, Q3o, 86o, J6o, J5o, Q2o, T2s, 94s, 93s, 96o, T6o, J4o
Top 80%	PN 3 or less	J3o, J2o, 53s, 76o, 63s, 65o, 92s, T5o, 73s, 52s, 75o, 54o, 62s, 83s, 82s, 64o
Top 90%		72s, 85o, 95o, 74o, 84o, 94o, 93o, T4o, 92o, 42s, 32s, 53o, 43o
Top 100%		63o, T3o, 52o, T2o, 73o, 42o, 32o, 62o, 83o, 82o, 72o

Appendix 4

ASSUMED RANK ORDER
FOR CALLING HANDS

Top 5%	AA, KK, QQ, JJ, AKs, AKo, TT, AQs
Top 10%	99, AQo, AJs, 88, KQs, 77, ATs, AJo, 66, KJs, 55, A9s, ATo
Top 15%	KQo, 44, A8s, KTs, A5s, A7s, 33, QJs, A4s, A6s, A9o
Top 20%	A3s, KJo, A2s, 22, QTs, A8o, JTs, K9s, A7o
Top 30%	KTo, A5o, QJo, A6o, A4o, Q9s, K8s, K7s, A3o, T9s, QTo, J9s, K6s, A2o, Q8s, K9o
Top 40%	K5s, JTo, 98s, T8s, J8s, K4s, 87s, Q7s, Q9o, K3s, Q6s, K8o, 97s, 76s, K2s, Q5s, T7s, K7o, J7s, 86s, T9o, J9o
Top 50%	65s, K6o, Q4s, Q8o, 96s, 75s, Q3s, T6s, J6s, K5o, 54s, 98o, Q2s, T8o, 85s, J5s, J8o, K4o
Top 60%	64s, 87o, Q7o, J4s, 95s, Q6o, K3o, 74s, 97o, 76o, T5s, 53s, J3s, K2o, T7o, T4s
Top 70%	Q5o, 84s, J7o, 86o, J2s, 63s, 43s, 65o, T3s, Q4o, 94s, 96o, 73s, 93s, T2s, 52s, 75o, T6o
Top 80%	Q3o, 54o, J6o, 83s, 92s, 85o, 62s, 42s, 82s, J5o, Q2o, 64o, 32s, 72s, J4o, 95o
Top 90%	74o, 53o, T5o, J3o, T4o, 84o, 63o, 43o, J2o, T3o, 94o
Top 100%	73o, 52o, 93o, T2o, 83o, 92o, 42o, 62o, 82o, 32o, 72o

Appendix 5

LIMITATIONS OF ICM

ICM isn't perfect, but it's the best model available that can be applied to a variety of tournament situations. Using ICM and knowing how changes in chip position affect equity is extremely important. But always remember that the "M" in ICM stands for "Model." We're only modeling the true equity and that model has a few shortcomings.

• It assumes all players are of equal skill.

• It doesn't take into account how soon you'll be posting your blind.

• It doesn't take into account the order of the stacks around the table (you're likely to do better if a big stack is on your right rather than on your left).

• It doesn't take into account the size of the blinds.

• It doesn't model the true equity of the stacks.

All of these limitations are real and affect your true equity. However, measuring these limitations precisely is difficult, if not impossible. Most people who've studied this problem agree that these factors make the model far from perfect, but it's still the best we have. If nothing else, ICM serves as a useful guide and as a starting point from which a player can make modifications. So how should these factors influence your play?

Skill: If you think you have a significant skill advantage over your opponents, you should play a more conservative game and not try to gamble when faced with close decisions. Your skill will be a continuous advantage and you don't want to take risks on neutral-EV situations, when more positive-EV situations will probably occur later. The better you are, the more important survival is to you and the longer you want the tournament to last. Push less often and call less often.

If you think you're one of the weaker players left, then you need to gamble it up more, push some risky situations, and hope to get lucky. If you're weak, time works against you and all-in confrontations, especially with the proper hand selection and with fold equity generally on your side, are the way to go. Weaker players should court the variance that strong players avoid.

Kill Phil was based on this philosophy. If you're not familiar with this strategy, we suggest you read and understand it thoroughly. It's your best shot at winning. Don't play small ball, allowing your more skilled opponents to outplay you. Make large and aggressive plays pre-flop. Push much more often than if you were equally skilled, but don't call more often. The first-in advantage is so great (since it gives you fold equity) that it's best to push much more, but not call more frequently, rather than to push *and* call more frequently. Precise ranges for both pushing and calling based on CSI are fully described in *Kill Phil*.

Blind posting: When you're under the gun, it means that you'll be forced to post the big blind on the next hand. Since that's a disadvantage, when we evaluate the *current* hand, we need to remember that folding is actually less attractive than the model predicts. Your true equity will be less than predicted, since you're forced to post the big blind on the next hand. This fact may sway you toward playing a marginal hand from UTG. How much has your equity decreased? Obviously, the loss is somewhere between no change and the equity you would have if you just automatically folded your blind next hand. It turns out that your equity loss is strongly tied to your bubble factor.

When you have a bubble factor close to 1, there isn't much disadvantage in having to post. You have more freedom in how you play your hand, so your EV in the big blind, while still negative, is not as bad as it would be if you folded 100% of the time.

As your bubble factor gets higher, it's incorrect to call as freely (negative equity), so your blind will be successfully stolen more frequently. The higher your bubble factor becomes, the closer folding that blind 100% of the time becomes the optimal course of action.

Note that in all cases, the presence of an ante reduces the effect of having to post a blind. The larger the ante, the less of a difference it makes being UTG.

Stack order: The stack order around the table should play a similar role to skill level. If there are big stacks to your right and/or short stacks to your left, you're at an advantage—you should play as if your skill level is higher.

The opposite is also true. ICM doesn't capture the fact that big stacks can push medium stacks around very effectively. There may be occasions that small stacks can increase their equity by more than two times by doubling up. This is because they didn't have any fold equity as a small stack, but are now more effective after doubling. The magnitude of this effect is one of those that's difficult or impossible to determine. A player simply has to rely on experience.

Size of the blinds: The size of the blinds isn't really a factor by itself, but rather influences the previous three factors. Since high blinds make the play more random, it reduces the effects of skill and the order of the stacks. This means the model becomes a more accurate representation as the blinds increase. However, the effect of posting your blind naturally becomes more significant when the blinds are large.

Doesn't represent true equity: There's another model that more accurately represents the true equity of chip stacks—the random-walk or diffusion model. This model assumes that chips move from one stack to another in a random fashion until a player has no more chips. The problem is that it's much more computationally complex than ICM, making it very difficult to solve for four players, and even more so for 5+ players. The random-walk model also suffers from the previous four issues, like skill level, in the same manner as ICM. Comparing ICM to the random walk does reveal that ICM tends to overvalue short stacks, suggesting that short-stack bubble factors should be closer to 1 than ICM predicts. This table shows various stack sizes and the chances that Player A will finish in the various spots according to ICM and the diffusion model:

Chips			Diffusion			ICM		
A	B	C	A 1st	A 2nd	A 3rd	A 1st	A 2nd	A 3rd
10%	10%	80%	10.0%	40.5%	49.5%	10.0%	41.1%	48.9%
10%	20%	70%	10.0%	23.3%	66.7%	10.0%	25.8%	64.2%
10%	30%	60%	10.0%	16.0%	74.0%	10.0%	19.3%	70.7%
10%	40%	50%	10.0%	13.2%	76.8%	10.0%	16.7%	73.3%
20%	10%	70%	20.0%	49.5%	30.5%	20.0%	48.9%	31.1%
20%	20%	60%	20.0%	33.6%	46.4%	20.0%	35.0%	45.0%
20%	30%	50%	20.0%	26.1%	53.9%	20.0%	28.6%	51.4%
20%	40%	40%	20.0%	23.8%	56.2%	20.0%	26.7%	53.3%
30%	10%	60%	30.0%	49.4%	20.6%	30.0%	48.3%	21.7%
30%	20%	50%	30.0%	37.6%	32.4%	30.0%	37.5%	32.5%
30%	30%	40%	30.0%	32.2%	37.8%	30.0%	32.9%	37.1%
40%	10%	50%	40.0%	46.0%	14.0%	40.0%	44.4%	15.6%
40%	20%	40%	40.0%	38.1%	21.9%	40.0%	36.7%	23.3%
40%	30%	30%	40.0%	35.5%	24.5%	40.0%	34.3%	25.7%
50%	10%	40%	50.0%	40.8%	9.2%	50.0%	38.9%	11.1%
50%	20%	30%	50.0%	36.3%	13.7%	50.0%	33.9%	16.1%
60%	10%	30%	60.0%	34.5%	5.5%	60.0%	32.4%	7.6%
60%	20%	20%	60.0%	32.7%	7.3%	60.0%	30.0%	10.0%
70%	10%	20%	70.0%	27.3%	2.7%	70.0%	25.3%	4.7%
80%	10%	10%	80.0%	19.1%	0.9%	80.0%	17.8%	2.2%

We've tested some of our recommended strategies using both ICM and the random-walk model. The choice of model makes very little difference in the solution; this limitation seems smaller than the others.

Appendix 6

RESOURCES

Supplements

Antioxidants, melatonin, etc.: Life Extension Foundation (www.lef.org)

Fish oil: Nordic Naturals (www.nordicnaturals.com)

Brain Entrainment CDs and Samplers

www.centerpointe.com (free trial CD available)

www.synchronicity.org (free online sample available)

Books

Brunson, Doyle. *Super System 2*. New York, NY: Cardoza Publishing, 2005.

Caro, Mike. *Caro's Book of Poker Tells*. New York, NY: Cardoza Publishing, 2003.

Harrington, Dan, and Bill Robertie. *Harrington on Hold 'Em. Vol 1, Strategic Play*. Henderson, NV: Two Plus Two Publishing, 2004.

Harrington, Dan, and Bill Robertie. *Harrington on Hold 'Em. Vol 2, The Endgame*. Henderson, NV: Two Plus Two Publishing, 2004.

Sklansky, David and Ed Miller. *No-Limit Hold 'Em Theory and Practice*. Henderson, NV: Two Plus Two Publishing, 2006.

Sklansky, David. *The Theory of Poker*, 4th ed. Henderson, NV: Two Plus Two Publishing, 1999.

Web sites

cardplayer.com
pokerpages.com
propokertools.com
twoplustwo.com

Software

Poker Academy has computer players for you to practice against with using real money (www.poker-academy.com/refer/ke.php).

Poker Tracker allows you to keep track of your statistics (and your opponents') from online hand histories (www.pokertracker.com)

Sit-n-Go Power Tools allows you to do complicated ICM calculations on hand histories and improve your bubble play (sitngo-analyzer.com).

Index

About the Authors

New Zealander **Lee "Final Table" Nelson** has been playing tournament poker for 10 years, with live-tournament wins in excess of US$2,000,000. His nickname was given to him by a tournament director who claimed that Lee made the final table so frequently, he was like "final-table furniture." Nelson won the 2006 Aussie Millions, taking down US$1,000,000 (A$1,300,000), along with the World Open in 2005 (US$400,000). He co-authored the highly acclaimed poker book, *Kill Phil*, and co-hosts televised celebrity poker shows in both Australia and New Zealand. According to Poker Network's rankings, Lee was the top-rated poker player in Australia/New Zealand for the period 2000-2006. He's a member of Team Poker Stars.

Tysen Streib has been a consistently profitable tournament player since 1998, both online and in live play. He specializes in the mathematical aspects of tournament structures and game theory. He has published several highly praised articles in *Two Plus Two Internet Magazine* and has experience developing artificial intelligence for computer poker players. Although his main passion is poker, Tysen has written articles about and analyzed other strategy games, such as contract bridge. He holds an engineering degree, as well as an MBA.

Kim Lee is a university professor. He designed the computer models used in *Kill Phil* and did the optimal departure analysis for Don Schlesinger's *Blackjack Attack*.

More great products to improve your Kill Phil play.

Now you can bring a condensed version of the Kill Phil strategies with you to live tournaments with our handy strategy cards: Kill Phil Rookie, Basic Live (including final-table/Sit-n-Go strategy), and Advanced Strategy Post-Flop Play. There's also a Basic Online card, for use as a quick reference when playing at home. Buy the set for $14.95.

Kill Phil Helper
(software download)

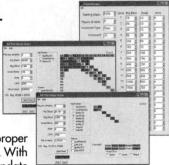

Assists you in using Kill Phil strategy while playing online Sit-n-Go's and tournaments, *Kill Phil Online Helper* stays open on your computer while you're playing, allowing you to input the tournament details and have the proper Kill Phil strategic moves at your disposal. With a few clicks of your mouse, you can update blinds, chip stack, and the number of players at the table.

KPOH also contains the new Heads-Up strategy developed by Blair Rodman and Lee Nelson that is not contained in the book. This alone will be worth the price of the program for many.

An excellent tool for those of you playing Kill Phil Strategy online. *Windows required.*

To order visit ShopLVA.com

ShopLVA.com
For Other Great
Poker Books and Gambling Products

Go to ShopLVA.com to find the best gambling books, software, DVDs, and strategy cards for all the casino games. All products at ShopLVA.com are endorsed by Anthony Curtis and the *Las Vegas Advisor* for their mathematical accuracy. ShopLVA.com is your source for the world's best gambling-strategy products.

For all of the best gambling products
on the market, go to www.ShopLVA.com.